THE DUKE'S

Georgian Hartington and Buxton
under The Dukes of Devonshire

Lindsey Porter

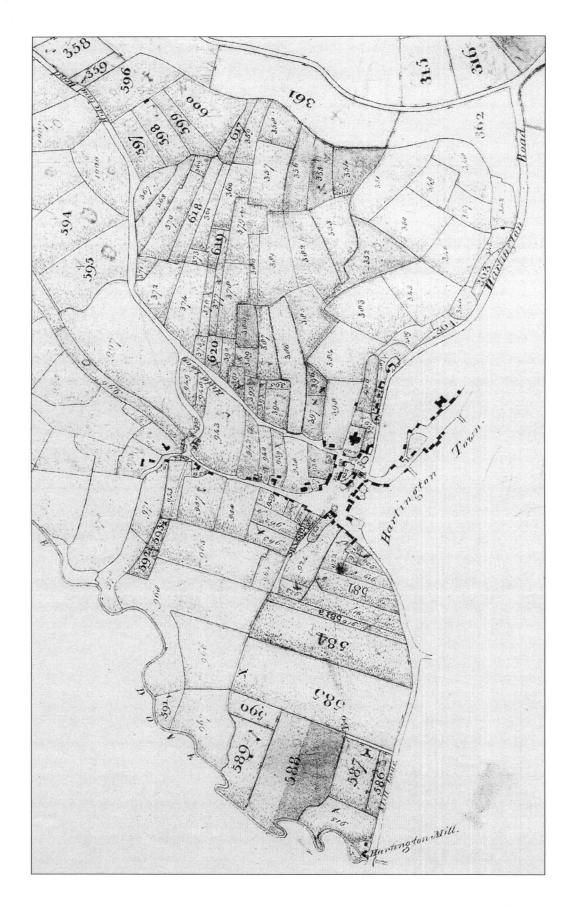

Hartington Mill.

FOREWORD

by

The Duke of Devonshire KCVO, CBE, DL

For over 500 years, my family seems to have thrown comparatively little away of its records. Today they represent an impressive archive of my ancestors: what they did, where they did it and how their activity wove itself into the historical fabric of many communities.

This is Lindsey Porter's second book drawing on the Chatsworth archive in the Georgian period, giving a detailed insight into aspects of the Devonshire influence on life and times of that era.

It reveals much new material on the business dealings of the 5th Duke. His life has clearly been misunderstood by historians up until now. His investments, fuelled by a massive capital injection from copper mining profits, reveal the sound financial acumen of his "Auditor", John Heaton and the support the Duke must have given him. Developing Buxton hamlet into perhaps Britain's first holiday resort was just one of the achievements.

However the research went much deeper than this, enabling us to understand the way of life in the Derbyshire Dales at that time. The changes occurring across the country from 1750 impacted on both Derbyshire and my family's estates – improvements in transportation, technology, plus the Industrial and Agrarian revolutions for instance all brought local change. It also saw the raw edge to life with worsening poverty in many villages as the national economy struggled with the effects of these changes, war and insurrection. It is a fascinating story, told here in such detail for the first time.

Stoker Devonshire

Guidelines Books & Sales
11 Belmont Road, Ipstones, Stoke on Trent ST10 2JN
Tel: 07971 990 649
Email: author.porter@gmail.com

1st Edition
ISBN: 978-1-84306-544-9

© Lindsey Porter, 2012

Design: Mark Titterton: Ceiba Graphics;

Editing: Eric Wood and Margaret Black;

Printing: 4edge Ltd, Hockley, Essex

Front cover: left: Glutton Farm; middle: The Crescent, Buxton; right: Ivy House, Biggin; background: Hartington from the 1880 OS Map showing many Georgian properties
Back Cover: Top row: left: Hartington's mere; middle: Buxton Church; Below: The Crescent, Buxton; Right hand side (from top): Former Common land at Heathcote, with meer; Hartington Hall; Earl Sterndale; Old Hall Hotel, Buxton
Page 2: Hartington in 1808(from the Inclosure Award). Reproduced by permission of the Chatsworth Settlement Trustees

If you have enjoyed this book you may like to know that a book on the Georgian period at Derby, drawn from the pages of the *Derby Mercury*, has just been published. It is *Bonnie Prince and Burning Rebel* by Harry Butterton, available from 37 Windley Crescent, Darley Abbey, Derby DE22 1BY or through local bookshops.

CONTENTS

1. SETTING THE SCENE

Until now, investment in landed property by the 5th Duke of Devonshire in the period 1773-1810 has been portrayed as encumbering the estate with debt. The full capital expenditure has not been appreciated previously, nor the fact that purchases between 1790-1810 were largely from income rather than from borrowings. The Duke's solicitor and Agent, John Heaton, has been described as being 'imbecile', an unfortunate misrepresentation now laid bare. Cutting his teeth in land management in Hartington Manor, Heaton was also responsible for The Crescent and other developments in Buxton, plus many more elsewhere, all aimed at increasing Cavendish wealth. This is a story of service and success, revealed in detail for the first time, along with much new information on Derbyshire rural life.

Unearthing long forgotten documents at Chatsworth enables a new light to be shone on how life played out in Georgian times on the Duke's principal revenue earning estate (after Weatherby and Richmond), based on Hartington Manor. With probably over 100,000 documents in the Chatsworth Muniment Room, the method of cataloguing means that much detail is not easily found. It is only after years of research that sufficient has been located to create this fascinating account also for the first time.

This book will enlighten the reader to a greater extent than perhaps is envisaged. There is a huge amount of new material within these pages. It is my hope that I have managed to present it in an engaging manner, although it is appreciated that some of the material is included for completeness, and not all of the subjects covered lend themselves to a light touch.

Through the system of manor courts, the Duke held a measure of control over the village and use of its huge common, one of the largest in the county. Although only a small parish in width – much of it being only a few miles – it was unusually long at about 20 miles/32km from north to south. Much of this was either common land or waste and most of it was owned by the Duke. It had been purchased from George Villiers, Duke of Buckingham in 1663 by the 3rd Earl of Devonshire, although some of it had been rented since the early part of the century. The Derbyshire-based Cavendish family knew Buckingham. Both George Villiers and Wm Cavendish, 1st Duke of Newcastle (and grandson of Bess of Hardwick) were members of the Order of the Garter in 1663 – Villiers from 1649 and Newcastle from 1650, so their aquaintance was a long one. The 1st Duke of Newcastle and 3rd Earl of Devonshire were 2nd cousins. The western boundary of the parish is the Derbyshire county boundary, the River Dove. In the north the parish looped around Buxton and continued northwards into the Goyt Valley to Errwood.

Just outside the parish and across the county boundary with Staffordshire rises the northern slope of an elongated hill called Ecton, the majority of which was owned by the Duke of Devonshire. Here in the mid-18th century was found a huge copper ore deposit. Fortune usually favours the brave but just as the wealth from this Eldorado was being established, the lease ran out, allowing the Duke to take possession from those who had risked all in finding it. Ecton became one of the richest, perhaps the richest, mine in the country for a few years. (1)

Hartington village lies on the River Dove, the county boundary between Derbyshire and Staffordshire. From the surviving records of village and mine, it is possible to piece together a good idea of rural life in a small village and its adjacent parishes in Georgian England. Important then because of the wealth the mine generated and important now because of the insight the records give us of what rural life must have been like in many parts of the

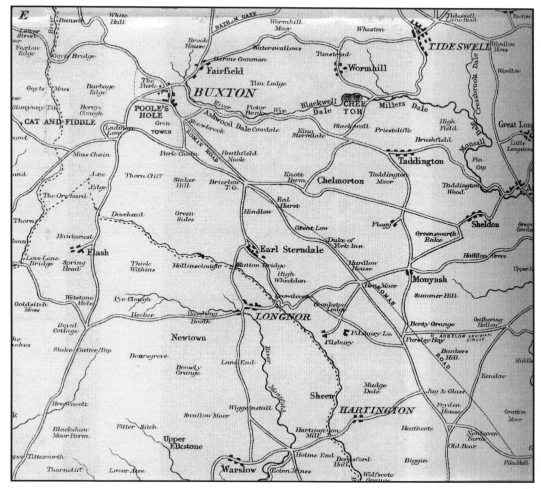

The Hartington and Buxton area. The map is taken from The Buxton Guide, 1868 and some spellings have changed

county. Arguably rural life would have varied little beyond the county. There are gaps in that knowledge, but some of these can be reasonably pieced together from details which have also survived of places and events nearby. This is especially of interest when these events are on the same estate. These events shared the result of the same way of working; the same all-pervading sense of paternalism threaded across the estate, and the influence of the same land steward. He exercised his influence and judgement in investment, assisting with special requests and needs from tenants and controlling day to day activity as was felt justified in the manor courts.

Hartington's site adjacent to the River Dove was of importance because it was also situated at the mouth of Hartington Dale, a deep, steep sided dale (or valley) which allowed a gradual ascent onto the Derbyshire plateau in an easterly direction. It was not however on any important crossing of routes. The two important north–south routes – the Roman High Street and the Via de Peco, a later route running towards Buxton, probably from Ashbourne – ran to the east of the village, high on the plateau.

However, Hartington lay on an important drovers' road heading for the Winster and beyond, coming from Cheshire by way of Meerbrook and Warslow in Staffordshire. It crossed over into Derbyshire at Hartington Mill. However it must have been the supply of water in the River Harding which caused the siting of the village to be where it is. This river now flows underground and is culverted across the Market Place as it heads for the River Dove. A section of it, known locally as The Stanner, is open at the top of Factory Lane. Here villagers could fill their buckets before heading back home. The culvert splits in the Market Place with a branch going down the side of the inn (now the Charles Cotton Hotel). Whether this was simply to supply the cold clear water to the inn, or whether the inn's position was determined by the pre-existing culvert branch, is not clear.

The village has a large pond – the Duck Pond – which had a separate supply of water. This was where animals were brought to be watered. Nearby, at the bottom of Church Street is the village pump where villagers would meet, gossip and fill their buckets for the kitchen. It presumably replaced the river water with a deeper, more permanent source of supply. Several of the larger houses, built or rebuilt in the latter half of the 18th century, have their own well. In a mining area perhaps this is not surprising and the nearest one to the village pump (in The Old Vicarage of 1789) is lined with stone and would have been sunk like a mine shaft by Ecton miners. This house was owned by the estate and in fact was used by the mine manager as his home from c.1800. The Duck Pond is not marked on the 1808 Inclosure Award plan, but another mere would appear to be shown on the north east corner of the cross roads at the bottom of Hide Lane.

The village had three large open fields where farmers tended their allotted strips, leaving one field fallow each year. The one between the village and the River Dove (? The Town Field) was crossed by the small River Harding (really just a stream) but some water was at least near to hand. The other two fields were on the hill top, one north and one south of Hartington Dale. Here, water supplies would depend on the rain. They were collectively called The High Field.

A large spring at Crowdecote must have had some influence on the siting of the village there, and the village mill was built just downstream of its confluence with the River Dove. To the north Earl Stendale had a large village mere also supplied by a spring. Why Biggin was situated where it is on the old drovers' road with no apparent supply of good water isn't clear. River water drove the waterwheel at both the Hartington and Crowdecote Mills, providing the power to grind cereals, chiefly oats and some barley. The latter was used to produce malt, having been roasted in a kiln before grinding. The miller would then have his round of pubs to visit, where the innkeeper would make his own beer. A visiting brewery wagon had to wait for a better road system in the late 18th century to enable any meaningful sort of distribution system. Once the Duke took over the running of Ecton Mine, a party for the several hundred workers or so was organised each year over the Christmas/New Year period – although only Christmas Day was a holiday. Various inns supplied a total of 120 gallons of beer for the event initially, before the mine bought in the malt and hops to make its own beer for thirsty workers.

The turnpiking of the road through the village, from Warslow and on to the Buxton-Ashbourne road, would have made access easier, albeit at a cost of the price of the tolls payable. Pedestrians and lime wagons went free however. Access by four wheeled vehicles and heavier loads would have been much easier. Use of other nearby lanes would then have become heavier as other users endeavoured to avoid the tolls. Although the Duke was an avid investor in local turnpike roads, almost as though he thought it was his duty, his mine at

Ecton studiously avoided using them whenever possible!

Use of the Great Drovers' Road from Cheshire would have seen many drovers and their animals coming through the village along with jaggermen and their Galloway ponies tethered nose to tail in long lines. These could travel relatively quickly, far faster than a one-ton capacity cart, although it needed ten packhorses to carry the same weight. However the nemesis of the packhorse arrived with the improvement of the roads and by the late 18th century their use had largely died out. One of the last exceptions were the pack mules which carried copper ore from the Ecton Mine to the Duke's smelter, about 8 miles/13 km to the south-west at Whiston near Froghall. (2)

Additional to the long distance drovers and jaggermen were the local traders, dealing in everything from candles to coal, salt to soap and so on. It is not clear how many shopkeepers there were in the parish. Hartington had a butcher as early as 1614, Wetton had to wait until 1796 for its shop. (3) In 1760, Thomas Barker, a baker of Parwich, some 3 miles/5 km to the south-east, attended the Hartington Small Court Baron. Two years later, George Lees, of the Bakehouse, Biggin, had to surrender the property to John Buxton, a grocer of Ashbourne, unless he paid the latter £15 within six months. These suggest that at least the village baker was a common feature. (4).

By 1836, the imposing colonnade-fronted store had been built in Hartington Market Place. Having later been The Volunteer Inn as well as a well-stocked supplier of provisions, it went on to be the Co-op for many years and is the 'village shop' to this day. However it sold much more than domestic items for the housewife. It also sold products needed by workmen, including gunpowder for miners, kept in a barrel in an outhouse. In the 1840s a trail of spilt gunpowder was ignited; three people died in the resulting explosion as the flame chased back along the floor to the barrel, see p. 39.

Less deadly, but no doubt equally profound, was the carefree enjoyment to be found in the village inns. By the 1820s (5) the village had three inns. They may well have been in existence for some time at that date. They were the Red Lion occupied by Anthony Gould, who was a farmer as well as an innkeeper (6). This inn was at the bottom of Hall Bank. Around the corner in the Market Place was John Lomas at the Three Stags Inn, probably now the Devonshire Arms, the Duke's crest being three stags' heads. Finally Henry Clarke was at the Bull's Head, probably now the Charles Cotton Hotel (previously the Sleigh Arms). In 1846, it was the Bulls Head and Commercial Inn run by Francis Clarke (6/1). This inn was enlarged in the style seen elsewhere in the village and dateable to the mid–late 18th century. The Bull's Head should not be confused with another inn of the same name in Biggin, kept in the 1820s by William Shaw (see p. 81). A short distance to the north of it, also on the Buxton – Ashbourne turnpike, was the Newhaven House, kept by Richard Shaw. Both of these inns offered accommodation. (No inn is recorded by Glover in Earl Stendale or Crowdecote although the inn at the latter is still known as The Packhorse).

In the late eighteenth century, the Hartington butcher was Thomas Fogg (7) and he is unlikely to have been the only tradesman. Other shops in the village in the 1820s were those of John Harrison, grocer and draper; Joseph Needham (the same trades); and George Sutton, grocer, draper and druggist. Sutton may well have had his business on the site of the current village shop, for a carving within the pediment depicts a pair of scales, possibly symbolising that it was a druggist's shop. It is probable that several wives supplemented the household income by bread, butter and cheese making (many households had a cow), and also selling vegetables, eggs, etc.

The 1808 Inclosure Award Map for Earl Sterndale (above) and Biggin (below) photo: Dec. Coll., Hartington Inclosure Award. Reproduced by permission of the Chatsworth Settlement Trustees

Top left: The 4th Duke of Devonshire, 1720-64; top middle: the 5th Duke, 1748-1811; top right: the 6th Duke, 1790-58; copyright Devonshire Collection, Chatsworth. Reproduced by permission of the Chatsworth Settlement Trustees

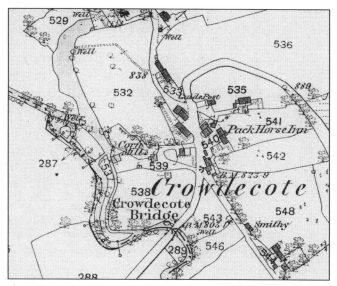

Crowdecote in 1880, showing the spring feeding the mill; the pub and the smithy

The manor included some large farm holdings called desmene lands, chiefly well cultivated farms which had originally been monastic holdings. These were Pilsbury Grange, Cronxton and Clementseats. These were all in the area between Hartington and Buxton and all were mainly on the limestone plateau above the river meadows adjacent to the River Dove. The only exception was part of the holding of Pilsbury Grange, which consisted of two farms (and two adjacent farmhouses) with some of the river meadow land. All of these holdings had been under Devonshire control from the early 17th century.

Additional to these holdings and during the late 17th century, the estate farmed land in the Upper Dove at Glutton and Harley. This practice may not have survived for long into the 18th century in favour of a more widespread practice of letting holdings on a 21-year tenancy agreement. The Agrarian Revolution focussed minds on increased yields and as a result, increased rentals. Better husbandry and soil enrichment followed. John Heaton (the Duke's land agent and lawyer) realised that much could be done to improve the virtually valueless heathlands by liming. Thousands of tons of lime were carted or carried by packhorse from Grin Quarry south-west of Buxton.

11

Using lime burned with Devonshire coal from Axe Edge and limestone from Grin, the heath lands were changed to farmland. The type of vegetation still surviving on Axe Edge above the current Leek – Buxton road formerly covered much of the land below that road and across to the current Buxton – Ashbourne road. It stretched south of Buxton to the Dove Valley and the desmene farms mentioned above. The green field landscape we recognise today resulted from the liming programme of John Heaton. Over time, increased rentals resulted. Improvements to farmhouses and farm buildings also commenced along with drainage programmes in the early 19th century. The population was growing too: in 1801 it was 1,812; in 1831 it was 2,103.

There was also another method of increasing the estate holdings. It was not necessarily cheap, but it did enable vast acreages to be bought freehold. This was the inclosure of common lands. In Hartington, the manor was increased in size to 13,192 acres/534ha. It cost £23,763 (£1.80 p.ac/£44.50 .p.ha) but this was partly how the Derbyshire estate as a whole grew to over 100,000 acres. The Hartington Manor was the richest part of the Derbyshire Devonshire estate in terms of rental income. It always seems to have been (bearing in mind that the lands at Chatsworth were farmed in hand). It is possibly the reason why the Dukedom also created the title of Marquis of Hartington for the eldest son, a title of course which survives to this day.

This book looks at the way of life in this Manor in Georgian times. It must reflect a similar experience for other Devonshire tenants in the county. Although the absent landlord always seemed to have exercised a paternal influence on his estates, the way of life could not have been much different for those who lived their lives off the estate. Equally, that way of life could not have been too different across county boundaries.

The enormous number of documents in the Chatsworth Muniment Room reveal a fascinating insight into that period. Although the records of the Ecton Mine are largely together (there are perhaps 4,000 of them in all), those relating to Hartington are scattered through the various series of documents stored in the collection. So much so, that most of them are not directly catalogued and many references have been found by chance. Even then, some areas of research have been restricted because of work by others. Fortunately these are in areas where the topic does not influence the thread of this story to any great extent. (8).

Consequently this story may be seen in a wider context of rural life in a part of middle England, drawing on the many surviving documents relating to Hartington and adjacent areas on the Devonshire estate. Additional study has unlocked the activities of John Heaton in the massive capital expenditure undertaken, particularly in the period of 1791–1810. Although a lot of this was as far away as Ireland and the Lismore estate, much of it was close to or in Hartington Manor), sufficiently close for the Buxton/Hartington revenues to be collected by the same rent collector as one rent collection area. The early development of Buxton has therefore been included herein.

Recent research on the troubled life of the 5th Duke's wife and the resulting film *The Duchess* did not portray any of the work produced here. Neither does research by others into the Duke's life and his finances. In fact his activity of huge investment has never been revealed in detail before. *The Duke's Manor* sheds light on his tenants and to a small extent on the man himself. It extends a little to the years before and after his time as Duke to help set the scene. The material on the Ecton copper mine is drawn on my book on the Devonshire activities there between 1760 and 1790. However for this book, it only covers the activities of the workers there.

Research for this work is largely confined to the manor and other Devonshire holdings. It is hoped that it creates a platform for further study on other aspects of the parish.

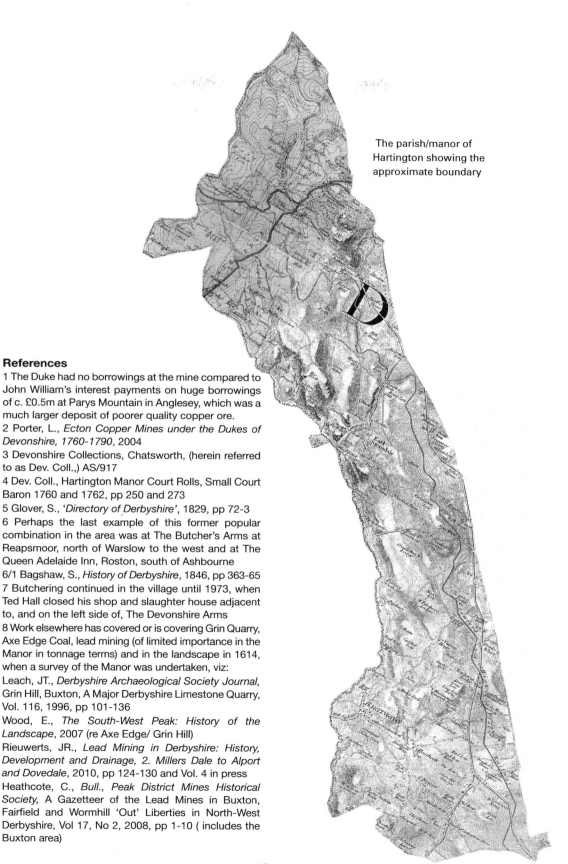

The parish/manor of Hartington showing the approximate boundary

References

1 The Duke had no borrowings at the mine compared to John William's interest payments on huge borrowings of c. £0.5m at Parys Mountain in Anglesey, which was a much larger deposit of poorer quality copper ore.

2 Porter, L., *Ecton Copper Mines under the Dukes of Devonshire, 1760-1790*, 2004

3 Devonshire Collections, Chatsworth, (herein referred to as Dev. Coll.,) AS/917

4 Dev. Coll., Hartington Manor Court Rolls, Small Court Baron 1760 and 1762, pp 250 and 273

5 Glover, S., *'Directory of Derbyshire'*, 1829, pp 72-3

6 Perhaps the last example of this former popular combination in the area was at The Butcher's Arms at Reapsmoor, north of Warslow to the west and at The Queen Adelaide Inn, Roston, south of Ashbourne

6/1 Bagshaw, S., *History of Derbyshire*, 1846, pp 363-65

7 Butchering continued in the village until 1973, when Ted Hall closed his shop and slaughter house adjacent to, and on the left side of, The Devonshire Arms

8 Work elsewhere has covered or is covering Grin Quarry, Axe Edge Coal, lead mining (of limited importance in the Manor in tonnage terms) and in the landscape in 1614, when a survey of the Manor was undertaken, viz:

Leach, JT., *Derbyshire Archaeological Society Journal*, Grin Hill, Buxton, A Major Derbyshire Limestone Quarry, Vol. 116, 1996, pp 101-136

Wood, E., *The South-West Peak: History of the Landscape*, 2007 (re Axe Edge/ Grin Hill)

Rieuwerts, JR., *Lead Mining in Derbyshire: History, Development and Drainage, 2. Millers Dale to Alport and Dovedale*, 2010, pp 124-130 and Vol. 4 in press

Heathcote, C., *Bull., Peak District Mines Historical Society,* A Gazetteer of the Lead Mines in Buxton, Fairfield and Wormhill 'Out' Liberties in North-West Derbyshire, Vol 17, No 2, 2008, pp 1-10 (includes the Buxton area)

2. VILLAGE LIFE

We are fortunate in that a cursory look around the area of Hartington Market Place reveals many properties which feature on the 1808 Inclosure Award map. It is similar in the other parish villages too. Although some properties were rebuilt and infilling has occurred, the basic scene is largely the same. There are notable exceptions such as the Hartington village mere, apparently moved to its current position in the 19th century and the substitution of thatch by roof tiles.

For a while your author lived at Knowl Cottage in the Market Place. It appears to have been in existence in the middle of the 18th century and was sold off by the estate in c. 1823. Around the interior of the top of the exterior walls pieces of thatch still exist. However it is of a smaller diameter than cereal stalks or reeds of today, being more of the size of rushes. If this shortened the life span of the roof covering, this may have influenced the change to tiles as these became widely available at an affordable price.

The building was originally lower and had a cruck construction, remnants of which remain, especially in the roof. It appears to have originally been two houses, following an extension on the west side. It is likely that the early stone built buildings in the Market Place and probably in other parish villages looked similar, either a typical 2-up, 2-down cottage with an outside privy (earth closet) or even smaller as this house appears to originally have been.

With the growth of a working middle class in the late 18th century, better quality houses were built. Five particularly come to mind. Two of them were probably built by the same builder/architect: Springfield, overlooking the current mere, and Watergap Farmhouse, just before Pool Hall. The latter was probably built by the Devonshire estate, as was The Old Vicarage of 1789, built on the corner of Church and Dig Streets. Finally, The Vicarage (now in secular use) was built behind the church. The living of the parish was in the Duke's gift (i.e. he appointed the vicar).

With such developments, the face of the village was beginning to change. At Earl Sterndale, even the church was replaced, but change, it has to be said, on the whole came slowly. The powerhouse of change happened beyond the villages, propelled by the Inclosure Award at the beginning of the 19th century. For a cursory look at village life, we need to go back a couple of centuries before that.

What then was life like in the Hartington area in the seventeenth century? A little information may be gleaned from the records in the Devonshire Collection and also from the Alstonfield Parish Registers. Although this work examines life in the Georgian period, a look at previous years helps to support a view of what life was like later. Surely the start of a new century or the Georgian period would not have influenced the way of life in rural Derbyshire. It was improvements in technology, transportation and improved farming practice which produced change.

Life was certainly more precarious in those days. From Chapter 9 it will be seen that a least five people (four of them women) died in wintery conditions – presumably in snow – and were buried at Alstonfield, the village to the south-west of Hartington. More graphic is the description of the drowning of Widowe Bailie at Lode Mill, (not then built), prior to the building of the bridge over the River Dove. Her body was carried away by the swollen river almost to the mill at Mill Dale, a couple of miles or so downstream. There is locally a traditional story of six packhorses and their owner (a jaggermen) being lost (i.e. died of the cold) in a snow storm. It was recounted by Nellie Kirkham, but she did not give the source of her reference. She states that it was in 1692, between Pikehall and Hurdlow – presumably on High Street, (1). The Alstonfield Parish Register records one such bad winter which affected the area for some time: *20th January 1614. The great snow began to fall, and so continued increasing the most dayes until the 12 of March.* It must have made life very miserable, not to say cold, for local people and the sheep and cattle caught up in it.

During the Civil War, Alstonfield must have had another worry when Ann, the daughter of Thomas Walton, died of the plague and was buried on 31st July 1646. The war had another effect too, for: '*in our warre-tym none would come to be married at the church between 23rd July 1641 and 5th June 1643*'. Although all of this was in a neighbouring village to Hartington, the way of life could not have been very different.

Amongst those with a trade were tailors (sic), weavers, a webster (a female weaver), a blacksmith and a button maker. (the Manor House, or Pepper Inn, at Back Ecton near Wetton, south-west of Hartington, was a button making workshop – factory is too strong a word, although one often hears it referred to in this manner). Hartington had a smithy in 1614 when Richard Milnes occupied the *smythforge* according to Heyward's map and survey. In 1684, the local smith, Thomas Malkin, was working at the mill and another smith, Joshua Greensmith was working at Crowdecote — perhaps from that village (which had a smithy much later) or perhaps from Longnor. No doubt there was a smith in most local communities, shoeing horses and attending to other local needs for iron work.

Officials in 1686 included Thomas Lomas, the Overseer of the Poor for Hartington Upper Quarter and Francis Norton, Constable. The vicar at that time was the Rev. Ralph Sterndale. Both the poor and the church held the right of an annuity levied on 65 acres of Glutton Farm, up-river from Hartington. In that year, 1686, the poor of Middle Quarter received 7d. per acre (£1. 16s. 11d.). The money was paid to the vicar, who may have been the Overseer of the Poor. The poor of Upper Quarter received 4s. 0d. In 1687, the sum of 10s. 10d. was paid '*for repair of the Church at Hartington*' representing 2d. an acre secured on Glutton Farm. An assessment was also made in 1684, for the benefit of the poor, on 'Hyde' Farm amounting to 4s. 3d. This farm is in Mill Lane, Hartington. A year earlier, £40 was allowed '*to ye curate of Edensor*' against the income from Pilsbury Grange. (2).

Glutton Farm seems to have been run by the estate rather than by a tenant and bills survive for various expenses incurred there during the 1680s, including mowing, ditching and fencing in 1684; thatching in 1687 and '*washing, shearing and blooding 30 eas*' (ewes) in 1688. There is little detail of the working activities of individuals from a commercial point of view during the 17th and 18th centuries. However the Hartington Rental of 1778 (3) includes the following reference: '*Thos Arden Butcher for the shop in the Barley Croft from Midsr (Midsummer) 1779*' at £2. 2s. 0d. (two guineas) per year. The Barley Yard was at Crowdecote. The same document records that George Flint, a butcher, paid rent for a house and shop, from Lady Day, 1779 at £3 a year, which points to him probably being the Hartington butcher (before Thomas Fogg). It also records Samuel Wardle renting a *slate delph* on Axe Edge from Lady Day 1779 at a guinea a year. Slates in this context would refer to stone shingles or tiles for roofing. The same year Cornelius Flint became the Manager at Ecton Copper Mine. His salary was £100 a year. In 1762, a George Lees lived at the Bakehouse in Biggin and probably made the village bread, oatcakes etc. (4).

The Manor Courts

Within the manor, civil administration of the area, virtually the parish, was controlled by the manor court system which consisted of two different courts together with a Barmote court controlling mining for lead ore.

The manor court consisted of The Great Court Leet which was held twice a year in April and October. It was used to enforce punishment for encroachment on the Common, nuisances, fraudulent weights and measures etc. This type of court usually served the local hundred, but as the Hartington court had its expenses paid by the Devonshire estate, was it concerned with controlling affairs in the manor? All residents (except peers and clergymen) were expected to do jury service. One court seems to have had jurisdiction over freeholders and another over copyholders. Copyhold was an estate in land. It was not as 'good' as freehold as it was subject to payments to the Lord of the Manor under certain circumstances (see below).

Cases were held before a Judge called the Steward, and Court administration was conducted by the Court Reeve. The local lead miners' court was also heard before a Steward (and still is under the *Derbyshire Mining Customs and Mineral Courts Act, 1852*). Both were held at the Newhaven House Inn. The Steward's feast was a feature of these occasions with 55 'gentlemen's' meals being served at the Steward's table in October 1759, plus 25 others (costing £6. 3s. 0d.). The Court Leet was clearly different from the Court Baron and records for it survive for this from 1659 to the 1720s (5).

The Court Baron consisted of two courts, The Great Court Baron and The Small Court Baron. Its jurisdiction was restricted in 1747 and 1833. By *The Small Debts Act, 1856*, Lords of the Manor could discontinue holding a Court Baron, but the Hartington Court continued until they were wound up in 1925. The Great Court Baron had an Inquest (otherwise known as the jury) of 13 men plus two officers. Its responsibility concerned the management of the Common and met in the spring and autumn. The Small Court Baron had a jury of 12 men who were known as the Homagers, also supported by two officers. It met once a year. This Court had the responsibility for appointing the Headborough, registering changes in ownership or occupation of copyhold land, including upon death of the occupier/owner – '*surrendered by the Rod according to custom*'. It included details of mortgages and entries carry the detail of when they were discharged. The Devonshire estate had a particular interest in recording these changes as they triggered the payment by the incoming party of a 'fine' or 'herriot' – see below – to the estate.

In 1756 it was recorded that the Court met at the Newhaven House Inn. This is the earliest noted premises for a meeting of the Court. The Court appointed four Headboroughs, one for each of the four Quarters (Hartington Upper Quarter, Middle, Town and Nether Quarters). The appointment was for a year the Headborough being the Constable's Deputy. The two court officers were The Steward, as noted above, and his Deputy. In 1762 Godfrey Heathcote, Agent for the Duke, was appointed Steward and Jonathan Lee his Deputy. The four Headboroughs fulfilled certain responsibilities for the Court. Meeting on 8th April 1763, the Great Court Baron decided to '*lay a pain*' of 10s. 0d. upon Francis Chapman, the Headborough of Hartington Middle Quarter '*if he does not set the pound in good repair betwixt now and the 1st May next*'. He was not, however, the pinner or pinder (as described in the court record) for this was Cornelius Haden at the time. Haden was responsible for impounding stray animals in the pound. Getting the annually elected Headborough to take his responsibilities seriously occurred again in October 1763, when Richard Goodwin of

Burbage, near Buxton, was fined 5s. 0d. for not even appearing at the Court to be sworn in.

On occasions there were clearly a lot of attendees at the court. In 1806 Timothy Greenwood, tenant of the Newhaven House Inn, paid for 307 dinners at 6d each *'being money collected from the persons who dined at the Newhaven Court for two years to Lady Day 1806, £7. 13s. 6d.'* (6). If this was good business for the owner, he had a good night in 1811 for which he put in a bill for *'Ale etc. given to the Inhabitants of Hartington on the Marquis of Hartington coming of Age £22. 19s. 5d'*. It was after all an event celebrated across the estates without regard to the cost. A few months later they would have been reflecting on the passing of the 5th Duke. Some tenants would no doubt recall that it was better than when the Marquis had been born; the estate having forked out £5. 5s. 0d. on that occasion. (7). See more on this on p. 43. Herriots, crist and other charges were levied by the estate especially, possibly exclusively, on the copyholders. They were receipts of unknown date of collection. This was levied upon events which happened from time to time:

> *'Of Widdow Wooddis for a Christ* (sic) *on ye death of husb[and] £ 0. 5s. 0d;*
> *Fine – Bennett Higton on a surrender for land in Biggin   £35.0s. 0d.'*

Both these were in 1785 and occurred upon the change of occupation. They could be quite onerous as Bennett Higton experienced. His payment was approaching two years' wages for a labourer. Although originally for goods and chattels, they were often commuted to a cash payment.

Detail of how Fines and Herriotts were assessed are also revealed in a surviving document (8):

'The Fines on Admittance of the Copyholders are uncertain, but it is usual on the Admission to take on a death about 1 year and a halfs [sic] Rack Rent. And on a purchase one year and a quarter Rack Rent. But the same must be varied taking sometimes more and sometimes less. Seldom twice alike so as to continue the Custom – And note that your fine may arise up to, but must not exceed, two years' Rack Rent. An [sic] Herriott is payable upon the death of every Copyhold Tenant vist. His best Good Quick or Dead. But this is Commonly compounded at about £3. 10s. 0d. sometimes more, sometimes less, sometimes twice alike; and to keep up the right of demanding the Herriott, the Herriott itself must sometimes be taken and a composition not always accepted'. These charges were still current in 1798 (9).

One of the largest Herriotts was charged on the death of Thomas Fletcher in 1733. By inference it was payable by Robert Bateman, and 10s. 0d. was paid for someone going to Uttoxeter to serve the charge. Later that year Bateman handed over a brown Bay Mare (no doubt with some displeasure) in lieu of the charge – here was a case of the *'Herriott itself being taken instead of a composition'* i.e. cash – see above. The mare was sent to the Chatsworth stables. (10). As if this was not enough, in 1742 a fine was levied on his estate of a further £92. 13s. 4d. – a huge sum. Bateman may have been from Hartington Hall and if so may well have had quite a large holding of land.

In August 1757 a tenant (Mr. Craddock) refused to pay the fine on his admittance to his farm, which had land in both Hartington and Biggin. The estate decided to test the issue in Derby Court. The case was found for the estate. Despite, the fact that Craddock had not taken up his occupation, the farm was not taken from him. The estate seldom insisted on retribution. Godfrey Heathcote undertook a survey of all the Duke's farms in Hartington as a result of this case *'and make new contracts with the occupiers'*.

Hartington School, Church Street, dated 1756

The Barmote Court

The other court, the Barmote Court, concerned lead mining. Each year a jury of 24 men (amended to 12 under *The Derbyshire Mining Customs and Mineral Courts Act, 1852*) was appointed to hear grievances between miner and miner, or between the Duke (the Lord of the Soil in court parlance) and miner. It used to meet in the spring and autumn. This court still meets, although at Chatsworth now, only each autumn. It is heard jointly with the court for the mining liberties of Ashford, Peak Forest and Tideswell. The appointment of the jury is made annually, although it is now rare for disputes to be heard. Details of mining royalties received are also recorded.

Ale, cheese, bread and butter is dispensed prior to the sitting of the court. After the transaction of the business, a meal is taken and clay pipes are laid on the table for each diner. Regrettably the recent smoking ban also affects one of the oldest courts of the realm. The court is held by the Steward (Mr. Michael Cockerton) assisted by the Barmaster (Mr. Edward Tennant). Other officials are the Deputy Barmaster or Bailiff (David Mort). The jury has a Foreman, elected by the jury. After the end of the court's business, the process is repeated for

Eyam and Stoney Middleton Liberties (also where the Duke is the Lord of the Soil) plus the court hearing for the Liberties of Calver, Hassop and Roland, where the Lord of the Soil is Mr. Henry Stephenson (referred to at the Court as being a *Gentleman*). Several records of the Hartington court survive from the 1720s and it is clear that the court procedure then was little different from today. The Court is not open to the members of the public as is the Wirksworth Court for the Soke and Wapentake of Wirksworth, which meets every April. The Barmote Courts are different from other Courts of the realm in that the jury is elected for at least a year and then until a new jury is elected.

Perhaps the oldest surviving record of the Great Barmote Court at Hartington dates from 29th July 1650. The Lord of the Manor was quoted as being Henry Marten. This document importantly states that the jury said on oath that the *'same customs of the myne and tyme out of mind have been used within the [?] of Hartington as have been used within ye Hundred of High Peak … and are [? returned] in an Inquisition taken the fifth day of September in ye two and fortieth yeare of ye late Queen Elizabeth'* [the date being 1600]. (11).

Taxes and Other Charges

Taxes, as distinct from manor fees and other charges, were also collected by the estate. An account of 1679 survives for 17 months tax collected for the building of *'thirty ships of warr'*. It was probably collected from just tenants of the demesne lands (the former abbey lands) of the manor, for the following were the only ones in the manor who were taxed:

Pilsbury Grange –	Mr. Bateman	£4. 3s. 4d.
	Thomas Rodgers	£4. 11s. 5 ¾d
Cronxton Grange	Edward Edensor	£1. 5s. 6d.
	John Needham	£1. 5s. 6d.
	Thomas Frogget	£0. 2s. 10.
Callinglow	John & George Brunt	£0. 18s. 10¾d

If paying for battleships was not enough, taxes were being levied for disbanding the Army: *'for halfe of ye 18 months tax for disbanding ye Army ended at Lady Day 1680, the summ of ten shillings …to his majesty'*. (12). Another unusual charge, in 1685, was *'By Militia Charges at ye Rebellion in ye west £23. 11s. 9d'*. It was paid for by the estate on this occasion. *Ye Rebellion* was that of the Duke of Monmouth, the son of Charles II, who rose against James II following the death of his father.

At the beginning of the 18th century, the Duke was paying a contribution of 50% of Parliamentary taxes on behalf of the tenants of Hartington, Pilsbury, Cronxton and Buxton House (the Old Hall). He paid 100% of the tax for those who leased the various tithes (not in Hartington parish, but in others nearby) and which were also accounted for in the Hartington manor collection. These ex-gratia payments were still being paid in 1718. (13). Nearly 100 years later, in 1806 a year's property tax allowance on the four Quarters amounted to almost £204 (14).

In addition to these national taxes as now, there was a system of local taxation. Rates were introduced by the *Statute of Elizabeth, 1601*, and the Headborough had, amongst other responsibilities, the job of maintaining the highways and levying an assessment on parishioners to provide the funds, although poor people were exempt. He also doled out ex-gratia payments to poor people passing through the parish (probably as a condition that they moved on, rather than become a further burden on his accounts). Featherstone reveals examples of this at Biggin, although his examples from the 1820s include a more urgent need for the persons concerned to move on: *'Gave a distressed man and his wife ill of the typhus fever'* and *'Paid 12 Americans some had typhus fever'*. (15) See also p31 for further detail on poor relief.

Controlling the Common

Beyond the cultivated furlong strips of the three village fields at Hartington, together with the land already enclosed as fields (chiefly enclosed prior to the 17th century) was the common land and the waste. All freeholders and copyholders had rights of common upon the 'common land and wastes'. The rights included pasture of animals, taking fuel (peat) and stone for personal use. Upon Inclosure, all of them were entitled to a portion of the Common. Others certainly kept a cow (at least) there, so these rights may have extended to all parishioners, but only landowners were entitled to an allotment of land upon inclosure. It was certainly an administrative function of the manor court. A list of 'rules' controlling commoners' rights on the common does survive and this was annually confirmed by the Court Baron.

The penalty for putting more sheep on the common than allowed incurred a fine of 40s. per score (20) animals. For horses or mares, the fine was 40s. 0d. per pair. There was a similar fine for putting horses or mares which were scabbed on the common. Tups or rigills had to be removed from the common by 1st September or risk a fine of 2s. 6d. per animal. For taking down the wall of the well at Heathcote Mere, or *'defiling the water in any manner'*, the fine was 2s. 6d. For taking heath or turf [for fuel] out of the jurisdiction of the manor meant a fine of 5s. 0d. per load. Enforcement of these and other decisions was the responsibility of the court.

In April 1746 Mrs. Brock was warned that if unworked shafts at the Goyt Head, Thatch Marsh and Ravens Collieries (on Axe Edge) were not filled up or fenced by 20th May (six weeks thereafter), a fine of 10s. 0d. would be levied. Another example concerned the commoners with land fronting Mill Lane, Hartington. Repairs to the *'long fence'* on the Mill Lane side had to be made good before 1st June 1746 or the commoners would face a fine of 2s. 6d. a rood length. This requirement was to crop up several times over the next couple of decades. One suspects that putting more sheep on the common might be a regular complaint, probably resolved by a warning. However in 1749 the court found it necessary to formally warn George Webster that he had 20 days to remove his flock from *'common land called Elack Low'* in the Nether Quarter or face a fine of £10. This indicates that he had some 100 animals grazing illegally on the common (16).

By 1751 other rules concerning the use of the common had been determined: *'[We] amerce John Hanson ten shillings foe breaking the pound and the same sum upon any other person that shall do the same'*. Anyone cutting fern before Michaelmas Day was amerced 10s. 0d. Abuse of any standing pools of water by unlawful means attracted a fine of 20s. 0d. Taking ducks and geese to Heathcote Mere was an example of this. Incroachment on the common resulted in a fine of £2, but as is shown elsewhere enforcement of this appears to have been weak.

Enforcing the repair of fences (presumably following representation) was a regular feature of the court proceedings, with a fine of 2s. 6d. if the work was not done. The system of fines was used to react to problems as and when they arose. In 1760, the Great Court Baron realised that the problem of the water being polluted continued and not through the activities of ducks and geese. Parents were warned that if they *'suffer or connive at their children guilty of such an offence'* i.e. fouling the water, the parents would be fined 10s. 0d. – and not just at Heathcote Mere either, the fine would apply to all springs or pools of water within the manor. It was quite a lot of money for an innocent child at play, but then no one wanted muddy water in the kitchen.

An even bigger fine was imposed in 1763 on anybody found pulling down the wall inclosing one of the wells on the common at Caskinlow (just under a mile due north of the later Hartington station). There was another good reason to ensure that children behaved on the common. In 1760 parishioners were warned that chasing sheep would invoke a fine of 10s. 0d. The same applied to adults too, and presumably their dogs. (17). Control of ducks, geese and even children highlight aspects of an ordered community life enforced by the court. It is a pity that the full picture of this is not clearer. One of the more amusing controls concerned *'swine rambling about'* which resulted in a fine of 2s. 6d. (18).

One of the biggest fines was £40 on Henry Bowman of One Ash Grange in 1757. He was fined for keeping sheep on Hartington Common. Although a tenant of the Devonshire's estate he clearly must have known what he was up to. However he, like everyone else, must have exploited an apparent loophole in that you received a warning first, which could give approximately a six months useage since the previous court session and a certain number of days to comply with an order.

All the above instances relate to the day to day use of the common, but occasionally the court deliberated upon events of a different nature. In 1765 for instance, a Mr. Davenport of Ashbourne was in the parish when his horse appears to have collapsed and died. Regrettably for him, he left it where it was, on the highway, and was fined by the court 5s. 0d. *'for letting a dead horse lye (sic) on the highway within the manor'*. These customs and procedure would have continued from one generation to the next. Their observance would have been the practice during the time John Heaton was the Agent. In 1816 he was called upon by miners at Tideswell to re-establish the Barmote Court there, 'according to ancient practice', which he duly agreed to. How long it had been in abeyance was not stated.

The Rise of a Working Middle Class

The eighteenth century saw the rise of both the Agrarian and Industrial Revolutions. Both increased employment, output increased wealth, especially for the land-owning aristocrat. Rental income increased dramatically and those with the resources to capitalise on this, such as the Duke of Devonshire, did so and saw rents increasing, particularly in the late years of the century.

It was in their interests to promote good farming practice, larger farms and land improvement through liming and better drainage. As a result, good tenant farmers became part of a strategy for estate revenue growth. With that, they in turn became wealthier, creating a wealth gap between themselves and those they employed. This in a lot of cases created a middle class who yearned to experience and be recognised as living above the salt.

Farey, writing in 1815, quotes Timothy Greenwood of Newhaven House Inn (who farmed

Dig Meer, now called the Duck Pond, Hartington   Hartington village stores, built in 1836

adjacent lands) and Joseph Gould of Pilsbury on wage rates, farming practice etc. Both must have been farmers with some status to have been interviewed about their practices. In fact both men appear in a list by Farey of the largest farms in Derbyshire (the only ones in the parish). Timothy Greenwood had a holding of c. 600 acres, but Joseph Gould's acreage isn't given (19). Greenwood also farmed Hand Dale Farm, situated on the B5054 below Hartington Station. In the Inclosure Award, the estate received (having sought it) 200 acres adjacent to the Inn to help create the farm.

In some instances, further advancement came from purchasing land as well as renting it. The Joseph Gould mentioned above was the son of William Gould. Both were initially estate rent collectors. William also acted as agent for the Duke of Portland who had married the 5th Duke of Devonshire's sister. He also rented one of the two farms at Pilsbury Grange and in 1786 bought Pool Hall Farm at Hartington. This is strange as the Duke also bought it. Gould may have bought a leasehold interest or perhaps because there are two properties – Pool Hall and Moat Hall side by side – they each had one of these farms.

Gould also owned Low End Farm between Hulme End and Sheen, with land running down towards the River Manifold.

Detailed below is comment on the rise of a professional class exemplified by Philip Heacock (see p. 24). Post-inclosure, larger, more profitable farms saw the rise of a more professional farmer such as Joseph Gould.. Using new technology on his farm and an enlarged acreage from former common lands, Farey details Gould's farming machinery and notes that he was also a Commissioner for Inclosure. From details of his farming activities it is clear that Gould knew and worked his farm using best practice for which he had become respected.

An example of this related to the method used to convert heathland to agricultural land. Timothy Greenwood sowed crops after ploughing the land once, but Joseph Gould ploughed and harrowed the heathland twice before sowing. He (Gould) was also very successful in draining land at Pilsbury and Low End Farm, laying dry some wells, which had to be sunk deeper (20). He improved Pool Hall Farm and also started planting trees on the poorer land (see also p. 67). On purchase, it was yielding only 2.5% and he was probably looking for an increase in capital and rental income from his investment. The demand for land from men like William Gould also pushed up demand generally and thereby land values. This depressed the return and improvements (to justify a rental increase) became important. Capital value increases also dragged up the return required to be paid and therefore the profit required by the farmer. However this was being met by a growth in the population, urban expansion and an increase in the cost of food.

Not only did estate rental income start to increase nationally in the last half of the eighteenth century, but in the quarter of a century from 1790 – 1815, the end of the Napoleonic War, rents doubled (21). In 1790 the Hartington rental was £2,718 p.a. In 1817 it was £6,800 p.a., although income from farm and other purchases, such as the Hartington Inclosure, needed to be allowed for. Unfortunately, the breakdown is not known of the 1817 rental, but the growth and its implications are clear nationally: It was bank-rolling significant development in industrial Britain. (22)

Revenues from land also improved the wellbeing of the country parson who relied on the return from the glebe lands and tithes as well as the Easter plate. In 1793 the Hartington vicar (23) took on the extra job of teaching ten poor children at the village charity school, to read and write for which he was paid £5 p.a. His successor in 1815, the Rev. William Davison, M.A., chose not to do this extra chore. However he had the benefit of 338 acres of glebe land owing to the loss of tithe income on the Hartington Inclosure and more certain revenue as a result of it being rented out to the Duke.

The Inclosure had provided an opening for William Fidler, farming as an estate tenant at Biggin Grange, bought by the estate in the 1750s. He persuaded John Heaton to let him have the contract for the road making and wall building (called fencing) resulting from the carve-up of the common. It cost thousands of pounds and must have made good money for him. Advancement did not always come by fair means either. Henry Bowman of One Ash Grange near Youlgrave, was fined £40 for putting sheep on Hartington Common as mentioned above. Knowing what you could get away with moved interests forward.

The landed class invested in industrial activity but not at the expense of getting their hands dirty. Massive mining success for the Duke at Ecton and the Pagets at Mona Mine at Parys Mountain on Anglesey, for instance, saw investment in mining shares unless you were lucky enough to draw a royalty from the mines on your own land at the expense of others. Not many had sufficient investments like the Duke to merit running coal mines to support other industrial concerns on the estate – the Kingsley coal mine (Hazles Cross Colliery) in N. Staffordshire provided coal for the Whiston and Ecton copper smelters, plus two mine brickworks while the Axe Edge Collieries aided the lime production at Grin Hill, Buxton. The Duke also held shares in many local turnpike trusts. Estate accounts reveal that by the early 19th century these investments totalled nearly £20,000 and this excluded canal shares e.g. in the Chesterfield Canal.

The investments in turnpikes were not high earners, indeed several were very slow in issuing the annual dividend (around 3%). However for a large estate the value of good communications clearly brought indirect benefits. This was especially true in the case of the royalty on limestone taken by the Peak Forest Canal Company from Peak Dale Quarry. In the period 1825 – 32 the canal tramway saw the removal of 601,740 tons of lime and road stone. It yielded a royalty of £2,562 to the Duke. (24).

There was however an opening for many to join the beginnings of the professional class acting as managers for aristocratic industrial investment or in other industrial activity (both with and without outside capital investment). In 1760, when the Duke took over Ecton Mine, castings had to be ordered from Walkers of Rotherham, but soon iron works and forges were opening for business much nearer the mine, satisfying increasing demand and using improved roads.

The Hurts of Alderwasley Hall near Wirksworth established a nearby iron forge (Alderwasley Forge) in the Derwent Valley north of Belper, Derbyshire. In turn, it was managed for them by the Wilkinsons of Chesterfield, who also supplied Ecton with gunpowder and through their bank, the cash the mine needed to pay a host of suppliers. Other local iron works supplying the mine were at Ashbourne and nearby Mayfield (run by Robert Longden and the Bassetts respectively); the Pethills iron works near Winkhill on the Ashbourne – Leek road; plus iron workers at Hathersage and nearby Abney, making sieves (riddles) used on the ore dressing floors.

On the Devonshire estate were several managers, initially the agent (men with a legal background, e.g. Godfrey Heathcote, succeeded by John Heaton) and the several rent collectors who also oversaw estate expense in their collection area and managers of particular concerns. The most important of these was Cornelius Flint who lived in Hartington and ran the Ecton Mine. Flint was responsible for exploiting the ore and smelting it. He was also responsible for employing c. 500-700 employees and running two brickworks, a coke works, a clay pit, stone quarries (for making sand as well as producing stone), two collieries (Kingsley and Foxt Wood), ore transportation to the smelter via a trans-shipment yard, paying wages and suppliers etc. He also was responsible for what may have been the deepest mine in the country (? anywhere), handling new technology (the first Boulton & Watt winding engine with its newly introduced sun and planet gearing in the Midlands and fourth in all) as well as rent collection in adjacent Staffordshire villages. His salary was £148 per annum from 1782 (initially £100).

Philip Heacock was the first of the estate professional managers and was appointed by the Duke in 1805. He lived at No. 1, The Square, Buxton, estate owned up-market apartments and lodging houses adjacent to The Hall Inn. He ran the Buxton estate and developments there, later taking over the Hartington rental too. In 1818 the Duke appointed John Taylor as his mineral agent for his various estates, notably Derbyshire and Yorkshire Dales. It was Taylor who advised the Duke to withdraw from running Ecton Mine and its associated smelter at Whiston and coal mine at Kingsley, all in North Staffordshire. Here was another example of the appointment of a professional 'agent' to oversee specialised investments. Taylor had been the agent at Wheal Friendship, one of the largest copper mines in Devon, in 1798. In 1813, he became the agent of the mines around Halkyn mountain in Flintshire for Lord Grosvenor. Lees–Milne in *The Batchelor Duke*, p 18, states that the age of the professional land agent came after the death of the 5th Duke, and he is not far out. However it would appear that the date may be moved back somewhat. Even as far as the appointment of Cornelius Flint (locally at least) in 1779, if the term *land* agent can be interpreted a little wider.

Other people willing to chance their arm at advancement through industrial activity were the Brocks and Dickenson families at the two lime works on Grin Hill. They both also controlled coalmines supplying the lime kilns (eventually purchased by the Duke). Of course there would have been a growing number of others too.

Beyond the Devonshire estate there were people such as Thomas Cantrell who opened a textile mill in Hartington's village square in c. 1777. Over in the Staffordshire Moorlands were the Gilbert bothers, Thomas and John, of Cotton Hall, who became land agents to the aristocracy. John was employed by the Duke of Bridgwater and had the idea of the Bridgwater Canal from the Duke's coal mines at Worsley to Manchester. They also speculated in various lead and copper mines (including one on Ecton Hill no less). Another copper mine in that area was the Mixon Mine south-west of Ecton, run by the Sneyd family of Basford Hall near Leek. Minor gentry, they were adept at getting involved in loss-making investments from Mixon Mine; the copper mine on Snowdon (where the main level is still called Sneyd Level); to the worst financial disaster in a Derbyshire lead mine at High Rake, Hucklow.

The burgeoning cotton textile industry gave opportunities to would-be entrepreneurs, although polarisation of the industry in Lancashire nearer to the sea and a coalfield was the ultimate fate and decline of many mills away from there (or Yorkshire in the case of wool). Local short-lived mills included Hartington, Brund Mill near Sheen, west of Hartington, Glutton on the River Dove, and Warslow just over the Staffordshire border. Clearly the good farm tenant and the professional managers were a less risky route to financial success and social advancement for those who cared or craved for it. This was especially so when the employer had a fine and stable financial background.

Hartington also had a long established family, initially yeoman farmers, who lived at Hartington Hall, building the south range and the initial side wings in 1611. This was the Bateman family. They did well out of the Inclosure Award increasing their land holding by 1,289 acres. It roughly cost them £1 per acre. Although the hall was put up for sale in the 1850s with some 3,500 acres, it remained in the family until 1948, when the house and 100 acres was sold for £10,000 to the Youth Hostels Association (who still own it). The hall had been rented by the YHA since 1934 and prior to that had been a hotel run by a Mr. Wardle in the late Victorian period. In the late 18th century, the owner, Sir Hugh Bateman, lived in Derby and the hall was occupied by the estate manager, William Bowman.

In the late 1850s after the attempted sale, there was a significant expansion, initially of the west and east wings plus a new range of farm buildings at the rear. This may well have been as a result of family occupation, but in the previous century, those creating an improved strata of local society seem to have done so without the Batemans being a part of it. In some areas, and this certainly included the northern part of Hartington parish, the land was too poor for there to be any landed estates or reasonably profitable agricultural holdings capable of supporting a resident gentleman farmer. In 1779, for instance, R. Weston wrote to Sir William Lee, Bt., of Hartwell, Bucks, having looked at the Grindon and Throwley Hall Estates near to the River Manifold, advising that the area was 'thin of people, especially gentlemen'. (25). This reflected low investment values, absenteeism, or both.

For social life, the Bakewell Hounds were in existence in 1757 plus the Chesterfield races by 1758. It is known that even some of the Ecton miners went off to Chesterfield Fair for a couple of days and that possibly might have included the races.

Even where it was not possible for a family to purchase a farm, a small area of land brought increased social status as well as the opportunity to feed the family and raise income from any surplus such as cheese, butter, eggs, vegetables etc. This was enhanced if rights of common permitted grazing etc. on common land in addition. It was also why pressure on the common was created by encroachment, especially if a relaxed view was taken of it. This did not happen in Hartington where records of encroachment were kept. In Grindon, south-west of Hartington, the whole of the common was encroached upon without resistance by the Lord of the Manor. No Inclosure Award was needed as a result. (26).

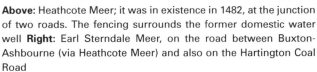

Above: Heathcote Meer; it was in existence in 1482, at the junction of two roads. The fencing surrounds the former domestic water well **Right:** Earl Sterndale Meer, on the road between Buxton-Ashbourne (via Heathcote Meer) and also on the Hartington Coal Road

Social Life

So very little survives of the nature of social life available in the Hartington area. William Gould's diary reveals that his social life chiefly revolved around house visits, often with an overnight stop. However the developments in Buxton must have brought a demand for events to encourage guests to choose Buxton as the resort town to visit although many people went for the 'cure'.

By the early years of the 19th century, a variety of opportunities for social activity had been established, no doubt available to local people with the money to participate. A Ballroom and Card Room existed at the Assembly Room at The Crescent. These were separate from the three hotels for they produced an annual income recorded in the estate accounts. Performances at The Theatre, leased to Williams and Martin, offered an alternative. This had opened at least by October 1796 when it was leased for 17 years having been purchased by the estate from a Mr. Brocklehurst. The Buxton Band seems to have been established in 1819. Well provided with instruments, each player having a uniform and cap, they gave performances at The Crescent, where a bandstand was initially erected. They must have been proficient; they played at Chatsworth for a Bow Group meeting in 1823. Presumably they also played on the quaintly termed weekly dress and undress (formal and informal) dance nights at the Assembly Room.

For the more adventurous, the Buxton Hounds had been established by 1815 under John Oakes, the Huntsman. The Buxton Races provided more excitement and the Duke of Devonshire provided a 50 guineas (£52. 10s. 0d) plate in 1821. Read Denham was its first winning owner. For those able to afford it, the provision of the hot baths in 1818 would have made *'taking the waters'* a more agreeable experience. There was a distinct policy of segregating the *'Buxton Experience'* for those who could pay, from those that could not. Poor people were not encouraged in the (later) Pavilion Gardens and presumably the earlier Serpentine Gardens, which snaked up the side of the River Wye, where recuperating patients could stroll. Separate baths existed behind The Crescent (the building still survives) for those of limited means.

A visitor to the bath in the early 1720 was Daniel Defoe. He found the bath very pleasant so much so that he could hardly be persuaded to leave it. The Hall Inn was the one place

26

offering a *'convenient lodging'* at 1s. 0d. per person. There were some other houses in the village which took in lodgers *'on occasion'*, but the facilities offered were not comparable to the Hall Inn, and of course, were not situated next to the bath. Defoe seems to have enjoyed his stay in Buxton and favourably compared it with Bath, about which he made some rather derogatory comments! (27). Even the Duchess of Devonshire referred to Bath as *'the most scandalous place in England'* in a letter of 6th January 1784 and for that matter also found Cheltenham Spa *'disagreeable'* in c.1787 (28).

Perhaps the town's Candlemass Fair (2nd February) would have provided some fun for local people. If Ecton miners went as far away as Chesterfield Fair and Ashbourne people walked to Tissington for the annual well dressing ceremony, a walk from Hartington up the river, or up the Coal Road via High Needham, to Buxton to reach the Fair would have not received a second thought. The estate paid for advertising the Fair in 1819.

The Rise of the Labouring Class

Until the mid-eighteenth century most of the parish would have only found temporary work. Most would try and grow enough to live on and to support a family. The larger farms no doubt had a need for a few labourers, but presumably much of that would have centred around the hay and any cereal crops.

The discovery of a major ore deposit at Ecton Copper Mine in c. 1750 would have found a need for more miners and ore dressers plus labourers: the wagon pushers in the mine, men on the surface with sledge hammers breaking down rock and ore etc. Even so, initially they would be feew in number. As output increased, focused on the termination of the lease in 1760, more workers would have been set on. It would have been these people that formed the original workforce when the Duke took over.

By 1780 some 500 people were employed with at least 350 at the mine and 150 at the Whiston smelter and the two collieries, Kingsley and Foxt Wood, both near to Whiston. For many of the workers, the concept of regular, weekly work at set hours per day would be entirely new. There would have been few skilled workers available and many would have to have been trained at the mine. There were small concentrations of workers in employment in the area, such as the Axe Edge Collieries and the seasonal employment at Grin Hill, Buxton, where a few men found work for 30 weeks a year at the lime kilns.

However, old habits die hard and the Duke was a benign employer. A close look at the dressing floor wage accounts shows that girls employed there often worked only about two weeks in four. Whether this was because they lacked the manual capacity or were needed at home is not clear. Regular work and pay would see improvements to the lives of many families although the combined wage of a man and wife might only be 2s. 0d. to 2s. 6d. per day for a 6-day week. (i.e. 12s. 0d. (60p.) to 15s. 0d. (75p.) per week.

Skilled miners earned more, as did the craftsmen, such as the carpenter or blacksmith. The miners (ie. the underground workers) fell into one of two main categories – labourers and contract workers plus copers. The contractors were paid by the fathom (6ft/2m.) e.g. for driving a level a set distance. Others were paid for the ore tonnage extracted, often working in a recognised group or company and known as copers. Initially, absenteeism after the pay day was a problem. This was not helped when the leader of a copers group (who received the payment for them all), dispensed it in a local ale house.

The women worked on the dressing floor, sitting in a building at a table beating the ore down to the size of a nutmeg with flat hammers and a long handle. They and the labourers worked a 10-hour day and then had to (presumably) walk home, unless someone ran a horse and cart as a kind of bus. For most of them, home was in one of the neighbouring villages, which (other than Warslow) was at least an hour away. There is some evidence to suggest that the miners worked a 6-hour day, but their work was more laborious and energy-sapping, let alone having to get to their work which could be in excess of a descent/ascent of some 600 ft./183 m. or more, and in their own time. Girls scurried around, separating ore into three different types of quality, topping up the tables and presumably carrying away the iridescent yellow, brass-coloured nutmegs. Boys pushed wagons underground and worked bellows delivering air to blind headings etc.

There were eight pay days a year; the concept of a weekly wage did not exist at the mine. Suppliers were also paid at the same time and it was usual to expect them to attend the mine in order to receive payment. This was usually accompanied for the suppliers by bread and ale, or even rum. For more detail on the mine, see chapter 6. Elsewhere, regular work, other than in agriculture was not so prevalent. The massive job of building all the stone walls following the inclosure (never enclosure) of the common was entrusted to William Fidler of Biggin Grange who had numerous gangs extracting stone and doing the building work.

Several people found regular employment doing specific work in a self-employed capacity. The jaggermen, running the mule trains loaded with ore to the smelter, bringing coal as back carriage were kept busy six days a week like everyone else (except the 7-day working pump men). There were carters such as William Mellor of West Side Mill (situated adjacent to the mine) who fetched clay and bricks from Newhaven and also supplies from further afield as occasion demanded. Other suppliers in the district made candles (10,000 p.a. were used), ropes, spades, hammers, sieves, provided oil and domestic supplies to the mine house etc. It was rare to find a self-employed woman, but Ann Newtown supplied candles from Ashbourne. Another woman, Frances Bassett, ran the Hulme End tollhouse. It still exists, a small stone-built building adjacent to the bridge over the River Manifold on the Hartington-Warslow road, west of Hartington. Mine invoices from both women survive in the Chatsworth records.

The Poor

For the labouring class, life did not hold a lot of surprises or prospects. There were few hills, let alone mountains, to climb or prospects to aspire to. In fact there was a singular, more immediate prospect – the need to even meet a level of income that would provide subsistence and support for life itself. There was so much that could unbalance the equilibrium: bad summers, bad winters, too wet, too dry and that was only the effect of the weather. Rising inflation, especially in times of war, plus other economic pressures probably rose above those most affected by it. The main symptom – the price of bread – had a more direct effect.

In 1764, when the 5th Duke succeeded to his title, the average price of wheat was 33s. 3d. a quarter (28lb). The actual price in 1800 was 142s. 10d. (over four times dearer) and a 4lb loaf in London cost 1s. 3 ¼d. (in 1803, it was down to 8 ½d.). Although war with France had created inflation, the rise in agricultural prices was even higher. Between 1773 and 1800, the price of oats had quadrupled and that of hay, it was estimated, had trebled. It was not just production shortages, for many farmers made matters worse by withholding what supplies existed to drive up the price, as if the prosperity of inflation was not enough. (29)

It seems safe to presume that the empty or part-empty stomachs recorded elsewhere during this period must have been well-known in Derbyshire, now remembered by the abstract accounts recording payments to various estate villages in the Chatsworth account book etc. Porter (30) records that the labouring class needed c. £30 p.a. to live on towards the end of the 18th Century. This equates to around 16s. 0d. per week. A male labourer at the Duke's nearby Ecton Copper Mine earned 6s. 0d. per week, twice that of a woman on the dressing floor. It was nowhere near enough to live on, yet the mine demanded attendance for ten hours a day, six days a week. It needed the wage of an adult son or two adult daughters to fill the table, to maintain body and soul. The alternative was to hope that Poor Relief made up the difference (it seems it seldom did) or take a second job. Some women chose the latter, spinning or weaving outwork from the new textile mills. Unfortunately, Hartington was some distance from such places on the rivers to the east or from Leek and Macclesfield. The factories at Hartington and Glutton would no doubt have provided some work but whether they had much impact, we have no idea today. The Brund mill west of Hartington opened to make use of the available labour from Ecton after the redundancies there and would have possibly provided a reservoir of outwork conveniently near to hand after it opened in 1790.

Presumably those fortunate to own a cow or a few goats could graze them on the Common; where they could also exercise the right of turbary – to carry peat away for fuel (so long as they could exercise right of common). A cow or goats meant not only milk, but cheese and butter for the table or market. A woman in the 19th Century used to walk from nearby Back Ecton to Leek every Wednesday to sell her butter at the Butter Market and then buy her groceries. The daily use of the Common – taken for granted for centuries – was to end in the first decade of the 19th Century as the land was inclosed. Inclosure brought short-term (walling, ditching etc.) and long-term employment (from larger and more profitable farm holdings) but this helped agricultural labourers (although there was less work in winter); it did not provide grazing for the cottager's cow or forage in winter. The Hartington hiring statutes fair for labourers etc seeking work was on the Wednesday before Christmas Day.

The loss of the labour pool at Ecton Mine in 1790 was not replaced by other mines in the area, although some work was found at the Axe Edge coalmines. The reality was that much of the lead mining activity in Derbyshire was passing its peak. Other mines in the parish (other than coal) were small and employed relatively few. Quarrying was beginning to take a hold but the basic problem was that the cost of food was outstripping labour rates. There needed to be a structural change to national food production, labour rates and more work for a growing pool of labour. The inhabitants of Hartington and other rural parishes of Derbyshire suffered until the national economy adjusted itself. This occurred in the early 19th Century, at least so far as wages were concerned (for eg. the wage for labourers at Ecton Mine had risen to 2 shillings (10p) per day). Even then, migration to industrial towns was often the only option available. Large industrial units in rural Derbyshire and North Staffordshire did exist, but there were few of them and even fewer near the Hartington parish. The full impact of this migration in the area has not been fully studied as yet.

Encroachment on the Common

One way of improving one's lot through self help was by taking land for one's own use from the Common. Incorporating land from the adjacent manor holding seemed to happen with impunity, which is not to suggest that it was all surreptitious. A list of encroachments of 1684 shows that a lot of people were doing it and the manor was keeping a close eye on it

Hartington Hall, built in 1611 and one of the finest yeoman farmer's houses in the county

— charging for each one. Presumably this is why the plan and survey of 1614 were made and ultimately covered its cost by the charges made. Although some were for 3 acres (and one for 4 acres) in extent, most were under two acres. Some were just extensions to gardens etc.

Regrettably, most encroachments are not described. One that is probably sums up most — Robert Bateman was charged 6d. for the following at Biggin: 'a *Garden Cote, Wainhouse* (wagon shed) *and a piece at his Paddock end*' (for half a year). Although assessed, many were unpaid and carried forward for years in some cases. Enforcement through the Manor Court does not appear to have been estate policy, probably restricted by cases of impoverishment.

In 1684 the charge was:

Over Quarter	£ 3. 12s. 3d.
Middle Quarter	£ 2. 2s. 0d.
Hartington	£ 2. 5s. 3d.
Nether Quarter	£ 1. 3s. 2d.
Biggin	£ 2. 14s. 8 1/2d
	£11. 17s. 4 11/2d = £23. 14s. 9d. for the year

Although impoverishment seems to have been sympathetically considered on Devonshire estates (see below), this was not always the case. An '*Account of goods taken for rent that was John Melors wish held parte of Hide Farme*' highlights this. The document is undated, but filed with documents dating from 1687. Items included in the distraint included Hay; strawe (sic); 40 pecks of meal; 3 cows (£9. 15s. 0d.); 2 horses (£2. 10s. 0d. & £2. 15s. 0d.); 3 sterks [stirks] (£5). The total came to £39. 14s. 4d. and the beasts were driven to Ashbourne Fair to be sold. (31). Distraint against one of the main tenants, William Harrison, in 1685, was more serious. A year's rent was £282 and the total expected by distraint was £256. 11s. 4d., showing a sizeable shortfall. Mr. Harrison is not listed in the list of tenants of 1685, but the sub-tenants of his holding based on the Glutton Farm lease are. Distraint at these farms may have been necessary because part of the rent went to poor relief (see below).

Poor Administration

The parish had an Overseer for the Poor, who collected income raised from landed property covenanted to the parish by benefactors. Land at Hide Farm at Hartington and at Glutton Farm was so encumbered as early as 1684. In that year, payment was made to the Rev. Ralph Sterndale *Oversee for ye Poor* of 10s. 0d. and an amount to Ralph Woodis *'for ye poor in Hartington'*, amounting to 2s. 0d. with an additional sum for the latter of 4s.3d raised on Hide Farm (32).

In 1687 circumstances appear to have been altered for 2d. per acre on 65 acres of Glutton Farm was paid for the repair of Hartington Church, whilst 4d. per acre was paid on 65 acres *'for receipt of the poore'* and was received by the Assessor, then John Nott [?]. The position of Assessor was an annual appointment, the appointee changing each year. Support for the poor can be traced back to at least 1649 for a trust existed which dated from the time of Charles I. The income from a parcel of land at Heathcote was given to the poor of Hartington and 18 new trustees were appointed in 1784 (33).

Rent increases clearly would have an affect on the poorer tenants and also any land tax which may have been due from them. The Duke paid the land tax (or a portion) for some tenants but it is not clear if this was for poor relief. In August 1757 following nearly a year of high food prices, there were food shortages and much discontent. This caused considerable unrest at least in the Bakewell and Crich areas, made more difficult by the demands of the new Militia Act on local men. A hungry mob marched from Bakewell to Chatsworth, but their fury was vented on being met by tables groaning under the weight of food and ale. Apparently the quality of the Duke's ale was not as good as had been anticipated ! (34).

There were some people living in the Hartington parish who could ill afford to pay rent. Pilkington in 1789 records ten 'dwellings' dug out of the ash waste adjacent to the Grin lime kilns. These were not unique to the area, for Daniel Defoe described one on Brassington Moor in the early 1720s. Farey stated that over 200 people lived in these dwellings at Grin, which is either wrong or the result of many more being created (35).

A letter written by Geoffrey Heathcote, dated 29th November 1766 (36) indicates that: *'the poor miners, men, women and children, have been always allowed to pick and dress lead ore out of the old castaway deads [waste rock] and hillocks after the owner of the mine had got what they could in the ordinary way of dressing'*. It was initially without payment, but a small payment had been made for ore obtained *'in later years'*.

At the other end of the scale, on 18th October 1788 and from Chatsworth, the Duchess wrote to her mother that her daughter, Georgiana, was making *'petty-coats for poor children'*; Lady Georgiana was five at the time (37).

There is no doubt that severe winters caused problems for the poor and in the main, this would have centred around hunger and the effects of the cold. The problem would have existed equally for farm animals too. In the winter of 1794-95, the winter must have been especially bad. The Hartington accounts record payments *'for the relief of the Poor during severity of last winter'* amounting to £23. 0s. 4d., a significant sum of money. The payments had been made in the parish by Mr. Thomas Lomas, Messrs. Bowman, Fogg, Fidler and Richard Gould. The same accounts record payments in Buxton, Fairfield and Hartington Upper Quarter by John Brandreath of £27. 19s. 6d. Smaller sums were paid in Youlgreave and Monyash (38).

Matters were worse in Wetton however. This must have been exacerbated by the failure of the nearby Ecton Copper Mine in 1790. An account of 10th February 1795 records that 18 households involving 76 people received, free from the estate, 456lb. of oatmeal per week from Wetton Mill for four weeks in all (over 16 cwt or 0.8 of a ton). Thirty two households received 1 cwt of coal per week, also for four weeks (6.4 tons) (39). This came from the Duke's colliery at Kingsley, near Cheadle.

Before memories had faded there was another poor winter in 1800 when Thomas Fogg received £14 expenses for *'His Grace's Subscription for relieving the Poor in Hartington during the Severity of the Winter'* [1799 – 1800]. Life in the parish must have been wretched for some. The severe winter of 1799 – 1800 and perhaps other problems had affected the poor well into 1800. The account for the Chatsworth Estate carried annual payments for the poor assessment for Edensor, clergy widows and orphans in Derby etc. However in 1800, there was a series of payments which indicates something much more serious. Payments started in April and continued until September. It is clear that the list (from the Chatsworth Estate Account for 1800) is not the totality either, for the Hartington payment of £14 mentioned above is in the Hartington Accounts and others may lie in other collection accounts.

Nonetheless, the following gives some indication that the area's poor were suffering in a profound and more serious way:

'April 23	*Towards the Relief of the Poor of Little Longstone*	£ 15. 0s. 0d.
ditto	*Ditto the Poor of Wardlow*	£ 10. 0s. 0d.
May 20	*Ditto the Poor of Ashford*	£ 42. 0s. 0d.
ditto	*Ditto the Poor of Sheldon*	£ 25. 0s. 0d.
May 23	*Ditto the Poor in the Hamlet of Newbold*	£ 10. 10s. 0d.
June 18	*Ditto the Industrious Poor of Beeley*	£ 8. 0s. 0d.
ditto	*Ditto Ditto of Pilsley*	£ 10. 0s. 0d.
ditto	*Ditto Ditto of Edensor*	£ 15. 15s. 0d.
July 26	*Ditto the Poor of Gt. Longstone*	£ 25. 0s. 0d.
Sept. 18	*Ditto the Poor of Brampton*	£ 10. 10s. 0d.

Total   £171. 15s. 0d'.

It is interesting to see the different description for the poor of the three Chatsworth villages. Thus the plight of many of the Duke's tenants was the inability to afford to eat. It is hard to see how a one–off payment really helped despite the fact that long–term, prices began to fall. Poverty, and in particular empty stomachs, did little to maintain contentment, but the effect on this in Hartington, let alone the rest of the Duke's Derbyshire and other estates, may now be difficult to assess.

A study has been made of the neighbouring parishes around the Manifold Valley, immediately west of Hartington parish and in particular the effect that the Ecton Mine had on local parish populations. It is an important study and its conclusions might well be reflected in Hartington parish and indeed elsewhere in the district. The mine had a positive effect on population growth from 1760 and although this mirrored the national trend, the increase in the area of the mine was higher than the national average. This growth was affected by the mine's failure in 1790. It had a pronounced effect on the local parishes and this must have included Hartington.

An analysis of the wage accounts indicated the mine employed a varying number of people. Some of these would have been children and some on part-time work. In the four years of 1782 – 85 the total (which would have excluded at least colliery workers) was 670, 773, 591 and 575. There were slightly more females than males.

Overseers of the Poor seem to have had a lot to do on behalf of their parish, with a significant number of illegitimate births. Certain families seemed to be prone to the problem to the extent that quite a few seemed to have a relaxed view of it, with grandmothers, daughters and grand-daughters maintaining an apparent family tradition. Elsewhere it may of course have been the result of partnerships rather than marriages where marriage was not an option or at least not a preferred option. Some unmarried mothers had to rely on poor relief, which was provided by the parish ratepayers. However the Overseer would pursue errant fathers to secure maintenance payments under a Court Order obtained at a nearby Quarter Sessions Court. They would restrain such culprits until appearance before the Court could be concluded. A case of pursuing one father to Macclesfield from Grindon is cited, followed by appearance at the Ashbourne Quarter Sessions. Such activity was not uncommon and also could result where the fathers were from outside the parish. There were several instances of this in Hartington Nether Quarter (40).

The parish would arrange apprenticeships of children on poor relief as soon as was possible, often in the textile trade. The excesses of harsh treatment of children at Litton Mill on the River Wye at Millers Dale, east of Buxton are well known.

As discussed above for quite a few cottagers, a most important possession was a cow and rights of pasture on the Common. This provided milk and butter for instance, and presumably a calf each year. The loss of the cow would be significant. The Chatsworth Estate account for 1759 records the payment of a guinea (£1. 1s. 0d.) to *'Widow Bark of Hassop on loss of her cow'*. The Estate accounts show many examples of a paternal attitude towards tenants in need (40/1). Sometimes one gets the distinct feeling that this approach was used to advantage by less than scrupulous tenants. In 1822 the Estate wrote off ten years' rent arrears for a cottage at £1. 5s. 0d. per annum from Lady Day 1811. The house was in Hartington Upper Quarter. As soon as possession had been relinquished, the house was taken down immediately afterwards. The tenant was Lawrence Wardle. Arrears were written off in 1825 at Wetton, in one instance being to *'a very poor man'* who had also lost a cow. In 1846, £2.12s.0d. was being distributed in bread every 2-3 weeks by the Hartington vicar.

There does not appear to have been much of an improvement in the welfare of the poorer tenants of the Derbyshire Estate. It does not take a great leap of imagination to suggest that this was a situation also prevalent over an area wider than the Devonshire holdings. Devonshire Accounts up to the 1830s are peppered with references to donations to the poor, reflecting the inadequacy of the poor relief system. Donations in 1831 to the *'distribution of blankets and flannel among the poor of Edensor, Beeley and Pilsley'* amounting to a huge sum of £120. 11s. 8d. reflected a typhus fever epidemic (see below). In the same year, £5 was paid to the Rev. S. Hey towards the relief of 'poor weavers' at Bonsall. The following year £5 was paid to *'the Rev. M. Mills …to a society for providing clothing for the poor in the villages of Gt. And Little Longstone'* (41).

The £5 payment seems to have been the policy elsewhere on the Derbyshire Estate for Sunday Schools with payments of this amount at Edale and Peak Forest in 1825. Ten pounds was paid to the school master, Ellis Woodroofe, at Peak Forest in 1825; towards the cost of erecting a Sunday School at Tideswell in 1825; a chapel at Flash in 1832 (to the Rev. James Roberts); with £5 a year later sent to the fund for erecting a Sunday School at Flagg. In December 1794, Joseph Gould (probably the Hartington Rents Collector, of Pilsbury

 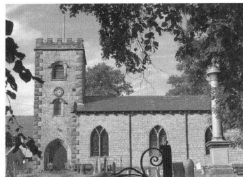

Left: Oldham Lane, the road from Hartington to Middleton (formerly Middleton Way) **Right:** Earl Sterndale Church built in c.1828 (finished by 1832)

Grange), paid £5, *'being a free gift from the Duke of Devonshire to the school of Great Longstone due Michelmas last'*, indicating that it was a regular donation.

At Hartington substantially more assistance was paid out: £100 to Joseph Turner & Co., towards the expense of erecting a school at Brand Side (on the east side of Axe Edge) in 1831. Construction of a new church at Earl Sterndale saw £100 being sent in 1828 to Anthony Broadhurst and George Wood, towards the cost of demolition of the old church and the rebuilding costs. The Estate even paid a guinea (£1. 1s. 0d.) for a *Ground and Gallery Plan* showing the pews etc. in 1832 after completion of the work. (42).

Despite the late date for the proposed Flash and Flagg Sunday Schools, the movement had reached the Peak in timely fashion; well at least by eight years after its commencement. On the 18th October 1788, the Duchess wrote to her mother to say:

'I have had a letter from Mr. Mower … he wants me to establish a Sunday School at Castleton. I perfectly agree with him that such an institute in ye Peak wd have good effect – likewise that I believe anywhere in the Peak I cd do it – but he likewise says Mr. Bagshaw, who has great property there opposes it …now Mr. B is a very old man, very strange and touchy …'

The Hartington Methodist Chapel on Hall Bank opened in 1809 and the Primitive Methodist Chapel at Biggin opened in 1835. Above (p. 23) was mentioned that the school master at Hartington received an annuity for teaching poor children. This was a charity school, supported by donations. The earliest reference to this would appear to be in 1726 when he was paid £3 per annum at Michaelmas. In October 1759 the school master was Robert Oliver. His receipt for the £3 paid that year states that it was a voluntary gift given annually by His *Grace 'for teaching six poor children to read'*. By 1765 the sum had been increased to £5 per annum. Oliver became the parish curate from 1760 – 1766. He was born of poor parents near Onecote, near Leek. After 1766 he took a living in the west of England (43). The school was on the north side of Church Street and the building is dated 1758.

In 1793, the Rev. Benjamin Hope (he had been a school master at Leek, Staffs) was paid £5 per annum for teaching ten poor children at Hartington to read and write. In 1816 no payment was made following the installation of a new vicar. (Rev. William Davison M.A., vicar from 1815 to 1826). (44). However the following year a fresh arrangement had been made and the education of ten poor children continued. It would appear that the new vicar had a different view of assisting the poor of his congregation. As early as 1712 James Hall left £2 pa to the school master for teaching 4 of the poorest children at Crowdecote. (43)

Whether anyone checked to see if the number being taught was higher or lower seems doubtful. It was more likely to be a contribution irrespective of the number of children turning up. Setting this in context, a similar sum appears in the Wetton accounts for 1825, being paid to Samuel Carrington, the local school master. In 1830 Joseph Vernon was paid £20 for the poor at Butterton, west of Wetton (45).

Public Health

In 1831 there was an outbreak of 'typhus fever' (typhoid) at Beeley and Pilsley. This would appear to have continued into the following year and also spread to Edensor. In 1833 there is a further reference in the Chatsworth Estate accounts of the disease in Beeley. In 1832 the accounts include an expense of £457 on the outbreak, being chiefly for meat, beer and coals plus £305 on medical attendance. Blankets and flannel (used to make clothes) distributed to the poor of the three villages may have been connected with the outbreak. Typhoid is transmitted as a result of poor sanitation contaminating the water supply.

Pure water was the main strength in maintaining a healthy level of public health. Hartington used the supply of water from the River Harding which flows down Hartington Dale into the Market Place, albeit now under the road. Adjacent to the village pond, the river may be seen flowing through 'The Stanner'. This shallow pit is open to the River Harding and enabled villagers to obtain their water, avoiding the village pond, which would have been used by the animals. Nearby is one of the village wells and pump but its age is late 19th century.

The Great Court Baron records for 1753 refer to two plots of land – Greater and Little Dig Mere. Herein must lie the name of the village pond – Dig Mere. It is situated in Dig Street, 'dig' being derived from ditch, c/f Dig Street in Ashbourne, which runs to the River Henmore. However it should be noted that the mere is not marked on the Inclosure Award map.

Crowdecote had three strong springs of water. In fact the mill was built just below the point where one of them reached the River Dove. Pilkington (46) states that in one of these three wells a few years ago, were found some small articles of silver, particularly pins and rings. In the Great Court Baron records for 1751, there is reference to a croft adjoining Fewell.

Earl Sterndale has a mere, like Heathcote, which may be an indicator of where this village found its water supply. Heathcote mere is mentioned in a document of 1482 (Derbyshire, Place Names Society) and is situated adjacent to an old drovers' road. However it also had a well and at least as early as 1745 the Manor Court annually decreed that a 2s. 6d. fine would be imposed on anyone taking down the wall of or defiling the water in any manner.

Public watering places were recorded in the Inclosure Award at High Needham (GR 115657); Hurdlow (GR 111675); Blakemere near the current Jug & Glass Inn (GR 155627); Cardlemere, east of Biggin (GR 172587). Heathcote Mere, and the village mere in Hartington are not mentioned presumably as they were not covered by the Inclosure Award. However the latter would appear to have been at the bottom of Hide Lane. Additionally, the little known well on the Common at Caskinlow north of the later Hartington Station, must not be overlooked.

These sources of pure water sustained the Hartington parishes and at least from Georgian times appeared to afford protection from typhoid and (later) cholera. It is worthy of note that the Ecton Mine manager, Cornelius Flint, settled in Hartington after his marriage to Mary Lomas in 1781. His son, Charles, 1789 – 1861, did not follow his father into mining for employment (he did invest in mines – or at least one – the Botstone Lead Mine at Wetton Mill in the Manifold Valley. Your author has a draft document of Flint's purchase of shares in this company). He went into medicine, becoming the Medical Officer for Health to the Board of Guardians at nearby Leek, Staffs.

Despite the experience at the three Chatsworth villages and the supply of *soft spring water* in 1820 – 21 to The Crescent, the Hall and George Inns plus nearby lodging houses owned by the estate at Buxton, it was 1840 before Buxton as a whole was provided with mains water. The supply of pure water was still being treated with lethargy at Ashbourne half a century later. Despite continuing calls for a public supply, it took a cholera outbreak and nine deaths in the town before anything was done. Here the water supply from a well in a yard off Dig Street was contaminated with sewage. The well survives in the yard at the Bridge Wine Bar, but its historic significance is not recognised there.

It is worthy of note that the Chatsworth typhoid outbreak nearly coincided with the first outbreak of cholera in this country (at Sunderland) in October 1831. The number of deaths reported in England alone reached 52,500 by the end of 1832. Some of the symptoms of cholera are similar to typhoid and both diseases are associated with poor sanitation and infected water. In 1752 the records of the Great Court Baron record a case concerning land at Doctor's Croft and Doctor's Barn in Biggin, which may indicate a doctor living in the parish.

Hard on the heels of the cholera outbreak was an epidemic of smallpox, although those inoculated against it were surviving it. (46). It seems hardly likely that many in rural Derbyshire would have been so protected.

Health & Safety

Additional to Public Health were the issues around health and safety, or the lack of it. Unfortunately few records of accidents and tragedy exist although there can be little doubt that they would have been a regular occurrence. Mining accidents must have been a particular area where the mode of work involved risk, although given the number of people working at nearby Ecton Mine, the number of fatalities or serious injury were few. This wasn't because the mine's health and safety record was a good one. Efford writing in 1769 stated that the descent to the mine bottom was hazardous and the risk of serious falls was high.

Dr. J.H. Rieuwerts has found a record of a mine at Newton Grange, south-west of Hartington in a case of *Robert Mowar v John Beresford*, 1686. A Matthew Beresford of Gateham, near Alstonfield, recalled an ancient mine at Newton Grange when he was 14 years old (in 1629). Although completely overgrown. at a depth of about 30ft/10m. they reached an old working with three skeletons in it *'one of which was of an extraordinary bignesse and some of the bones were very greate ones'* (47). When the Ashbourne – Buxton railway line was being constructed, in digging foundations for the viaduct just to the north of Hartington Station, an old mine was broken into which contained the remains of more entombed miners. (48)

At the Hayesbrook Mine, north of Warslow, c. 3 miles/5km. west of Hartington, miners were apparently working on a vein which rose upwards into shale. When the shale was reached there was an inrush of water and six men had to run for their lives, leaving their tools behind. This is a traditional oral story, not yet confirmed by documentary evidence but is not likely to be unique in the area. In the 1930s men working in the bed of the River Manifold, again west of Hartington near to Thors Cave, looked up from the hole they had dug to see the dry river bed changing, with a wall of water rushing towards them (49), so the dramatic effect of water was not confined to affecting local workers underground.

The loss of 'Widowe Baylie' at Load End (now Lode Mill in all probability) in the swollen waters of the River Dove in 1658 is covered in Ch.9, *'the watter being verie bigge'*. Victims of other circumstances, e.g. bad weather and robbery etc. are also mentioned therein.

Events at mines are better documented than perhaps the more general accidents which occurred. Mining activity was sometimes recorded in the mine records, *The Mining Journal*, or in the records of Barmote Courts. Perhaps one of the most famous – it is still referred today as the case of the Redsoil Murders – occurred just to the east of Hartington at Magpie Mine near Sheldon. Here the veins of two separate mines merged creating a lot of bad feeling and action at the Barmote Court. In 1833 matters boiled over and the Redsoil miners lit fires underground hoping to smoke out the Magpie miners who had broken through into the Redsoil workings. The draught changed and the smoke – from timber and tar – infiltrated the Redsoil Mine, aided by more fires set alight by the Magpie miners. The shafts belched smoke out of the Redsoil shafts over the weekend. On the Monday morning, the Redsoil mine manager descended the initial shaft and declared the workings free from smoke.

The lower workings were not inspected and were full of gas. Three miners suffocated to death. The inquest was heard by Ashford Barmote Court (not the Coroner, whose writ did not run under Derbyshire lead mining law and custom, codified in 1288). Six Magpie miners were indicted for murder before Derby Crown Court, where they were found not guilty.

The effect on the affected miners' families would have been profound of course, not only for the widows and children but also the rescuers, for clearly several were affected by suffocation. Probably an 1830s equivalent of a disaster fund was opened, for contributions were made by the Duke:

'Payment to widow of Thomas Wager, destroyed by suffocation in the Red Soil Mine on 2nd September [1833] £50; Pd to widow and children of Isaac Bagshawe, late of Sheldon, miner, who was killed at the same time, £30; To widow and child of Francis Taylor, late of Bakewell, who was killed at the same time, £20; Pd £15 to rescuers suffering from effects of suffocation at Red Soil Mine'

The last item probably covered time off work and medical expenses. (50).

A chaleybeate spring used to exist in nearby Butterton, south-west of Hartington, issuing a mineral water. It was close to the ford across the Hoo Brook. In 1840 a mine shaft was sunk next to the spring. The latter was situated at the far side of the little croft on the right as you leave the stream and start up the hill towards Grindon. The spring had been bubbling to the surface since at least 1680 when it was recorded by Dr. Plot in his *'History of Staffordshire'* (published six years later). At the time the shaft was sunk, it was said to be giving off the smell of bad eggs (i.e. hydrogen sulphide, a toxic gas, even in small quantities, e.g. 1% in air can be lethal).

A bed of iron pyrites (fool's gold) was reached, which may been the source of the gas which was being given off by the water and which *'had a violent effect on the miners' eyes'*. The mine had been closed for some time when a boy, Joseph Shenton, entered it on 30th August 1842. The ladder was still in the shaft and he descended it with his playmate. A report of the accident states that the boy reached the bottom of the ladder and said *'I am dying'*. His playmate gave the alarm to a group of men working nearby on the highway. As they stopped work and went to investigate, none could have foreseen the tragedy unfolding.

One of the men descended the ladder to rescue Joseph Shenton and fell from it into the water. Two more men tried, one at a time, trying to rescue those who had made the descent ahead of them. A fourth man was prepared to descend the shaft but was restrained. (51) Three men, Joseph Wood, Rowland Cantrell and William Hambleton had, despite a dangerous

The current officers of the Hartington Barmote Court with The Steward (M Cockerton (left); E Tennant, Barmaster, middle; and D Mort (Bailiff) on the right. The standard lead ore dish dates from 1513 and is full of Peak Forest galena. (Strictly speaking it is the dish for the Low Peak, based at Wirksworth). Photo: A. Goodman

situation, in a gallant and selfless act, made the descent of that lethal ladder to save those in the water. The mine was sealed and the bodies were never recovered. Only a plaque in the church records the names of those who died that day, placed there by '*an eye-witness of this noble Christian deed*'.

Forty-four years' later, there was another tragedy at the first cottage on the left-hand side beyond this mine and the same Butterton ford on the Grindon road. Gunpowder was readily available in grocers' shops and as will be seen below, Hartington was no exception. In the later years of the 19th Century, gunpowder (commonly called black powder) was replaced by gelatine cartridges, a form of dynamite. In the right hands the cartridges could be used for a variety of jobs – even lighting the fire at home. It was an effective but expensive firelighter!

William Fearns, a miner, had taken a couple of cartridges home in order to blow up a tree for fuel. It is likely that he worked at Ecton Mine, then the only one still working in the immediate district. It also seems likely that he left the cartridges outside, maybe in the privvy (outside toilet) and that there was a frost that night. In the morning he placed them in the kitchen stove to soften them, and went outside for a few moments, perhaps to dig a hole under the tree in which to place the warmed cartridges and insert the fuse. There was a huge explosion and he ran back into the house. The iron grate had been blown to fragments, acting like shrapnel, killing his mother, wrecking all the furniture and the windows. His sister, although blown off the sofa, miraculously survived with only a few cuts. The gelatine is thought to have frozen, causing the explosion. A simple act such as leaving it outside on a frosty night was unwittingly the likely cause of the tragedy, probably only because Fearns could not insert the fuse before lighting it.

Hartington was not free of accidents. Unfortunately, the detail is lost, except for one which also involved gunpowder in a spectacular, if innocent, tragedy which must have rocked the village in more ways than one. It happened in the summer of 1838 (52) at the grocer's shop (the one with the arcaded front). A 2 cwt barrel of gunpowder was kept in a rear shed to supply local miners etc. The shop keeper's 33-year old son, John Harrison, and the latter's son, Dick (aged 10) were playing with a servant boy, Hugh Glenn, aged 19. Presumably at John Harrison's suggestion, they decided to have what they termed 'a fizz', with some loose powder which was scattered on the floor. Unfortunately, there was more powder than they realised. An explosion occurred and the roof of the building rose as high as the church tower. The three were killed and 4 – 5 tons of hay was scattered about.

Two years before, the keeper of the Butterton Moor tollgate survived a similar experience. He was about to retire to bed when he realised that there might be two men at the Royledge Copper Mine to the west of his home. Knowing that there wouldn't be anyone to draw them up the shaft he went off to do it – it was no short walk either, especially in the dark and was probably a couple of miles away.

Upon getting there, he found they had already got out of the mine and he (also a Royledge miner) decided to sharpen his tools in the smithy, as the fire was still lit. He put gunpowder on it to raise the heat, leaving a trail back to the barrel. He too saw the 'fizz' before the explosion which blew off the smithy roof and left him badly burnt and hoping, one supposes, that someone would be roused by the bang (53).

If it was not gunpowder, an equally potent medium likely to lead the unwary into trouble was, of course, alcohol. The wagon driver who upturned his wagon breaking two pier glasses worth £500 was probably under the influence, as the estate held him responsible for the accident (see Ch.9). Another accident, recorded in graphic detail, shows that today's driving under the influence is nothing new. It relates to the crack *Telegraph* coach bound for London from Manchester. It was a journey completed in 18 hours 17 minutes including breaks for two meals. It came to grief on Swinscoe Hill, descending (now the A52) from Swinscoe towards Ashbourne, 12 – 13 miles south of Hartington. It was New Year's Day, 1830.

'The coachman was accidentally thrown off his box and pulled a passenger down with him. The horses, experiencing liberty, went down the hill at full speed, crossed the bridge at the bottom, and carried the coach with great violence against the corner of the public house [now the Royal Oak Inn] *on the opposite side, forcing off one of the wheels. They then galloped towards the toll-bar* [at the turning into Green Lane] *where the coach came into contact with the gatepost and was dashed almost to pieces ... The guard and coachman, it is feared, were far from sober, as they had called at many inns on the road to drink, in commemoration of the day.'* (54).

These instances are more than anecdotal. Most of them can be interpreted as self-inflicted, perhaps influenced by naiveté. Five of these events occurred in the years 1830 – 42 involving the death of ten people. Accepting that these did not include domestic or agricultural events, let alone others, one wonders just how many more such as those recalled took place. The actual number per annum could have been considerable.

Do these represent the tip of an unknown iceberg, showing the rawness of a way of life now long gone, that accepted and took within its stride accidents, tragedy and death at a level we cannot comprehend and which today we could not countenance?

Wages

At the Ecton Mine, in the 1760s, a labourer could generally earn about 1s. 0d. per day. This varied a little according to the nature of the job and whether there was an element of responsibility attached thereto. In 1811 at Bakewell, William Greaves revealed that he used to pay labourers 1s. 6d. per day until the Inclosures commenced in about 1805, but since then the rate had risen to around 2s. 0d. – 2s. 6d. per day. This rate was reflected at the mine too, but had risen to 10s.0d per week (for six days) as early as 1786. (55). Farey records that the following was paid at Pilsbury:

'Mr. Joseph Gould, from the conclusion of Harvest till Lady Day pays his Labourers 2s. 2d. per day; thence till the beginning of Hay-time 2s. 4d. per day; and during the Hay Harvest 2s. per day and Board and Lodging. The cutting of his Corn is done by his Yearly Servants, and by Labourers employed to reap by the Thrave, of 24 Sheaves (each a yard in circumference); a Kiver or Shock is half a Thrave.' (56).

However, emoluments were sometimes provided, with a lower daily rate as a result. Farey goes on at length citing wage rates throughout the county and another local example highlights the point about emoluments:

'At Newhaven, Mr. Timothy Greenwood, to two regular Labourers who occupy cottages on his Farm, Rent free, he pays 7s. and 8s. per week; fetches their Coals; supplies them with Oatmeal at 1s. per peck; keeps a Cow for each of them, and finds ground, prepared, for planting their Potatoes; besides which, they have the Plucks of the Sheep killed for the use of his Inn' [Newhaven House, adjacent to his farm]

Working hours were usually from dawn until dusk, sometimes as the dew permitted. Beer was on occasion provided too. Judging by other figures recorded by Farey, Joseph Gould seems to have paid well, but then one wonders if he matched the emoluments offered elsewhere. Servants were usually hired on a 12 monthly basis. The pay in one instance was 15 or 16 guineas a year, in another it was 10 to 12 guineas per annum and for a woman, 4 to 5 guineas per annum. (57). Earl Chesterfield complained that *'the Public Statutes for hiring (i.e. the hiring fairs) occasioned strangers without characters* [references] *to be hired; and that after Michaelmas, numerous servants ran away from their places'*. Confirmation of Farey's comments about the wage paid to women survives in William Gould's diary entry of 1st October 1785. An Ann Hardwick attended a job interview at the Gould's Welbeck (Nottinghamshire) home, for the position of housekeeper to their son Joseph at Pilsbury. Mrs. Gould engaged her at £5 per annum. She was a replacement for a Miss Froggott, who left the previous April as part of a cost-saving measure and who presumably was being paid more. Gould's diary states that Ann Hardwick was from "Thirkby" which Michael Hanson interprets as being Thirkleby, 3 miles south-east of Thirsk in North Yorkshire. Mobility of labour is often thought of as being a more recent feature of the labour market.

The local newspaper announced that at Ashbourne *'a statutes shall be held for the hiring of servants on the first Tuesday in October and to be annually continued'*. (58). This seems to suggest that the hiring fairs were generally infrequent. Ashbourne had many annual fairs (?14) and the report below might relate to one of these:

'Fair at Ashbourne (beef and other stock).
Unexpected number of servants appears in the Market Place seeking fresh engagements, displaying blue ribbons upon the occasion. The fair was well attended by more young people than at the great pleasure fair in May' (59). Presumably hiring also took place at the Newhaven Fair which was always a popular event.

One essential service in the community, as now, was that of the rat catcher, now the pest control officer. The Devonshire Estate used one and payments to him in the 1750s survive (they no doubt occur regularly, but this particular one highlights a specific point). It was difficult to work out the payment structure until it was realised that he was being paid the price of a pint of beer per rat killed. What a wonderful incentive designed to ensure diligence and a high success rate. From the rat catcher's point of view, the job also had permanence of some measure, no matter how successful he was. Another method of killing rats other than by snaring was by poisoning them. Arsenic was a tried and presumably trusted agent. In Chester in 1661, arsenic was put in the papier mache paste used to make 'giants' in a street pageant. It prevented them from being eaten by rats (60). It is difficult to imagine that a rat catcher wasn't generally available in the Hartington communities.

In fact William Gould must have cursed rats in June 1784. Although he planted many young trees near to Pilsbury, they did not take well and the healthy plants were moved to create a new wood at Ludwell Farm, probably on the Staffordshire side of the valley. The original site was later planted with acorns which Gould had brought from his home at Welbeck, where he had a position under the Duke of Portland (additional to his work on the Devonshire Estate). Much of the crop was eaten by rats (61).

Festivities

Church holidays – Christmas, Easter and Shrovetide particularly, were a time for celebration, with Shrove Tuesday being an afternoon of fun. Bull-baiting, cock fighting, dog throwing and football being the main ways in which it was expressed nationally. Pancake races were an extension of using up food not eaten during Lent. Despite the suppression of bull baiting in the 1830s, Ashbourne was claimed to have possibly been the last place in the country to abandon the practice, in the early 1840s.

At Shrovetide in 1697, the vicar of Leek spent 2s. (10p.) ensuring that his church remained 'safe against the rabble'. In all likelihood he was trying to prevent a cockfight being held in his chancel. A hundred years later (1797) a son of Sir Richard Arkwright wrote home from his boarding school (The Grammar School) at Ashbourne, seeking more pocket money from his father. The letter, sent on Shrove Tuesday, told his parents that the school master had provided a football for the day. Local boys had demanded the ball, but declined an invitation to come and take it. The goals would likely to have been the church gates and the Hall gates. It was also recorded as being played in Wetton and Ashford–in–the–Water. No records of activity in most of the Peak District villages was recorded but doubtless similar events were enjoyed annually. (62)

Plot in his *History of Staffordshire* (he visited the county in 1660) records that it was an annual custom to decorate wells with boughs and flowers (e.g. May blossom) in the Staffordshire Moorlands. The custom was accompanied by cakes and ale, music and dancing. He ignored the practice across the Derbyshire border, where well dressing is now well known. It is still observed at Endon in North Staffordshire, but only since 1845. Well dressing in Derbyshire died out with the exception of Tissington. Its revival would appear to have started at Wirksworth in 1827 and Youlgreave in 1829 with the introduction of the village water supply. In Hartington current observance started in the late 20th Century.

The practice of pressing petals into clay probably started at Tissington prior to 1837 and possibly as early as 1817. By 1830 it was regular custom for people from Ashbourne to walk or get a lift if possible, on anything passing with wheels, to visit Tissington for the well dressing. It seems unlikely that a few branches laid by the well would be the inducement. Either conviviality and the 'new' custom of images created by flowers pressed into wet clay to create a design or

Left: Buxton House Inn/ or Hall Inn (now The Old Hall Hotel), showing its proximity to the original bath, The latter was later extended and called The Natural Baths

Below: The original building finished in 1572. It was later extended either side and the bays added. It is one of the oldest continually operated hotels in the country

scene was the motivation. The earliest image of well dressing shows a well at Tissington in 1837. (63). Buxton celebrated its new water supply in similar fashion to Youlgreave in 1840, although mains water was laid onto various hotels on the Devonshire Estate in 1820. This included *'water closets'* – w.c.s – as well as tap water indicating the establishment of a new drainage system too. The innovation is not recorded as being extended to the Newhaven House Hotel, where a lack of an adequate water supply may have been the problem.

Coronations and some royal weddings were also a cause of celebration too. At Ashbourne, the wedding of the Princess Royal in January 1858 was celebrated by Shrovetide-type football. There is some evidence (persuasive to your author) to suggest that it was preceded by a similar game in 1797 on the marriage of the then Princess Royal when as an experiment, the game was played between Sturston and Clifton Mills. It was found to be more enjoyable than playing across the local River Henmore. It was adopted at the following Shrovetide and has been played in that manner ever since (64).

The Estate was clearly keen to ensure the tenants celebrated the Coronation of King William IV in 1831. It made a donation of £7. 10s. 0d. *'to enable the poor inhabitants of Ashford to celebrate the Coronation.'* On the Devonshire Estate, the birth and marriage of each successive Marquis of Hartington seems to have been celebrated. The liquidity of the 5th Duke (wealth as well as wine) perhaps permitted his greatest extravagance on the occasion of his son's 21st birthday although the Duke would not have seen it in that light (see below).

Other customs surviving locally include the Rush Bearing Service at Forest Chapel just beyond the upper reaches of the Devonshire Estate at Macclesfield Forest. A little nearer to the Estate is the annual Tea Pot Day at Flash, celebrated at the Traveller's Rest Inn on the Leek-Buxton road, although whether this dates back as far as Georgian times isn't known. Many villages still celebrate a day which saw its origins in 19th Century village lodges attached to the Oddfellows or Foresters organisations including Hartington. In Castleton the Restoration of Charles II is observed with the Garland celebrations on Oak Apple Day. Ashbourne's Shrovetide football game probably commenced on the first Shrove Tuesday, in 1661, after the Restoration.

The Coming of Age of the Marquis of Hartington, May 1811

It is widely known to this day that the Duke celebrated his son's coming-of-age without regard to expense. The extent of this has never been fully revealed. A copy letter survives written by John Heaton to Thomas Knowlton with just over four weeks to go before the birthday. It sets out Heaton's initial thinking on how the Duke's intentions could be implemented (65). Knowlton was the Duke's Steward at Chatsworth.

"
Burlington Street
18th April 1811

Sir

I have received your letter of the 15th Instant. There is no time to be lost in making preparation to celebrate the Marquis of Hartington's Birth day, on his attaining the Age of 21, on the 21st day of May next. Beer, Brandy, Rum and Wine, must be laid in at all the places where this event is to be celebrated. The Duke thinks there was some Beer brewed at Chatsworth, when Lord Hartington was born, and His Grace recollects to have tasted the Beer, which was brewed on Lord Titchfield's birth, to be drank when he came of Age and says that it was the worst liquor he ever tasted, nothing like Beer, but something like bad strong wine, without flavour. As far as I can learn, how best to make use of this strong Beer will be to mix it in the drawing with other Liquor, but as the whole of the Strong Beer will be consumed with a much larger quantity you will have to distribute, probably you may find it convenient to mix the whole of this Strong Beer in Vessels with New Beer, so as to draw off the whole with one tap as both will be consumed. All the Drinkers will understand that they are drinking Beer brewed at Lord Hartington's Birth.

There was some offence given, I understand, on Lord Milton's coming of age, by putting the Beer into Troughs, where each Man might fill his Mug, instead of having it drawn from the tap, or delivered to them out of large Jugs. To be delivered in pails is in drinking something like roasting a whole Ox at once in eating; the lower orders of the English People are civilized enough, not to be well pleased with that mode of entertainment.

I have seen the Duke to day, and laid before him your letter, and I have suggested to His Grace what appeared to me to be some improvement on your plan. Your plan for Chatsworth I think is very good, that is, to entertain the Duke's principal Tenants, and any Gentlemen who may chuse to join them, in the Entrance Hall, with a good Dinner, Beer, Punch and Wine. But the Duke feels some difficulty in the invitations to Gentlemen – He wishes them to be there, if they chuse it, but to have it understood that they will not be shewing want of attention and respect to his family if they should not make parts of so large a meeting where they cannot have those attentions he wishes them to receive, whenever they are pleased to favour him with their company.

Your plan to entertain other part of the Duke's Tenants of the next order, in the Quadrangle, seems to be very good. They should have Beer and Punch. In case the weather should be bad, you should be prepared with canvas and poles to cover them from it.

Your plan likewise for entertaining the Populace in the Outer Yard is very good. You should however be prepared with Canvas and poles to cover them also in case of bad weather.

Tables, made of Boards upon Tressels, in those places will be sufficient; and you will be able to borrow knives and forks and plates in case you want them making a list of what you borrow, and taking care to send back as much as you may have borrowed, by buying new things to make up for loss and accidents. Of Men, which you will want as Waiters, and to preserve order in the Management of the entertainment, you have all the Duke's Tenantry at your command, and perhaps, the circumstance of your being a military man, will be of use to you in producing a plan for subordination in that description of Assistants.

The Duke's Tenantry, if they should all be invited to come to Chatsworth and Hardwicke, might make a point of going to one of those Houses, however inconvenient to themselves, and the number of them alone certainly would not be less than 2,000 – I should think if each of them took with him one of his Neighbours, not the Duke's Tenant, you might have 4,000 people to entertain at those two Houses –

I have therefore suggested to His Grace a plan, which he wishes you to consider, whether it would not be more convenient to the Tenants and better upon the whole to have other places as well as Chatsworth and Hardwicke, fixed upon to entertain the Tenants, and such Gentleman as might chuse to attend, in the same manner as they would be entertained at Chatsworth or Hardwicke. The plans I have thought of would be Staveley (where the Colliers would be kept from Hardwicke), Shottle (to which place many people might chuse to go from Derby) and at Buxton –

In consideration with Mr. Heacock and Mr. Clarke whether this, or any other division of the places of entertainment, you will be able to decide, would be best.

When I hear from you again, I will write a letter to you, to enable you to give proper directions for the management of this Festival, throughout Derbyshire, and perhaps it may be best that directions from you should go from Chatsworth to the Revd Mr. Carr, Agent for the Duke's Londesboro' and Bolton Abbey Estates, to Mr. Lockett, for the Duke's Wetherby Estate, where he may entertain all Knaresboro; if they chuse to go, and to Mr. Maynard, Agent of the Duke's Marton on the Moor, Baldersby and Rainton Estates.

I will write however to Mr. Carr, Mr. Lockett, and Mr. Maynard, to apprize them that they will receive a letter from you to say what the Duke has ordered to be done in Derbyshire, and to wish them to make preparations for doing something of the same sort upon the Estates in their respective collections.

In managing this business, you will see that Mr. Heacock and Mr. Clarke, should consult with the principal Tenants in their collections so as to fix the plan of entertainment in such way as may best suit the wishes of the County, and that the entertainments should be given as far as they can be sensibly, and with as much attention to prevent waste, quarrelling and trouble, as may be. Great waste there will unavoidably be on this occasion, but the expense is not to be considered even in Hundreds of pounds at each place. The great consideration will be how to please the Country with as much sense and economy in doing it as can properly be introduced.

After what I have said you will find that you have business enough upon your hands, fully to employ your mind and activity from this time forward 'till the Birth day arrives. The great difficulty I think will be how to provide enough for eating and drinking, and particularly in procuring a sufficient quantity of meat, cooked, to be served up cold to the populace.

at Chatsworth and Hardwick I think you should begin cooking many days before the Birth day and I think you will have nearly the same thing to do at Shottle, where people from Derby will go, and in my mind it would be better that there should be an Ox too much, than there should be any want of meat. The Fragments may be given to the poor people on the following day. Bakers who likewise be employed to provide a quantity of Bread. You can provide Mustard and Vinegar, but I am afraid you will not be able to give them potatoes.

It occurs to me that if the Beer was drawn out into small casks, of which there are many at Chatsworth and Hardwicke of course, and those casks carried out to the place where the populace are to dine, they might have as much Beer as they might like to drink. They cannot all sit down to dinner together and when one set goes out to let in another to eat, they would have as much more Beer as they chuse to drink given to them at the Outer Gate.

In this Scene of Festivity, Ladies and Females wd derive no comfort or amusement, but if Lord Hartington at any future day, shod chuse to give Balls to the Ladies and Balls at different places to the Tenants' Wives and Daughters, and Young People, it may be done with infinitely more satisfaction to those who wish to have the pleasure of Dancing, than it possibly could be on the same day that Men meet to celebrate His Lordship's Birth on attaining 21 years of Age.

I understand from the Duke that the Marquis under His Graces' advice, has given up his intention of being in Derbyshire upon the occasion of this great Festivity.

I am …'

If this is how the event was celebrated, it must have been a really good party, divided up into various events across all the estates. One wonders if the 'Ladies and Daughters' got their event too! The Chatsworth Accounts for 1811 carries the cost of purchasing 1,000 knives and forks, which were used for the event held at Devonshire House. It was certainly celebrated well at Hardwick Hall, where William Howitt, researching a book on customs and celebrations, gate-crashed the event.

He had walked over from Mansfield and arrived at the Hall shocked from what resembled the dead on a battlefield, with the dead-drunk liberally scattered everywhere. A band played folk music for the benefit of any capable of appreciating it, with various throngs of revellers scattered about.

From the spigots of huge barrels, ale cascaded out with men in need, or in the case of many, no longer in need, trying to catch it in their hats. In some cases two or three men were trying to drink out of the same hat. Others felt an even greater need to drink directly from the gushing spigot. Servants stood at the garden gates repelling all comers without a ticket trying to gain access to the house. They were beaten back by hefty men with staves amid fighting and scuffling, clamour and confusion. Staves rained down on skulls; no wonder the bodies from the battle were to be encountered everywhere.

Howitt did not have a ticket but managed to slip past the uplifted arms of one of the burly stewards about to mete out more persuasion with his stave. This was hardly the hospitality that the Duke had in mind. In the house, those with a ticket (and there were scores of them), were liberally feasting on chunks of roast beef and plum pudding off heavy pewter dishes and drinking equally liberally from leather jacks and tankards. Footmen tried to contain the demand for more food and foaming ale. In the kichens, ranks of cooks battled on to try and feed all those in the house and those housed under canvas, as Heaton had suggested, in the forecourt. Here many more sat at long tables. These were *'the Duke's tenants of the next order'*, the more important tenants and other guests of similar rank, no doubt hoping that the line at the gate would hold the mob at bay.

Many of the latter had climbed up onto the garden wall, abating their curiosity and creating a cacophony of demands for food to be thrown up to them. Beef and pudding sallied forth by the handful. Other hands tried to catch it with much hilarity. Under the weight of the numbers, a finial on top of the wall collapsed with a man clinging to it. Under the weight of stone, he was killed on reaching the ground. Servants carted the body away and the festivities were rejoined. Ale, wine and spirit flowed, food flew though the air towards the wall, and no doubt everybody with a ticket was glad the house had cooked that extra ox.

Jostling for position on the wall, another man jumped for what was perceived to be a better position on a lower wall. Fortune favours the brave but not the brazen. Clearing the wall, instead of landing safely on it, he plummeted down a steep drop on the other side and was also killed. By now, however, the level of intoxication meant that few knew, let alone cared. The populace of dead-drunk warriors beyond the gate were now being joined by battle weary ticket-carrying intoxicants within the courtyard and the house itself, with bodies everywhere as the incapable joined the insensible. John Heaton had wisely speculated: *'In this Scene of Festivity, Ladies and Females wd derive no comfort or amusement'*. The Duke had worried that some of his gentleman friends might prefer not to attend. Both were correct but Bacchus would have been content; thousands had the binge of a lifetime, even if the reason for it was lost in the mists of an alcoholic haze that lasted far longer than originally anticipated. One is left to speculate how the Buxton and Hartington guests and *populace* also responded. (66) The following day was a Wednesday; mass male absenteeism from work must have been endemic across the entire estates. The true cost of celebrating the birthday must be beyond calculation; this, for those present, was Cavendish largesse in its finest hour.

Although the cost of absenteeism is not known, the costs of the celebration in the Hartington – Buxton area are known:

'Expenses of the dinner and liquer at the Great Hotel	*£78. 2 2*
Ditto at St Ann's Hotel	*53.19.8*
Ditto at The Centre Hotel	*48. 2 .6*
Ditto at The Hall Inn	*49 6 0*
Ditto at The Eagle Inn	*50.10.8*
Ditto at The George Inn	*40. 2 .0*
Ditto at The Shakespeare Inn	*38.14.0*
Josh Francis bill for ale given to the populace	*70.13.4*
Muscicians bill	*7. 0. 0*
Fireworks had at Buxton and paid for by Mr Knowles	*20. 0. 0*
Timothy Greenwood's bill for two sheep and two hogsheads of ale etc given to the inhabitants of Hartington	*28.19.5*
For a dinner for the tenants in the Tutbury Collection and for ale for the populace	*50. 0.0*
Mr Flint by Mr Heathcote Dinner and ale for the populace [of Wetton and Kingsley]	*40. 0.0'*
Total	*575.9.9* (67)

Note: A hogshead holds 52.5 Imperial gallons. Therefore two held 840 pints of ale. It would therefore appear that at a conservative estimate, not much short of 10,000 pints was consumed in this district alone.

The birth of the 6th Marquis must have been quite an event too. Lord George Cavendish wrote to his sister-in-law, Georgiana, the Duchess of Devonshire saying; *'People of all descriptions have rejoiced without measure in Lord Hartington in many parts of Derbyshire. The balls would not let people sleep in their beds for several nights.'* (67)

Newhaven Fairs

Newhaven Fair was held on the large triangle of land which used to be between the Ashbourne – Buxton road, the Ashbourne – Bakewell road and the Newhaven – Cromford road. The road layout is different now, presumably in the interests of road safety. The Fair site is clearly marked on the relevant plan covering Newhaven in the Inclosure Award document in the Chatsworth Muniment Room. It had an area of 7 acres. Newhaven was well known for its fair (mentioned above). It was being used by the Estate as early as 1682 or 1683. An account records to helpers *'to hold ye sheep* [from One Ash Grange] *at Newhaven Fair 1s. 6d'.* If the original Fair was in October, the year would be 1682. (68).

In 1798 Timothy Greenwood, the landlord of the Newhaven House Inn, was paid his expenses for holding a meeting at Newhaven *'to establish another Fair there'.* Glover (69) in 1829, states that there were two fairs at Newhaven, so clearly the second fair was established. In fact they were held on the second Wednesday in September and on October 30th (for cattle).

In 1830, Mr. Hall, the Primitive Methodist preacher of Hognaston, east of Ashbourne, went to Newhaven Fair and *'changed a £5 note to speculate on the thimble-rig. He was soon eased of two sovereigns (£2) and on reaching home, found two more were bad ones'.* Such were the vagaries of life, then as now, with forged £1 coins circulating in Ashbourne in 2004 (70). Just when the cattle fair commenced is not clear, but in the Chatsworth Estate Account for October 1801, fifty Scotch bullocks were purchased at Brough Fair. In October 1804 (the accounts for 1802 -03 seem to be missing), 8 oxen were bought at Ashbourne Fair. The following year, 2 oxen were paid for in May bought at the fair at Matlock and 5 more at Bakewell fair in the October. Six more from Ashbourne fair were paid for in the following month plus 40 Scotch bullocks (no other detail given), but Brough seems likely. In 1806, 6 oxen were bought at Tideswell Fair (paid for in September) and more in the November from Brough Fair. Despite a regular pattern of purchase from local annual cattle/oxen fairs, there is no mention of Newhaven. Hartington Fair may date back to the grant of the market in 1203 and was a 3-day affair at the Festival of St Giles. Other Hartington fairs were held on 12th February, 2nd April and the Wednesday before the last Thursday in April for cattle and pedlary but this had been 'long dicontinued' by 1846. The annual Hartington Feast was held on the nearest Sunday to 12th September. (71)

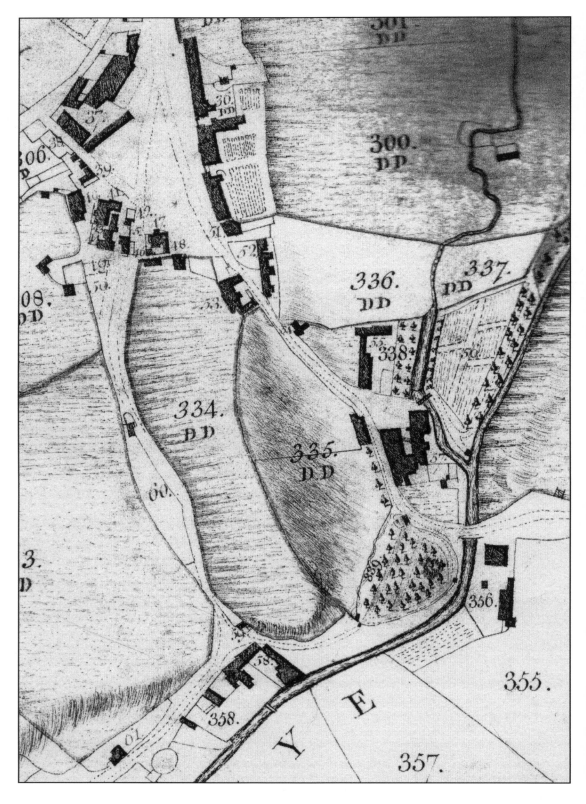

References

1 Detail from the Alstonfield parish registers are drawn from extracts taken by Tim Eades of Hope Marsh, Alstonfield; For the loss of the Jaggerman, see Kirkham, N., *The Perambulation of Hartington* Pt 2, Derbyshire Miscellany. 19XX, p 26

2 Dev. Coll. AS/95

3 Dev. Coll. AS/1401

4 Porter,L., ibid, 2004, pp 40 &42

5 Dev. Coll. Hardwick Papers, No.450

6 Dev. Coll. T-Series Box No 1-7

7 Dev. Coll. AS/1300

8 Dev. Coll. AS/1053

9 Dev. Coll. AS/1222

10 Dev. Coll. AS/1371; The Fletchers had a large estate at Earl Sterndale

11 Brit. Library, Wolley 6682, ff. 76-79. Thanks to Dr. J. R. Rieuwerts for this

12 Dev. Coll. AS/363/4

13 Dev. Coll. AS/437

14 Dev. Coll. T-Series, Buxton and Hartington Accounts, 1806

15 Featherstone, P., *Biggin and Hartington Nether Quarter,* 1998, p 63

16 Dev. Coll., Brooke-Taylor docs. Book 8, pp 10-11, 85

17 ibid. Gt. Court Baron records, 1760, p 240

18 ibid. 1761, p 262

19 Farey, J, *General View on the Agriculture and Minerals of Derbyshire.*, Vol.2, 1815, p 25

20 Farey, J., ibid, pp 96 and 393

21 Porter, R., *English Society in the 18th Century*, 1991

edit., p 66

22 Some care has to be taken in using these figures as the farm rents (including cottage and copyhold rents) in 1793 were £2,484. In 1801 it was only £2,702. There had been a 21-year rent revision c.1798. In 1804, with Inclosure rent rises, it was £5,412. Dev. Coll. AS/1056; T-Series Bundle 3; AS/1247

23 He was the Rev. Benjamin Hope, vicar 1790-1814, succeeding the Rev John Bullock, vicar 1755-1790.

24 Dev. Coll., T-Series Bundle 3

25 Wm. Salt Library, Stafford, 63/2/41; even the Hurts of Castern(e) Hall, opposite Throwley, had moved from there to Alderwasley after the estate there had come to them through marriage in 1690. (Wain, D., *The Hurts of Derbyshire*, 2002, p 25). There is a wonderful oral tradition, preserved to this day in the family, that when they moved from Castern to Alderwasley, they drove their deer herd there with them.

26 Bromfield, P., ibid. Ch.4, p 9

27 Defoe, D., *A Tour Through England and Wales*, Everyman Edition, 1927, p167

28 Dev., Coll., 5th Duke's letters, letters from the Duchess to her mother, Countess Spencer,

29 Watson, J.S., *The Reign of George III, 1760 – 1815*, 1960, pp 519 -520, also quoting Clapham J. H. *Economic History of Modern Britain*, Vol. 1, p 602

30 Porter, R., *ibid*, p 92

31 Dev. Coll., Hardwick Papers No. 450

32 as 31

33 Wm. Gould's diary, 1782 – 1788, 2/1/1784

34 Derbyshire Arch Journal, Vol. LXXII, 1952

35 Pilkington, J., *A View of the Present State of Derbyshire*, Vol. 2, 1789, pp 289 – 292; Defoe, D., *A*

Opposite: Buxton in 1777. This fascinating map shows the village prior to the development of The Crescent. The large building left of the confluence of the two streams is the Hall Inn. The Square was built over the stream confluence. Over the bridge is a square-shaped building, which is The George Inn. The building behind it is either the inn stables or possibly the (later) Theatre, with five poor cottages arranged either side of it. However, whether it was open in 1777 is questionable. The road between the two inns was the main way out of the village to Whaley Bridge. This was abandoned when the development of The Crescent commenced, although Hall Bank is a remnant.

At the time of the development work alluded to, in 1780, 'the greater part of the grove or avenue of trees was cut down'. This probably relates to the trees marked left of The George Inn and is probably how The Grove Hotel got its name. The Hall Inn had a Bowling Green and some of the trees were left standing to protect it from north winds. Presumably the building closest to the stream (and not fronting the road) was the Stables. The original Hall Inn was the part of the building complex with the double three story bay windows. Presumably the inn's original entrance fronted the former road.

In the Market Place, so named in 1813 when the Market was granted, are three groups of buildings on the right side. The middle one is presumably The Eagle and Child Inn (now The Eagle Inn) with its stables extending out at the rear. The Inn was let with a farm and presumably field 300 was a part of that. The Duke's land is marked DD. Photo: Chatsworth, Dev. Coll., Map 2049

Tour Through England and Wales, Everyman Edition, 1927, pp 162 – 163; Farey, J., ibid, p 22

36 Dev. Coll., AS/1353

37 Dev. Coll., 5th Duke's letters, No. 915, letter from Duchess of Devonshire to Countess Spencer

38 Dev. Coll., T-Series, Bundle 3. In Youlgreave Mr. Barker and Wm. Bridden had spent £5. 15s. 4d. and in Monyash, Ebenezer Bowman had spent £3. 3s. 0d

39 Dev. Coll., AS/917

40 Bromfield, P., *Industrial Workers in a Peasant Community: Manifold Valley parishes in the 18th Century with special reference to workers at the Ecton Mine* c. 1760 – 1820. Keele University library

40/1 Dev. Coll., AS/1062

41 Re bread distributiuon: see ref 71; Chatsworth Accounts, 1831 – 32

42 Dev. Coll., T-Series for the village and date for Edale, Peak Forest and Tideswell; Hartington references in the Buxton Accounts (T-Series, Bundle 14). Flagg reference in Chatsworth Estate Accounts for 1833. The Sunday School movement started in 1780 so it had taken 40 – 50 years to reach Flash and Flagg The Gt. Longstone reference is from Thornhill, R., 'About a Derbyshire Village 1790–1820', 1958, p 30

43 Lysons, D&S., *Magna Britannica, Vol 5, Derbyshire*, 1817; Dev. Coll., AS/1013 and 1126. No payment was recorded in 1724; AS/371/1/2; AS/98

44 Dev. Coll., T-Series, Bundle 3; Devonshire Collection Series of MSS, List of vicars, filed under H (not to be confused with the main collection of documents)

45 Dev. Coll., T-Series, Box 8 – 15, Buxton and Hartington etc. Accounts; Bagshaw, see ref. 71

46 Pilkington, J., *A View of the Present State of Derbyshire*, Vol.2., p.289 – 292; *Where Truth Abides, Diaries of the 4th Duke of Newcastle-under-Lyme 1822-50*, edit., J. Fletcher, 23/8/1833. He lived at Clumber Park, Nottinghamshire

47 Porter, L., & Robey, J. A., *The Copper & Lead Mines around the Manifold Valley, North Staffordshire*, 2000, p 194

48 Bentley JM., & Fox, GK., *Railways of the High Peak, Buxton to Ashbourne*, 1997, p 76

49 pers. comm. the late John Bonsall, Apes Tor Cottage, Ecton, one of the men nearly caught by the oncoming water

50 Dev. Coll., Chatsworth Account Book, 1834

51 Local oral tradition, supported by Garner, R., *Natural History of the County of Stafford*, 1844, p 541

52 *Derbyshire Chronicle*, 4/8/1838

53 *Mining Journal*, July 1836

54 Dodd, A.E., & E.M., *Peakland Road & Trackways*, 2000, p 146

55 Porter, L., & Robey, JA., ibid, p 99 and Farey, J., ibid, p 186

56 Farey, ibid, p 188. Joseph Gould was the son of William Gould, both Collectors of Rent for the Duke

57 Farey, ibid., pp 184 – 189

58 Hanson, M.J. (see below); *Derbyshire Courier*, 4/4/1829

59 *Derbyshire Courier*, 18/12/1830

60 Strutt, *Sports and Pastimes*, 1834 edition, pp x/iii/xlv

61 Wm. Gould's diary, 20/6/1784. The new Ludwell Farm wood was known as the Isle of Man. Some eight trees from this planting would appear to have survived on the Staffordshire bank of the River Dove opposite Ludwell Farm. (Hanson, MJ., William Gould's Diary, Version 1, 2001, p 292).

62 Leek Church Register and *Shrovetide Football and the Ashbourne Game*, Porter, L., 2002, p 23 & 39; Roberts, J., *A History of Wetton, Thors Cave and the Ecton Mines,* 1900. For bull baiting see Porter, L., *Victorian Times in and around Ashbourne*, 2000, p 46

63 It appeared in *The Mirror* of 20th May 1837 and is reproduced in Naylor, P & Porter, L., *Well Dressing*, p 10

64 Porter, L., *Shrovetide Football*, ibid. p 45

65 Dev. Coll., 5th Duke's series, letter No. 1997

66 Lees-Milne, J., *The Batchelor Duke, 6th Duke of Devonshire*, 1990, pp 14-15, quoting Howitt, W., *Rural Life of England*, 1840

67 Dev. Coll., AS/1510. P Heacock's letter books 24/6/1811; 5th Dukes's letters, No 1056.1, 9/6/1790

68 Dev. Coll., AS/403. This account also records the payment for washing 662 'old sheep' and 197 lambs at One Ash

69 Glover, S., *Directory of Derbyshire*, 1829, p 72

70 *Derbyshire Courier* 6/11/1830

71 Bagshaw, S., *History, Gazetter & Directory of Derbyshire*, 1846, pp 363-65

3. RUNNING THE MANOR

Developments at Buxton

The village of Buxton adjoined the parish of Hartington Upper Quarter. In fact the southern half of the current town is on land once within this parish. Although there were some ancient enclosures (i.e. fields) much of Buxton, consisting of the four small villages of Buxton, Staden, Sterndale and Cowdale was common land or waste. The Duke of Devonshire owned some of the ancient enclosures with others and this entitled them to rights of common pasture on both the common and waste land. These extended to 800 acres on land owned by the King (through the Duchy of Lancaster) as Lord of the Manor of High Peak. The Duke's lands had been purchased by Bess of Hardwick and her husband, the Earl of Shrewsbury, and handed down the Cavendish line of succession.

Additionally, William Henry Cavendish, Duke of Portland, owned the *'great tythes'* within the hamlet of Buxton. The Duke of Devonshire owned all tythes or tenths (*? The great tythes*) of corn, grain and hay in the three other above named villages. The Dean and Chapter of Lichfield owned the tythes of wool and lamb, while the Vicar of Bakewell was entitled to the 'small tythes' of Buxton liberty. (1)

As a result of this, in the late 18th century, the Duke had to buy land in Buxton to build The Crescent and other developments. He did not have a large holding of land here as in Hartington parish where he, not the King, was Lord of the Manor. He was allocated only 24 acres in the Buxton Inclosure Award. Major acquisitions included Sir John Edensor Heathcote's estate at Buxton and Hartington for £8,000 in 1782; Robert Longden's land at Fairfield and Hartington for £4,000 in 1788; William Gould's estate at Buxton, Staden and Hartington for £8,100 in 1788 and land at Fairfield from Isherwood's trustees for £4,080 in 1798. The full picture is explained in Chapter 4. However this was the tip of the iceberg. The Duke's investments in Hartington parish and Buxton (and especially at the latter) between 1776 and 1805 amounted to £208,645.

However the Cavendish interests in Buxton had begun in 1569, when Mary, Queen of Scots, had been placed in the custody of Bess of Hardwick's husband, George Talbot, Earl of Shrewsbury. Coincidentally (or perhaps not?) in 1571, she requested that she would like to visit the Buxton bath. Langham and Wells record that the Earl had received treatment at Buxton in 1569 and benefited from it. They state that the Scottish Queen's request in 1571 and 1572 were refused on the grounds that the Hall was being built and was unfinished. The property had been purchased from a Mr. Robert Cotteril by the Earl of Shrewsbury in 1571 together with the Buxton Wells plus St. Ann's Well and the single bath. In 1573, a further request to Queen Elizabeth I to permit a visit to Buxton, with the Earl also stating that his own health would benefit from taking the waters, was granted. (2)

In 1695-96, improvements were made by the tenant, Cornelius White. Langham and Wells state that improvements were made to the bath and an overflow installed to another bath (called White's Bath) for the *'poor and impotent'*. Both had a large drain to the River Wye to empty the bath. It also appears that a pump was installed to stop the cold springs reducing the warm water in the Ladies' Bath. Bathers apparently entered the water naked by this time. (3)

However, c. 1697-1703, Celia Fiennes stayed at the Hall Inn, Buxton and was not impressed. She described it as being the largest in the village but *'not very good'*. It was basically an inn, not an hotel. There was no overall price for your stay with each meal and drink – including

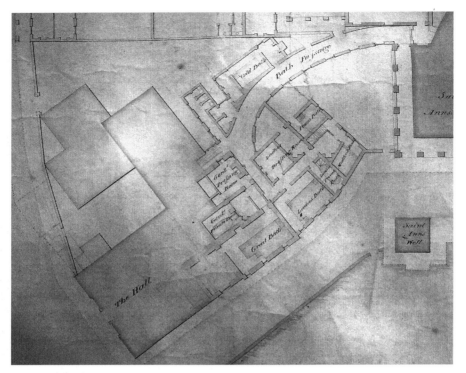

A Chatsworth plan of 1806 showing the Hall Inn and the Buxton Baths. There was access to the Baths from both the Inn and The Crescent. Note St Ann's Well, bottom right. Reproduced with permission of the Chatsworth Settlement Trustees

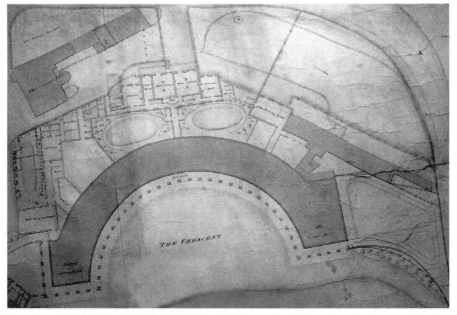

The same Chatsworth plan of 1806 showing The Crescent and its gardens to the rear. Note the rear access road and the George Inn (top left). Reproduced with permission of the Chatsworth Settlement Trustees

The Chatsworth plan of 1806 (see also opposite page) also includes a proposed elevation for The Square, built adjacent to the Hall Inn and The Crescent .It was actually built with 11 columns, not 17 as seen here. There was a house where the Victorian letterbox now stands and presumably the owner would not sell, resulting in the smaller Square. Reproduced with permission of the Chatsworth Settlement Trustees

that for the servants (probably meaning the latter had an inferior meal) – paid for separately. The beer accompanying the meal *'is so bad that very little can be dranke'*.

The accommodation was not to her liking either: *'you pay not for your bed room and truly the other is so unreasonable a price and the lodgings so bad, 2 beds in a room some 3 beds and some 4 in one roome, so that if you have not company enough of your own to fill a room they will readily put others into the same chamber, and some tymes they are so crowded that three must lye in a bed ... few people stay above two or three nights'*. She had to stay a second night by reason of one of her party being ill, but it was much against her will.

There was also too much noise from people going in and out of the bath, described as being about 40ft/12m long by 20-30 ft./6-9m wide. It had 10 – 12 springs that bubbled up the luke-warm mineral water, (*'not as warm as milk from a cow'*). It was not a *'quick spring'* either and therefore did not replenish the bath water quick enough for her liking. It was warm enough to open the pores but not enough to induce sweats. It also made her shake, (considered by Morris, the editor of her Journal, to be a result of lead poisoning, which is not substantiated). Although covered over, the bath which lacked a proper ceiling had a central ventilation shaft which poured cold air *'down onto your head'*; more likely to make you shake than water flowing through lead lined pipes on so transient a visit.

There was a stone floor with stone seats on one side of the bath. Surprisingly, you had to have *'a guide that swims with you'*. It was shallow enough to be neck deep (say 5ft./1.5.m) where you *'may stand and hold by a chain'*. Elsewhere in the bath *'it was very deep and strong, it will turn you down'* presumably above the outlet. She also describes St. Ann's Well, situated in a building with an arched roof. She wrote that the water was not unpleasant but rather like milk and was thought to be a *'diaretick'*. It was not as warm as the *'Somersetshire Baths and Springs'* i.e. at Bath. There were several other places to stay but all were *'ordinary entertaining houses'* – i.e. inns.

By the time Daniel Defoe reached Buxton two-three decades later, Buxton Hall had been improved. He described the lodgings as *'convenient'*, the food *'very good'* and use of the bath at a shilling (5p.) *'convivial'* He wrote: *'here* [in the bath] *you are never tired and can hardly be*

Left: The Square, Buxton. The original plan showed a longer building with 17, not 11, columns as built
Right: Flagg Sunday School, built in 1833, see page 33

persuaded to come out of the bath when you are in'. There were several springs including '*on the sides of the hill*', which may include the source of the water used for water closets etc. at the Duke's hotels in 1819–21 (see below).

Defoe speculated that if there was better provision for the nobility and gentry *'and suitable entertainment'* as he put it, Buxton would be *'frequented'*. He liked the open and healthy country *'fit for the ladies to take a ring upon their coaches'*. He compared Buxton with Bath. He described the latter as *'more like a prison than a place of diversion, scarce gives the company room to converse out of the smell of their own excrements and where the very city itself may be said to stink like a general common shore.'* (4) The improvements to Buxton Hall mentioned above, occurred in 1710. (5)

Defoe's comfortable experience would appear to have been as a result of various changes, which occurred after the visit by Celia Fiennes. In 1711, John Barker a *'joyner'* was paid on account (i.e. a part payment) of £200 *for 'building four new rooms, a staircase and stables'* at Buxton, which must relate to the Hall. Barker built a three storey bath (with a roof this time) at a total cost of £400. Langham and Wells include drawings of this building and describe Barker as being an architect of Rowsley, south of Chatsworth. (6) So much for the Chatsworth book-keeper calling him a *'joyner'*! In 1726-27, a John Smith was paid for *'severall journeys to Buxton to view the Hall and direct what Repaires Mr. Norton [the tenant] must be at the charge of'*. Later, further work was done in 1744-46 totalling £600. It was described as being *'the new building at Buxton Hall.'* The completion of this coincided with the tenancy commencing for 21 years by Brian Hodgson's father (see below). (7)

After 1772 and the *Buxton Inclosure Act*, the St. Ann's Well was to be left unenclosed for the use and benefit of the neighbouring inhabitants and all other persons resorting thereto for their health or otherwise. The local inhabitants were to appoint at a Vestry Meeting, to be held in Easter week at the Chapel of Buxton, a poor person of the four hamlets (Buxton, Staden, Sterndale and Cowdale) to attend and take care of the well and assist and hand the water to anyone requiring it. This is why we can all obtain mineral water at the well free of charge today. Young (8) makes it clear that the method of payment experienced by Celia Fiennes was widespread. Writing in 1771 he stated that '*Matlock is by no means a disagreeable spaw (sic) to spend a short time at, for viewing the country around. Each person pays 1s. 0d. for dinner, as much for supper and 8d. breakfast. Servants in proportion and horses at the common price (sic), the rooms gratis. There are billiards and music.*'

On 16th August 1773, Godfrey Heathcote wrote to the Duke from Hardwick (9). His letter suggested two significant courses of actions, one concerning development in Buxton village which initiated capital investment there, albeit slowly. Heathcote reminded the Duke that Buxton (including Cowden, Staden and Kings Sterndale) contained about *700 acres of inclosed lands* and about *900 acres of common* or waste land. Other action was in Hartington.

Hartington contained a much larger acreage, with about *800 acres of inclosed land and some 12,000 acres of common* or waste land. It is clear that development was already being considered: '*Both Buxton and Hartington are at this time objects to your Grace of very great importance and requires a very particular and serious attention. The former (i.e. at Buxton) on account of the necessary improvements which are absolutely wanted by both your Grace's tenants and by all persons that resort to the place either for Health or pleasure*'.

The Duke had in 1773 two commercial properties in Buxton – the Hall Inn and the Eagle & Child Inn. Heathcote pointed out that the prospect was available for further baths from the outflow of the first bath. The Hall had been occupied from 1746 by Brian Hodgson's father on a 21-year lease. Brian Hodgson was the tenant by 1773. His tenancy also included other lands and Fairfield Mill, the total rental being £280. 4s. 0d. at that time. (10)

The Eagle & Child Inn is in the Market Place, purchased in c. 1748 from a Mr. Newton, with a tenant at that date called Moorewood. Along with rents on additions to the buildings provided at the Duke's expense, it returned £218 per annum in rent. The Eagle & Child would appear to have been extended in 1765 when payments were made to John Wheeldon towards the building cost. It is still called The Eagle today. (11) At the '*foot of a close*' belonging to this rental and near to St. Ann's Well were two '*pretty strong springs*'. One was a warm spring similar in temperature to St. Ann's Well and the bath's water at the Hall. The other spring was a cold one. It was considered by Heathcote that both would make good wells of commercial importance, especially as other speculators were being attracted to Buxton. A '*house for entertainment* (another pub) *is now erecting by one Dakeyne of Warrington within Fairfield, close to the River Goyt*' for instance. Presumably this was the George Inn. Fairfield parish was on the north side of the River Wye i.e. immediately behind The Crescent. The reference to the River Goyt is wrong.

The springs mentioned above must relate to the Pump Room spring, although the current building dates from 1894. Four additional baths were constructed by John Carr between 1786–88, three of them on the land between the Hall and The Crescent. These were the Gentlemen's Private Bath, the Ladies' Private Bath plus the Matlock Bath (with a lower temperature, similar to that at Matlock) and a cold bath at the rear of the site. In 1809 a pump was purchased for the Gentlemen's Bath '*which I think will be found particularly useful to those bathers that cannot bear to be exposed to the cold air, which they are pumped upon*'. Either warm air was being introduced or the cold air directed away from the bathers. (12)

Ward states, writing in 1827, that there were two public baths and one private for gentlemen, one public and one private for ladies and one for the poor. The springs issued about 60 gallons of water every minute and took two hours and fifty minutes to fill the baths. There was also another bath at the end of Serpentine Walk which followed the infant River Wye upstream. Its water temperature was only 64°F, compared to the Buxton Bath's 82°F. Additionally Ward noted the Hot Baths (see below). (13)

St. Ann's Well, Heathcote noted, had *'for time immemorial'*, through *'grace & favour'* of the Duke, been available for the public use for drinking. It still is. He also suggested that more baths be built. However it was over a decade before The Crescent was built (also by John Carr) and the four additional baths provided. He had suggested a covered walkway from the Hall Inn to the bath to give an edge against the new inn being built. The Duke's eventual response was incredibly far-sighted.

In 1780 work started on the development of The Crescent, a semi-circular building with a colonnaded front and side to reach the bathing area between The Crescent and the Hall based on Heathcote's suggestion. William Gould, the estate's Hartington rent collector, recorded in his diary that in 1783 the roof was being constructed. This development included two hotels, the St. Ann's at the western end and closest to the Hall and the Great Hotel at the eastern end. There were seven apartments including a town house in the middle of the frontage for the Duke and shops in the colonnade. It has been claimed, this was Britain's first holiday resort. The centrally situated apartments did not last for long, demand for rooms saw them (including the Duke's town house) converted into yet another hotel – The Central.

The Crescent's hotels opened for business in 1786. However, the Devonshires did not use their town house there until December 1786. On the 17th December the Duchess wrote to her mother to say that a planned visit had been delayed *'til we know if the fever is safe there'*. A previous letter to her mother dated 25th October 1786 may indicate that it was not finished at that time. The surviving letter is not complete and the locality is not confirmed, but the Duchess wrote: *'I got up this morning at 9 and went into the cold bath. I walked a great deal and cours'd a great deal on horseback. My horse (the chestnut) carrys me with ye greatest safety. In the eve'g we played cards as usual.'* She went on to add *'I believe this place as beautiful as the weather looks, is growing unwholesome. I know D- [the Duke] thinks our Derbyshire valleys are very unwholesome from ye fogs, so late in the year. I have strongly recommended to the children and to Bess* [Lady Elizabeth Foster] *be out only in ye sunshine.'* If they were in Buxton (which seems likely) they must have been staying at the Hall Inn.

On 23rd December 1786 the Duchess wrote again to her mother announcing their arrival in Buxton: *'Here we are and have found the house more comfortable than we expected – a decent parlour and good bedrooms. Lady Warren be praisd (sic) is gone and there is nobody we know but Dr. Denman and the Heatons, Mr. Shaw Stuart and his newly marryd wife, Lady Maxwell and her daughters and a few more, but we can keep quite clear of them as they all dine in their own rooms. I bathe tomorrow having had a good deal of pain and drink two glasses* [of mineral water]. *We shall live the wholesomemost of lives here, dine out and go to bed at 11, up at 7.'*

The Duke was not keen on going at all; on 17th December the Duchess had written (again to her mother) saying *'I am afraid going to Buxton is very disagreeable to him* [the Duke] *but he is so set on it for me'*. On 19th June 1787, the Duchess wrote saying that a new warm spring had been found at Buxton. This discovery would appear to have not been documented previously. (14)

The Ballroom (Assembly Room)

The Great Hotel was adjacent to the Adam-style ballroom (which survives and was restored by the County Council when in use as a library). It apparently still retains its original chandeliers. Here, ladies would take to the floor with their husband, daughter or maybe a son – or a gentleman who had caught her eye. Other men able to divert away from a pretty face, figure or finery could spend time chancing their arm or wallet in the nearby and elegant card room. Buxton became a premier destination for the social elite.

The Ballroom was also known as the Assembly Room and was run by the estate, making income from lettings, dances etc. A reference in the accounts for income from the Coffee Room in 1810, related to another innovation. (15) Participation in these events was governed by expensive subscriptions and entry fees. Langham has shown however that the income from the subscriptions to the Ballroom began to decrease after 1796 and never recovered the popularity of the early years. Divine Service was held in the Assembly Room on Sundays until St. John's Church was completed.

The decline in popularity must have been quite a disappointment to John Heaton. It is not hard to anticipate his expectations for the Buxton developments. The creation of a fashionable spa, spared of the excesses so despised by the Duchess at Bath, must have seemed a certainty for him. The presence of the Duke and Duchess would have seen a steady procession of Britain's aristocracy to The Crescent, followed by countless other visitors. However the Duke appears not to have been keen on the place. His townhouse in The Crescent was little used and eventually became part of another hotel as Heaton accepted the reality that Buxton was where people came for the cure rather than the conviviality of aristocratic social life. He would have found it ironic that his attempts to maximise the return on investment, which must have looked like a safe speculation, was frustrated by the Duke himself. By 1810 the party was over, the Duchess having died in 1806. Twenty years before that, however, The Crescent must have been Heaton's pride and joy!

From June to October three assemblies were held in the Ballroom every week; casual dress on Monday and on Friday (referred to oddly today as the undress ball) as distinct from the dress ball held on a Wednesday.

Other Diversions

By comparison, the card room was open every evening, including Sunday. There were several billiard tables in Buxton, an excellent one being Billings' opposite the Hall (presumably on or near Hall Bank). The theatre had performances on Tuesdays, Thursdays and Saturdays. *'For the diversion of gentlemen, a pack of carriers is kept by subscription and to enjoy the amusement of shooting, many resort to the neighbouring moors, on which are found grouse, snipes, plovers and that singular bird, the dotterel'.* Hotel guests kept in touch with home via the post office which was in the centre of The Crescent. It was kept by a Mr. Moore who was a bookseller and stationer who also had a reading room, supplied with papers. Under the piazza adjoining the Hall was Mr. Bright's jewellery shop, also selling cutlery and plate, both places being popular with hotel guests. (16) The Crescent's architect was John Carr, of York.

In March 1811, there was consternation at the kennels for the Buxton Hounds. Some of the dogs were suffering from a disease thought then to be hydrophobia. It was wondered if the dogs had developed some kind of madness. There being a full moon did not help the speculation (literally). Some visitors to Buxton had been bitten by the dogs including Mr.

Sherbrook Dell, south
east of Buxton, drawn
c. 1820 by F L Chantrey.
It was a popular outing
for visitors to Buxton

Oaks, a kennel hand. Destroying all the dogs was considered against the possibility that visitor numbers to Buxton could be affected by wild and unsubstantiated rumours circulating in the town. Mr. Oaks had gone to Liverpool '*for the purpose of bathing and drinking the saltwater*'. A week later after keeping the dogs locked up, the position seemed to be recovering as were the bitten visitors. As for Mr. Oaks, Heacock wrote that '*I am surprised* [that he] *is not returned from Liverpool*'! (17)

By 1811, there were six baths served by natural hot water at 82°F, with the cooler Matlock Bath at 68°F. A reminder that the King, not the Duke, was Lord of the Manor in Buxton (in his capacity as Duke of Lancaster) came in 1812 when an application was made to the Duchy for a grant of Fairs and Markets. (18)

At the end of 1812, Heacock wrote to Heaton with his idea for a hot bath. '*it has been suggested to me by the Medical Gentlemen who attend this place during the season that Hot Baths would be extremely desirable. Hot Baths … would benefit this place in as much as they would bring very considerably in as much as they would bring a great many of the better kind of company who are obliged to go to Bath and elsewhere.*'

Following the consecration of the new church in 1813 (see below), the Duke asked Heacock to accompany him the following day to set out a significant area to be planted with trees. The Duke mentioned his intention to set out the land opposite The Crescent (now The Terrace) with shrubs and '*in other respects ornamented*'. This piece of ground was described as being '*a most unsightly-looking foreground to so palatial a structure*'. He also mentioned that he would like to purchase the Grove Inn and adjacent property opposite his own. In the event it rained the following day and he returned to Chatsworth saying that he would be back the following May, which appears not to have happened.

However his ideas on planting timber seems to have been implemented. Although hindered by a shortage of cash, this suggests that the Duke was still spending with caution but was already formulating plans for Buxton, which came to fruition some five years later. His need to focus his mind on the issue was soon to become apparent. A couple of months later in May 1813, Heacock reported *'All the new buildings at this place are completed and the expenses of them are comprised in the Bills paid to 31st December last … The balance in hand including the receipts of the Baths and Rooms to the 20th of August next will not be sufficient to meet the expenses to that period.'*

It took until 1816 before an innovative scheme was launched *'for supplying spring water and erecting a warm spring–water bath at Buxton'*. However Heacock had suggested a couple of baths for individuals adjacent to the existing baths. This new scheme was for the erection of Hot Baths (where the water was heated by coal) to the right of The Crescent. This was however only a part of the plan for invigorating Buxton's trade. In 1817 Mr. John Chatterton was paid for his assistance in furnishing a plan and estimate for supplying Buxton with soft water. This probably related to the hotels. It was 1840 before mains water was supplied to Buxton (which by then had become a town with a population of 1,500). Some £400 was spent on the hot baths in 1817 and £1,230 the following year, excluding £7. 13s. 3d. spent on tiles from Josiah Wedgwood. A further £1,530 was spent on creating the Terrace Walk laid out by Jeffry Wyatt, (Sir Jeffry from 1827) opposite The Crescent, the urns thereon coming from Londesborough Hall in Yorkshire. In 1819–21, some c. £2,000 was spent on further work at the hot baths and in supplying soft water (brought in earthenware pipes purchased from Samuel Bagshaw) from a spring in Manchester Road to water closets in The Crescent's three hotels, the Hall Inn, the George Inn and the *'new lodging houses'*. The Hot Baths were the work of Charles Sylvester of Derby, who was paid £86. 18s. 0d. in 1818 for *'drawings and attendance'*.

The Hall Inn water closets must have been added at this time but are not mentioned in the accounts. Presumably the landlord paid for them. It is inconceivable that they would not have been provided. The Terrace Walks became an integral part of the *'cure'* being sought by the gout-ridden patients or those afflicted with arthritis etc. Exercise was taken on the paths of The Terrace; reaching the top being an indication of success of the treatment. (19)

Langham states that these baths *'helped to keep the town at the forefront of advances in water medicine.'* With the use of coal-fired boilers, steam was used to increase water temperature above the heat of the natural hot water. Presumably by the time it had travelled in pipes to the far end of The Crescent, it had cooled too. A covered way was built between The Great Hotel and the Hot Baths. The latter also helped to maintain the reputation of Buxton as a centre for hydrotherapy and to protect estate revenues. The addition of quality housing and lodgings did too, especially in the fashionable and upmarket apartments in The Square at the side of the Hall Inn, built in 1803-06.

A further development was the rebuilding of the Chalybeate Well near to The George Hotel in 1819. It had been out of use for at least 27 years. Later redevelopment at the Natural Baths (those adjacent to The Hall Inn) saw two rooms provided where water could be drunk. The original St. Ann's Well (on the corner of the building, to the right of the former Tourist Information Centre) was in one room and a Chalybeate Drinking Well behind it in another.

Chalybeate was used in water treatment and not least as a tonic and was of a different chemical composition apparently to the mineral water in the St. Ann's Well. The estate had purchased The George Hotel in 1804 from Messrs. Dakin (sic) alias Dakeyne above, for £6,000. However, revenue generation had been checked after the death of the 5th Duke in 1811, bolstered by industrial unrest.

Buxton was part of the combined Buxton and Hartington Rental Collection controlled by Philip Heacock. In 1824 it was worth £33,604 per annum of which Buxton was the most important in terms of value – £7,934 per annum. However, arrears in Buxton, of which the hotels were a major contributor, totalled £8,006 (out of a collection area arrears total of £8,866. (20). This was serious and Heacock would not have let it get to this position if it was felt that there was an alternative. Because of the downturn in business, since 1809 the hotel and inn rents had been collected by instalments, but still arrears had accumulated. It came at a time when the 6th Duke was in deep financial difficulties. In that same year, he was forced to dispose of his Weatherby Estate, the very one which had been his father's principal source of revenue. It was sold for £160,000, although part had been sold in 1814. (21)

Heacock wrote to John Heaton in mid-season (July) 1812. He commented on the trade downturn saying that because of civil unrest, people from Lancashire and Yorkshire who used to frequent Buxton were staying at home. He also stated that *'the place has not been of late years much frequented by Irish visitors'*. General Maitland, who was commanding troops in these areas, was staying at The Great Hotel, which was weathering the storm better than its competitors. Fortunately for the landlady, Mrs. Hall, he had made her hotel his headquarters. (22) Ironically her hotel had an extension in 1809 to create a new dining room. The stone landings and flagstone came from Halifax, possibly Halifax, Nova Scotia, for Heacock wrote *'even including the expense of carriage at a less price than in this country'*. (23) The downturn in business took its first major casualty in September 1813 when Mr. Edward Anthony of the Hall Inn went into receivership. The irony was that after four indifferent seasons 1813 had turned out to be a good one. Some 75 people (important local tenants and local gentry) were cheered up by a dinner provided on the day by the estate to celebrate the opening of the market. This was on 30th October 1813, the first fair being two days earlier. On 1st September, 1814, Heacock wrote to John Heaton stating that he *'never knew the place (Buxton) so full of Company'*. One wonders whether the civil unrest had abated to the benefit of the hotel trade.

In 1828 the position had not materially improved and the arrears were written off. Matters were to get worse for in 1833, James Muirhead, the proprietor of the Great Hotel was declared bankrupt, which cost the estate over £4,000.

Langham has shown that subscriptions to the ballroom declined after 1791 and profits on the Natural Baths after 1811, despite a resurgence in 1815–16. However the Hot Baths must have accounted for some of the decline in popularity of the Natural Baths. The decision to build more than the two baths requested by Heacock had been a good one. Although by and large, the extra income provided by the Hot Baths remained fairly level for twenty years or so, it pushed total profit for the Buxton Baths to over £1,000pa, the Hot Baths contribution being c. £300pa.

Heacock was one of the first of a new profession of men who became agents of the land-owning aristocracy, starting his employment in 1805 on a salary of £560pa. He continued the work of John Heaton in improving rental income and pressing for improvements. However after the death of the 5th Duke in 1811, very little capital was available for further schemes. Perhaps Heacock's greatest contribution was St. John's Church, completed in 1812, but started under the 5th Duke. It was largely finished by 1810 as the accounts for that year record the cost of £6,757. 18s. 4¼d.

In 1809, Heacock was experiencing profound problems which must have made him concerned he would ever get the church finished. Furthermore, the site of the church was on unsound ground: the building work being delayed until the insertion of 2,200 (sic) wooden piles each 16 feet long had been completed. (24)

Initially he had difficulty getting stone for the masons, several of whom were called up for 28 days Militia duty in Buxton. Unable to replace them with local men he was forced to send a man (Bramwell) to recruit from Yorkshire. However, he was not so lucky regarding the stone and even less so with his search for timber. He had his eye on stone for the columns for the portico from near Devonshire Bridge or Wirksworth or Elton, and eventually made an offer for some stone at the latter village. However the quarry owner linked the sale to a sale of the quarry itself and ended up in losing the order.

After a five month delay, he was able to report that with a month of '*remarkably fine weather*' his new masons (and the Militia men now back at work) had the columns rising with stone from near Chatsworth. With all the timber being grown for sale on the estate, you would have thought that there was ample for the church roof, but it was not long enough. Eventually, timber from Quebec in Canada was purchased from a Liverpool merchant and delivered to Whaley Bridge Wharf, where it languished for weeks as the merchant would not provide details of the cost and Heacock would not move it until he was sure he was not being cheated. In the end it cost him £13 a load which was 13s. 0d. (65p.) cheaper than timber from Hull (presumably from Norway). (25)

As the year 1810 came into focus, Heacock could see his 'chapel' (as he called it) getting ever closer to completion, although continuing delays were to thwart him until the 1812 official opening. No doubt replete from a barrel of oysters, a Christmas present from the contractors, White & Co., he wrote to them on 1st January 1810 about the building:'…*it will be a most elegant piece of architecture and will prove a most useful, as well as ornamental acquisition to the place,* i.e. Buxton. It still is.

Although the slaters were busy on the roof, as winter approached Heacock had the western end thatched to keep out the weather and allow work to proceed on the interior! The church was consecrated on 9th August 1812. It was the end of March 1813 before the Duke saw it, attending Divine Service. He said he felt highly pleased with it and also with the surrounding grounds, although he felt the coat of arms could have been larger and better displayed. If only he had known the aggravation Heacock had experienced. Even getting a black marble top from Mr. Brown at Ashford Marble Works went awry. Ordered in late August 1811 and required in ten days' time, it still had not been delivered six months later.

At least the Hall Inn took lettings of pews in the new church. It took pews 24 – 31, eight in all which took five people each. (26) The churchyard yews were planted in 1822. The former village chapel (which still exists as St Anne's Church) was converted into a school.

Despite the presence of the various hotels, a few weeks later, (1812) Heacock declared his preference for accommodation in Buxton when he recommended '*Mrs. Cummings' house …a very comfortable one*'. At the time there was plenty of room in the hotels. Several lodging houses had been built by the estate and some of these let out accommodation (rather than serve as what we now call second homes). It was a condition of the leases of these premises that hirers could not have dinner served therein. The estate wanted the visitors to eat in the

St John's Church, Buxton. The opening was delayed until 1812, the year after the rather large date stone of 1811 (MDCCCXI) because of delays in getting stone, finding enough masons and timber long enough for the roof

estate hotels or inns. From the estate's point of view, profitable hotels and inns could afford good rents.

Langham & Wells, (27) fortunately include a letter from a lady visitor writing to her sister about what she and her brother did in the first week of a three week stay. Her parents had come to take the water cure. They stayed on Hall Bank, built to John Carr's design as a row of lodging houses. Arriving on the Saturday, the first excursion (on the Monday) was to Castleton, setting out at 6 a.m. They spent an hour at the Ebbing & Flowing Well, east of Barmoor Clough, just north of Dove Holes, and also diverted to check out Eldon Hole, arriving at Castleton at 10 a.m. The Ebbing & Flowing Well rose and fell twice while they were there. These days it does not ebb and flow at all.

They saw the Speedwell Mine, Mam Tor, Peak's Hole (now Peak Cavern) and the Castle before continuing to Bradwell. Here they spent 30 minutes at Bagshaw Cavern (no longer open to visitors) before returning via Tideswell. They attended the Assembly Room in the evening. On the Tuesday they went to Poole's Hole (now Cavern) and saw the lime houses (dwellings dug out of lime ash nearby) in the morning. It rained in the afternoon so she (her name is not given) walked along The Crescent arcade and called at Mr. Moore's lending library. Her brother went to the Billiard Room. After tea they went to the theatre (describing the exterior as *'looking like a barn'*). It was to their enjoyment notwithstanding and they went again on Thursday and Saturday. It was situated at the rear of the George Inn. Apparently its appearance was not helped by being adjoined by *'a number of very poor cottages'*.

Wednesday was wet in the morning and later they went to a popular feature at that time – the Lovers' Leap at Sherbrook Dell, situated below the hairpin bend on what is now Duke's Drive above Ashford Dale. In the evening there was a dress ball (formal attire) at the Assembly Room *'... Buxton having within these few days had a number of arrivals of the first fashion, the Assembly Room appeared to me to be uncommonly brilliant'*.

Thursday morning saw them at a concert and horse riding in the afternoon. There was another excursion on Friday to Chee Tor (Chee Dale) and Millers Dale on the River Wye, down river from Buxton. Saturday was a twelve-hour trip to Chatsworth, setting off at 6 am and returning via Hassop, Great Longstone and Monsal Dale. The following week, trips were planned to Dove Dale; Diamond Hill (a small knoll now called Countess Cliff, south of the town and near to the industrial estate at Harpur Hill); and the Marvel Stones, limestone outcrop at nearby Peak Dale only protruding some 4 – 5 feet out of the ground and 200 feet long. Life would appear to have been much slower then and expectations for diversion lower.

Langham gives the impression that it was John Heaton who was responsible for the lack of further investment, but Heaton must have felt frustrated as much as Heacock. However further investment would have required borrowing and it is unlikely that Heaton would have recommended it. (28) At the end of August 1813, Heacock was appraised of the reason for the lack of further investment. However it did not prevent him recommending a new theatre, two hot baths (adjacent to the existing baths) and a Market Hall, once the grant of fairs and markets was made. He was quite specific about how the latter should be built too, seemingly one suspects, having seen or heard about the huge Market Hall previously built by the estate at Weatherby.

Bathing arrangements

Godfrey Heathcote's letter of 1773 (see above) goes on to describe the bathing conditions and practices which visitors had to endure. They provide a unique and fascinating insight of what visitors to Buxton wishing to 'take the waters' could expect. It was a far cry from the new facilities initiated by John Heaton in the 1780s at great expense and financed by increasing output at the Ecton Copper Mine from 1780.

Not only were more baths (or at least one) needed but the prices, times and manner of bathing needed regulation. The bath was under the control of the Hall Inn, where Brian Hodgson was the landlord. He charged 1s. 0d. (5p) for all users of the bath unless they were residents (and took meals) at the Hall or at his own (recently erected) lodging house (these he charged 6d. (2½p). Guests at the Eagle and Child Inn (where Mr. Wheeldon was the landlord) were given preference to other visitors not staying with Hodgson. Hodgson and Wheeldon had other business interests together, hence the preference.

Hall Inn guests could bathe in the morning and other people thereafter. People were therefore having to wait, and at least another bath for ladies was needed (with an undressing room attached) so that they could bathe at the same time as the men. Further, the ladies (or men) had to wait 'with indelicacy' on going in or out of the bath, as the other sex came out.

Further the bath was situated adjacent to the privy (toilet), bakehouse and brewhouse. The privy was 'intolerable offensive both to the eye and air of several passages, lodging rooms', etc. What was needed, Heathcote recommended, were two privvies, one for each sex 'with private convenient passages to each'. He further suggested that removal of the bakehouse and brewhouse would enable the rooms to be added to the bath area (as undressing areas etc.) or added to the hotel where other changes were needed as the dining room was no longer big enough. It was just short of fifty years later that the smelly earth closets were replaced by water closets. (29)

Plans for the two new hotels in The Crescent must have come as quite a shock to the Hall Inn. Although there were several inns in town, none were adjacent to the bath until then, and of course, the estate had the money to ensure guests in The Crescent found the new hotel facilities to their liking. Enlargement of the bathing facilities also ensured that The Crescent hotels' guests were not disadvantaged.

Threats from The Stuarts & France

Taxation causing estate payments for specific and unusual occurrences feature elsewhere in this book and were sometimes for military matters, such as building ships and the standing down of soldiers. Another event was the 1745 Rebellion. In response to this, the Duke of Devonshire paid for the raising of troops – he paid for the expenses of arming and kitting out 122 men, 12 horsemen and various officers. His expenses totalled £2,169. There was clearly concern for the security of Chatsworth. Gathering intelligence was helpful and payments for this were made. The Duke was the Lord Lieutenant for Derbyshire and his security concerns would have extended beyond Chatsworth.

Before it was clear which way the Scottish Army would march from Stockport, the Duke took responsibility for the *'breaking up [of] the turnpike between Whaley and Buxton and for Ale'*. Payments amounting to £62. 11s. 11d. were made for this, together with *'several bills for trees cut down and for damages done ye fences etc. £4. 16s. 0d.'* In the event the Army went to Macclesfield and then Leek. Hugh Travis was paid £28 for setting the road in good repair again. Presumably this attempt at blocking the road would have been where the road narrows just north of the junction with the road to Castleton, north of Dove Holes at Barmoor Clough. It is difficult to image the panic created by the Young Pretender, but clearly the Duke took the threat very seriously.

Hartington Hall has a small chamber (bedroom) known as Bonnie Prince Charlie's Room. Clearly the Prince did not stay here, but it is possible that the house played host to an unwelcome visitor, perhaps associated with movement of men on the flanks of the main body of the Army. To that extent it is possible that the Devonshire Estate was touched by events out in rural Derbyshire as well as in Derby itself, where the Duke had a townhouse. Here the Prince decided to retreat to Scotland and a life abroad following Culloden.

It may have cost the Prince a throne, it certainly cost the Duke a fortune. (30)

What of the bedroom at Hartington Hall? It is likely to have been one of the smallest in the house. In December 1745 it would have been rather cold as it did not have a fireplace. It was hardly a room the Prince would have chosen given the choice of any in the buildings. Whether the name of this small room indicates that the looting to feed the Army reached the village is no longer clear and remains unrecorded. The estate records would seem to suggest it did not happen with no details of payments by the Duke to assist those in distress as a result.

Concerns about the Jacobean Army were real enough. From Stockport, it proceeded via Macclesfield, Leek and Ashbourne to Derby before retreating back by the same route. The innkeeper at The Royal Oak, Hanging Bridge, on the River Dove near Ashbourne (close enough for comfort) was shot and killed for refusing to hand over his horse.

At Leek, Prince Charles Edward Stuart lodged for the night on the outward journey at The Vicarage in Church Street. The Vicar's wife was ill and suffered a relapse from sheer fright of later retribution for doing so. On the return journey a room was denied for the Prince and he slept next door but one at the top of the Market Place. The relapse was real and the poor lady died shortly afterwards.

Over at Swythamley, close to the Staffordshire border with Cheshire, William Trafford at Swythamley Hall hid his horses and livestock in a small secluded valley off the River Dane downstream from Danebridge. It is/was known as Meal-Ark Clough. Army scouts found the Hall deserted except for the squire. He was dressed in labourer's clothes and was threshing grain by hand. With each stroke he uttered the words *'now thus'* and was taken for a 'simpleton'. Saying nothing else, he was left alone. His grave in Leek Parish Churchyard (near the east window) bears those words.

A further threat to British sovereignty arose at the beginning of the 19th century with a perceived threat from France. The number of militia was raised to 100,000 men and the civilian volunteer force reached 410,000 men. In Derbyshire, the Chatsworth Estate accounts show that on January 8th 1804, Shaw and Ashby were paid £472. 16s. 0d. for cloth for the Chatsworth Battalion of the Volunteer Infantry. It was to be used to make uniforms. Muskets, steel bayonets, scabbards and shot were also purchased. The cloth was turned into 234 *'suits of uniform'* for the Chatsworth Volunteers.

Additionally the Duke made donations to companies (of the Hundred of High Peak) for Hathersage; Bradwell; Hope; Woodlands and Derwent; Edale and the Glossop, Padfield and Hadfield. Further donations went to the Buxton Company and various others in the east of the county. Well over £2,500 was spent in 1804 alone. Conspicuous by its absence was any reference to Hartington, unless it was incorporated into the Buxton Company, where the donation was £172 in May 1804. (31)

Collectors of Rent

In the 17th century, rent collection may have been more relaxed. In 1682-6 arrears of tenants were to be collected at Bakewell fair. (31/1) In the 18th century the Devonshire estate had several men who were responsible for the collection of rental income for a specific group of estates and for the disbursement of any expenses relating thereto. William Gould's diary gives some indication of the work involved. He was continually on the move, usually on horseback, trying to avoid a soaking in wet weather. His job included being prepared for mail arriving by a variety of carriers (usually connected with Chatsworth), requesting his attendance by John Heaton and others at short notice. He was used to carrying money, especially on rent collection days, which were twice yearly. Staying away overnight was a common part of his life. It was usually at the home of colleagues and friends and he reciprocated freely. When staying in Buxton, it was at The Eagle & Child, never it seems at the Hall Inn; presumably his expense allowance did not stretch that far.

Like other visitors to Buxton, William Gould sometimes found it difficult to obtain a bed for the night. In August 1783 he wrote in his diary that *'the town is very full of company, scarce a bed to be got'*. It probably was behind his decision to return to Pilsbury that night, after dinner. It was not however before he had noticed the new Crescent being roofed over. It was to open with two new hotels for guests before too long. His responsibilities included notifying tenants of the date for rents to be paid and preparing the accounts. The Michaelmas Collection was the same day as the Manor Court and was held at the same venue, the Newhaven House Inn. Clearly chasing up arrears followed and also obtaining the charges for encroachment, although this was never particularly successful it seems, judging by the lists of amounts carried forward for years. His son, Joseph, collected the rents due from the lower Dove Valley (Marston on Dove estate) at the time of one of the Ashbourne Fairs.

Left: The Ballroom, The Crescent. Photo: Trevor Osborne Property Group **Right**: Mining exploration work at the north end of Long Dale. There is a significant amount of surface remains of this activity down the dale **Below**: The Eagle Hotel, Buxton, bought by the estate as the Eagle and Child and extended in 1765

William Gould enjoyed the trust and the confidence of John Heaton, who regularly sought his opinion and on occasions would call him to London or send him further afield to act on his (Heaton's) behalf. Conversely, Heaton could trust Gould to be 'straight' with him. When Heaton was wondering about offering Joseph Gould the steward's position at Chatsworth his father advised not, on the grounds of his son's lack of experience. Heaton did go on to appoint Joseph as a Collector and must have been satisfied with his appointment, for additional areas were added to his responsibilities, including Hartington and the Granges (Meadow Place, One Ash and Calling Low) at a salary of £65 per annum. In October 1786, Joseph bought the 38 acre Pool Hall estate in Dig Street, Hartington, for £1,100 from Mr. Firchild. It was let to John Allen, the former village constable, at about £28 per annum.

By 1793, father and son were jointly responsible for the estates at Hartington, Sterndale, Meadow Place, the Rectory of Youlgreave, Biggin, One Ash, Callingloe (sic) and Conxbury (sic) Granges, still at the payment of £65 per annum. The account was signed by Joseph Gould, which may indicate that his father was not as well as he might have been. He died in 1795, aged 55 years. His diary entries in the period 1783 – 88 frequently record his tiredness at the end of the day. His hours were frequently very long, travelling on horseback until late into the evening. Michael Hanson, who transcribed the diaries in 2001, records that he rode his mare between 1,100 and 2,250 miles a year, in all weathers. His son, Joseph, lived to be a little older than his father, until his 60th year (1765–1825) and became agent to the 6th Duke. (32)

In March 1812 Joseph was returning home from Leek Market in the evening when he was thrown from his horse *'with such violence as to give the surgeon who were (sic) called in on the occasion very little hope of his recovery'*. Made of sterner stuff, he recovered. However Heacock wrote that *'his face is cut in a dreadful manner and that several bones were so injured so as to render it necessary for the surgeons to take them out before they closed the wounds'*.

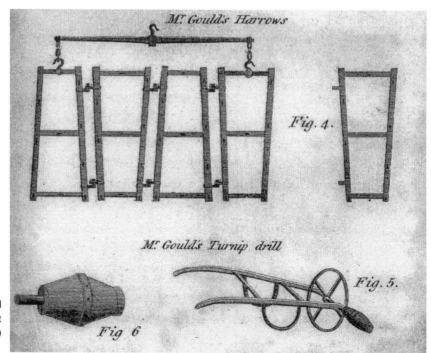

The harrow used by Joseph Gould at Pilsbury (see p. 73)

William was also the agent for the Duke of Portland for his Welbeck estate, covering both that position and the work for the Devonshire estate at the same time. He was always keen to see the personal Pilsbury farm accounts kept in order and up to date. He complained in his diary on several occasions about his son's tardiness in maintaining them at times. The farm was profitable and he usually seemed content with the amount, although he never stated what it was. He kept servants at the farm and seemed to live reasonably well.

A Helping Hand

It is clear that the Rent Collectors did work with a social conscience however. Philip Heacock confirmed in February 1812 to Cornelius Flint, Collector for Wetton and Kingsley in addition to his duties at Ecton Mine, that *'the person you have recommended to the use of the Bath and benefit of the Charity belonging thereto (both free) shall be admitted immediately on his arrival.'* The charity covered accommodation and all overnight visitors of any means were asked to contribute one shilling (5p.) to the Charity. By September 1812, Heacock was reporting to John Heaton that more poor people seeking treatment *'have been relieved this year than in the preceeding ones'*.

Heacock came to the assistance in February 1812 of one of the ladies running a lodging house. He complained to the manager of some workmen abusing the lady where they lodged *'in a very shameful manner'* and clearly without paying, seeking restitution of what she was owed.

A couple of months later he was involved in looking after the affairs of a Mr. Royston, one of the Duke's innkeepers who had felt the wrath of a creditor. Heacock poured oil on the waters, prevented a prosecution for debt and put the man's affairs in order. While all this was going on the estate was contemplating taking in hand the Ashford Marble works. Heacock recommended Mr. Hartley (who had looked after the Buxton building work) as the works manager. At Buxton he wrote, for Mr. Hartley *'there is now so little to do'*.

It is true that Heacock had more of a role as estate manager than the other Rent Collectors because of the nature of the development work in Buxton. He regularly used large sums of money, ordering cash from Mr. Toplis of the bank Arkwright, Toplis & Co., probably of Bakewell, specifically asking for their notes. This would be because of the *'great many forged notes in circulation'*. He would write requesting the money to be sent the following day by the *Nelson coach*, confirming receipt thereafter.

Inclosure of the Common

Inclosure of Hartington Common would appear to have been first mooted virtually 50 years prior to the passing of the Act. Godfrey Heathcote, the Duke's Agent, wrote to the Duke on 27th December 1756 stating that inclosure was agreed *'by the gentry, but not by tenants and persons of inferior circumstances'*. Although initially in favour, Hugh Bateman of Hartington Hall turned against it and would not give his reasons for it. Bateman even called a meeting in Ashbourne of landowners, when several objections (the substance of which is not known) were made. However it was felt that these would not defeat a Bill before Parliament.

Despite Hugh Bateman not stating his reasons, Heathcote wrote to the Duke stating *'I can hear 'em elsewhere and Your Grace shall know 'em when I come to town. He was extremely urgent to have the application to Parliament deferred for one year and sayd if not complied with, he hoped Your Grace would not take it amiss if he and about a dozen more whom he named made an opposition to it.'* Heathcote recommended that the application be deferred for a year.

By July 1757, Bateman's concerns seemed to have been resolved. He stated that he would not oppose the Bill for Inclosure if he was involved in swearing the commissioner, i.e. appointing him together with agreement that the allotment of the common lands in each Quarter should be to the estates lying in each Quarter. These were not in the Duke's best interests, the latter because it was without precedent *'because it will be found to be impracticable if equality in the division amongst all persons concerned is to be observed'*. (33)

There is no further mention of Inclosure by Heathcote and it would appear that the matter was dropped for half a century. However, it was not far from the mind. In August 1792, a Mr. Fletcher of Whitwell (also manager of Chatsworth) and a Mr. Renshaw of Owthorpe, an Inclosure Commissioner, inspected the estate freeholds and the improvements made through liming. They were of the opinion that the Duke *'should lose no time in endeavoring to obtain an enclosure'*. It was anticipated that the rental would increase by £1,700 p.a. (34)

There must have been significant interest amongst the copyholders (35) and others in enlarging their land holdings – at least from those whose income would stretch to the cost of a mortgage. Consolidation of land holdings elsewhere, the liming of heath land and other poorer soils south of Buxton in the 1780s etc. was bringing increased revenues to those who farmed such lands. The Inclosure of Commons nearby must have focussed minds upon the huge area of Hartington Common. Here was a substantial area of land where strips could be consolidated into fields surrounded by fences or stone walls. Commoners had at least the right to keep a cow and other animals on the common, but this and their rights to dig peat for fuel, carry off wood etc. were lost upon Inclosure. Only those with an interest in land or tithes received an allotment of land, but some poorer people could not afford to fence or improve it. This gave opportunities for others to further develop their holdings by buying such allotments.

The vicars' tithes were also treated in the same way, being commuted to a cash payment paid annually, or by an allotment of land – the glebe land – which was given to the vicar in the case of Hartington. However for the Inclosure process to start, it required a petition to Parliament, signed by 80% of those affected. The Hartington copyholders tried to use this requirement to gain more advantage for themselves, to no avail (see below).

In 1830, the Trustees of Sir Hugh Bateman realised that a Quit Rent of 6s. 8d. per annum due under the allotments scheme had not been collected for 27 years (sic). It was due in lieu of corn tithes *'within the Parish of Hartington'* from the Duke. The claim was accepted in full and a payment of £9 was made to the Trustees. These payments are recorded as being due on Lady Day 1818 (sic), which is rather confusing. (36)

Glover (39) records that in 1829 the Lords of the Manor of Hartington were the Duke of Devonshire and the Trustees of the late Sir Hugh Bateman, who owned Hartington Hall. Under a list of gentlemen's residences, Hartington Vicarage was mentioned by Glover, but not the Hall, for Sir Hugh appears to have resided at Derby. In the 1780s the Hall was occupied by 'Mr. Bateman' (see Improvements in Rental Income below). (37)

At a late stage in the preparation of the case for Inclosure prior to a Bill in Parliament, which was due to be presented in 1798, several of the copyholders threw a spanner into the works. They were entitled to a proportion of the Common according to their rights. Therefore the proposals were on the basis that the land would be copyhold. However they sought enfranchisement of the land to freehold. The Duke in lieu of his rights to tithe on the Common was to receive a proportion of the Common lands together with 1/18th extra for his 'right to the soil' and for his Consent to the Inclosure. Despite the fact that agreement between the Lord of the Manor (His Grace) and the Commoners had been reached some time previously, the copyholders called a meeting on 11th April 1798 to press their ambitions. In the event of no agreement, they were suggesting that the Commissioners appointed to oversee the Hartington Inclosure should make some allowance to the Lord in compensation for the enfranchisement.

This was completely unacceptable to the estate and Counsel's Opinion was sought prior to the April meeting of the copyholders. This upheld the view that there was no case to answer and that the claim should be resisted. The reason for wishing to resist the claim for elevation of copyhold interests to freehold was the loss of fines and herriots upon a change of occupation due to the Duke as and when that occurred. To get around this, the objectors had originally suggested at a meeting in Buxton that the Duke should receive a larger proportion of the Common but that must have been rejected too. It is likely that one of the most vociferous opponents of the Duke of Devonshire on this issue was Sir Hugh Bateman of Hartington hall. The Hall, grounds and orchard were all copyhold. The rear barns standing on freehold land. Copyhold land extended to a total of c. 2,850 acres.

It is not clear where the Hartington tithe barn was (if one existed) and there is not even a record of it in the surviving records. Youlgreave had a Tithe Barn and there is a record of this being repaired in 1689. (38)

The *Hartington Inclosure Act* received Royal Assent in 1798. It states that the Commons and Waste amounted to 12,000 acres or thereabouts. The principal *'proprietors of the common open fields, mesne inclosures and waste lands'* were the Duke of Devonshire, Sir John Edensor Heathcote, Hugh Bateman and Thomas Fletcher (plus several others unnamed). Additionally, William Lygon (later Lord Beauchamp) was the Lay Impropriator of the Parish of Hartington and as such wa*s 'entitled to certain tythes, both Great and Small, from all titheable lands within the Parish and also to certain Glebe Lands and Right of Common'*. (39) The Parish Vicar, Rev. Benjamin Hope, is confirmed as having entitlement to *'certain Glebe Lands and Rights of Common'* (similar to Mr. Lygon) and also to certain payments and Easter dues.

Under the Act, three Commissioners were appointed to take responsibility for all aspects of the Inclosure. They were Henry Bowman of Knockin, Shropshire, John Renshaw of Owthorpe, Notts., and Joseph Outram of Alfreton, Derbyshire, all described as *'gentlemen'*. These three had to commission a land survey. They also had to *'ride or perambulate'* the boundary of the parish. If there were any disputes concerning the boundary, they had to appoint arbitrators in order to get them settled. They had to ensure any disputes were settled which concerned rights of common. They also had the responsibility of setting out any roads which they thought were *'necessary and proper'*. Additionally, they had to provide *'bridle roads, footways, drains, watercourses, bridges, stiles etc.'* as they thought fit. They could also stop up any roads which were being replaced, but excluding any turnpike roads. An example of a new road was the Hartington Coal Road from Axe Edge via Harley, Earl Sterndale, Wheeldon Trees and Vincent House to Hartington. This made parts of the earlier coal road redundant, which then reverted to agricultural land, e.g. to the east of the Leek – Buxton road near the head of the River Dove.

The costs of all this were to be *'borne and paid for by the several owners of the lands intended to be divided and inclosed'* (excluding Mr. Lygon and the Vicar), a rate to be levied according to their respective rights and interests and respective proportions. The new roads were to be kept in repair in the same manner as the other public roads in the parish.

Not a lot seems to have been overlooked, the Commissioners being even charged with setting out public watering places for cattle. They were not to exceed 20 acres in total. Places for digging and getting stone, gravel etc. for making or repairing bridges, highways and roads within the manor and parish were also to be set out. They also had to make an allotment of land to the various granges *'in satisfaction and compensation'* for the loss of common right or tithe-free land.

The Act confirmed the entitlement of the Lay Impropriator and the Vicar to an allotment of land as compensation for all of their unenclosed Glebe Lands and right of Common. Additionally, the Vicar was to receive a further allotment for the loss of revenue amounting to £7. 3s. 4d. payable on undisclosed lands, which were to be lost, together with an allotment of land to the yearly value of £50 for the loss of tithes etc. (but excluding the Easter dues etc. which he retained).

Mr. Lygon was also to receive 1/9th of the residue of common land and waste to a value equal to 1s. 0d. per acre on all lands on which he had had the benefit of tithes now lost. In the final assessment, William Lygon received:
An assessment of 1,148 acres of freehold land, plus:

'For the 1s. 0d. per acre on the Titheable Common and Open Fields
Mesne Inclosures & Ancient Inclosed Lands' 819 *acres* (freehold)
[and] *'for Moduses'* 79¾ *acres* (freehold)

Farey, writing in 1814, stated that the tithes of Hartington parish were worth £120 at the most prior to Inclosure. However the owner (he does not mention Lygon by name) sold the allotment made to him for £28,000 *'when ring-fenced'* against an income of £1,280 p.a. (40)

The Vicar, Rev. Benjamin Hope, received a total of 207 acres (freehold) including:

'For Augmentation	- *109 acres on the north side of Oldham Road*
	and also 40½ acres on Phillimoor Edge
For Annual Payments	- *14 acres at Caskinlow* (north of the station)
For Glebe Lands	- *23 acres at Moneystones'*

Oldham Road is the green lane to Middleton which crosses the A515 just north of the Jug and Glass Inn. Its extension westwards from the A515 towards Hand Dale was called Phillimoor Lane. The Edge is likely to be the high ground to the north of here.

A key section of the Act from the Duke's point of view was that the allotment of land was to be the *'same tenure as the lands for which they are alloted'*. In other words, the attempt to enfranchise copyhold land to freehold land had failed. As discussed elsewhere (under Administration of the Manor), changes in ownership of copyhold land attracted a fine payable to the Lord of the Manor. This was restricted to a nominal 6d. (sixpence) on Inclosure.

Any encroachments made after 1st January 1768 were to be treated as part of the Common and valued as if unimproved. If it had been improved and was to be allotted to a third party (excluding the Lord of the Manor), the latter was to pay compensation to be determined by the Commissioners.

Mr. Lygon's and the Vicar's lands were to be fenced with 6 feet high by 2 feet wide (at the base) stone walls and a good oak gate hung on stone posts to each allotment (field) at the expense of the owners of the lands to be allotted. Out of the Duke's allotment, a minimum of 200 acres was to be adjacent or as near as convenient to the Newhaven House Hotel. All rights of common on the allotted lands were to be extinguished. Presumably, they continued on any unenclosed lands.

Allotted lands were to be *'inclosed, hedged, ditched, drained and fenced'* at the cost of the new owner. The Commissioners were empowered to do the work and claim the cost by default. Interestingly, meerstones could be erected where a hedge, ditch, wall or fence was considered impractical. Was this when the Elliot Stone above Dove Head Farm was placed? (See detail on the parish boundary at Appendix 1) Any lands being allotted which were let at a rack rent would only continue to 25ᵗʰ March 1799. Any trees or hedges passing to a new owner had to be paid for, or taken away by the former owner.

Out of a total allotment, which was finally made, the Duke received 13,192 acres, valued at £8,468. The total value was £14,140, the Duke's share being 59.9%. A total of 144 people received land and 622 parcels of land were allotted. The Act also covered 62 cottagers and others occupying 5,916 acres of land in all plus 382 acres in hand by the estate. (41)

The cost of this to the Duke amounted to £14,255, being £8,644 in the money paid to the Commissioners and a huge sum of £5,611 on land improvement (e.g. the erection of stone walls). Some drainage costs followed, but this affected only a few farms and the land tenanted by the proprietors of some of the Buxton hotels.

What seems strange is that the old inclosures – those lands inclosed for many years prior to the 1798 Act, were included in the scheme. However it seems that this might have been done as a vehicle to ensure that minerals thereunder were reserved to the Duke (except lead ore). There could be no arguement over ownership if they were allotted under the Act. The value to the estate of the allotted lands is not known. However it is possible to obtain some idea. A rental document for the Buxton area also gives acreages and the rent paid per acre. It generally varies between 15s. 0d (75p) and 30s.0d (£1.50) per acre, more for good land. These figures are supported by Young (42). If an average of say £1.25 per acre is taken covering say 12,000 acres (allowing for the wasteland on Axe Edge and land improved by the tenants, although there was no security of tenure beyond current leases) at 4.5% a figure of £337,500 is derived. This ignores any value for mineral rights, some of which already were in hand.

All minerals (excluding lead ore) including stone under the 'old' inclosures were reserved to the Duke. With the new inclosures, all minerals excluding stone were also reserved to the Duke and this was common to both freehold and copyhold land. Compensation for any surface damage would have to be paid. No doubt the detail of this was to prove important as aggressive quarrying progressed south of Buxton on the Duke's land.

Although the Common ceased to exist (except perhaps for a few areas classed as waste), the Manor Court continued with its function of issuing herriots, fines etc. upon death and sale etc. of copyhold properties. The function of controlling the use of the Common and issuing fines for abuse ceased in the Great Court Leet, although its other functions (see Chapter 2) continued. All holdings created under the Act of copyhold land had to be registered with the Court, although as noted above, a fine for so doing was limited to 6d. The *Hartington Inclosure Act* is registered as 38 Geo III 1798, so it took ten years or so for the Commissioners to fully implement it.

In December 1809 it was realised that £235 due to the Duke from Sir Hugh Bateman (at the order of the Inclosure Commissioners) had not been paid. Phillip Heacock urged the Commissioners to demand that the payment be paid but it appears that it was possibly

William Lygon who owed the money and Bateman remained silent on the matter. In 1813 Bateman not only refused to pay but raised questions on the validity of the Order, no doubt as a smoke screen. A lot of John Heaton's time seems to have been taken up with issues like this. In 1810, it was realised that iron ochre was being raised and sold in Derby by Bateman from land allocated by the Commissioners to him near Biggin. However the mineral rights remained with the estate and had not been allocated under the Inclosure Act, Bateman eventually paying the receipts over to the Duke. (43)

Working the Land – Post-Inclosure

Post-Inclosure at Hartington, the Duke had over 13,000 acres of freehold land better off. Farms were enlarged, new ones created (e.g. Newhaven House (Inn) Farm), and most importantly, total rental income began an upward surge. Farey indicates that the area had two of the largest farms in the county. The Devonshire estate had spent large capital costs improving land especially on the old established farms. This was recovered by improved rentals.

With Inclosure, a large area of several thousand acres was available for improvement. However the investment policy of the 5th Duke was cancelled (by and large) by the 6th Duke in 1811. It was left to those farmers with the wealth to make the investment themselves. A substantial acreage was improved by liming in this manner. One of the new era farms was Pilsbury Farm occupied by Joseph Gould. Farey gives a good impression of the investment made there, embracing new technology.

Gould had a Rotherham Swing Plough, which was nothing new, having been introduced in the 1720s, although no doubt his plough would include any subsequent improvements. He used it with two horses working side by side, ploughing one to one and a quarter acres per day. Although ploughing with oxen had died out some time previously, Farey records that it was making something of a comeback. Most Derbyshire farmers preferred a two-share plough (44) and wheeled ploughs. Ploughing is followed by harrowing and Farey was sufficiently impressed with Joseph Gould's 'machine' that he included a drawing of it (and a turnip seed drill). It consisted of four separate rectangular frames. These were replaceable if they became damaged or broken and lasted longer than larger types.

The days of broadcasting seed by hand had been replaced by a long wooden box. It was filled with seed and was distributed through holes. One supposes it was a little like an elongated colander. It was nine feet long, made in Norfolk and would cover 8 – 10 acres a day, pulled by a horse. His turnip drill was described as being *very simple and effective. A more simple and yet efficient machine than this I scarcely ever saw'*. Having been cut by scythe or sickle and dried in the field, cereals were no longer thrashed by hand.

Bigger farms (Farey gives a list of 20 of them) were beginning to invest in a thrashing mill. There were a few manufacturers of these and most farms in Derbyshire were using a mill made by Thomas Noon of Burton-on-Trent at £50 each. Joseph Gould however was using one made by William Moire of Shropshire. It was dearer at £87 and was the only one listed in the county. Worked by three horses, it thrashed, cleaned and winnowed the cereal crop.

Gould had also gone out of the county to a Mr. Darley of Worksop, Notts., for his chaff and straw cutter. It cut the stems of the crop for animal feed. Timothy Greenwood had one from Lintons of Church Gresley. Even Gould's sack filler (for the corn) was described as being *'a very simple and good contrivance'* at Gould's *'new farm'*.

Although William Gould (Joseph's father) complains in his diary that Joseph was a little slack in keeping his farm account books up to date, he had clearly become a respected professional farmer with good working practices. Farey makes a comparison of how Gould and Timothy Greenwood treated the heath land to convert it to good agricultural land. Greenwood's heath land would appear to have thinner soils but he did not treat it with as much lime, manure etc. as Gould (45).

Oat production was an important aspect of the farm economy, and farm enlargement following Inclosure helped this with good-sized fields and the abandonment of the strips in open fields. Oat production has completely finished today, replaced by pasture and some crop production including rape – unheard of two hundred years ago in this area. Although the profitability of Pilsbury Farm post-Inclosure is not known, it is known that in the 1780s, Joseph Gould's father, William, confided to his diary that a *'tolerably good profit'* had been produced on more than one occasion.

A greater acreage and improved machinery etc. must have improved efficiency and profitability, one may think. Equally importantly, and in a wider context, what Farey was showing in his descriptions of Pilsbury Farm (the detail is separated out under different farming practices e.g. ploughing, sowing etc.) is that good practice and success could be found in the higher lands and upper reaches of Peakland rivers. Over a hundred years before, Plot had reported that the lower Dove Valley was valuable cereal land, yet the inference by Farey was that Pilsbury was not only one of the county's larger farms, it was comparably efficient. Curiously, Farey did not include the Chatsworth Estate Farm or the large acreage of One Ash Grange and Meadow Place Farms (for instance) east of Hartington. It is likely that Pilsbury was therefore not the only example (with Newhaven Inn Farm) that Farey could have cited.

A little later, in 1834, the Chatsworth estate paid for mowing 275 acres of grass and 84 acres of oats on the home farm. Oxen were being reared (and had been for many years) for the beef and a herd (possibly of around 30) were kept at Cracknowles north of Bakewell. At Christmas 1831, the Duke (then Lord Chamberlain) presented the King at Brighton with a sirloin of beef *'being part of a famous ox grased at Cracknowles'*. The ox weighed 1½ tons. Pilsbury was not the only good sized farm in the Derbyshire Peak, but it did have a more challenging profile, with river meadows giving way to thinner soils on the steep valleyside and more exposed lands above, again with soils thinner than in the river meadows.

Reclaiming Common Land

The processes used to turn the heath lands of the Common into farmland were not much different between Timothy Greenwood and Joseph Gould and therefore probably reflect the method employed across the former common. Gould applied more lime per acre and used manure which Greenwood was not recorded as doing. The latter may have been a little more careful with his expenditure for he had a tenancy of 600 acres of ex-common land to treat and convert to agricultural land. Greenwood described his common land as being heath (*erica vulgaris*), moss and mossy hillocks. Gould's description being 200 acres of short heathy, and 70 acres of hillocky dry mossy land. Both burnt off the vegetation, limed it at 120 bushels per acre (Greenwood) and 120 – 160 bushels (Gould) and ploughed. Farey, in a separate note, records that Gould ploughed and harrowed twice. In another note, Farey reveals that there were three bushels per horse load (see p. 115). Although the liming was done for three years in the liming programmes elsewhere on the estate prior to Inclosure, this does not appear to have been quite the case with Greenwood and Gould.

The latter (after the second ploughing) planted turnips, then white oats (with some black oats on poorer soils). Another crop of oats followed and then the land was left fallow for a year when it was dressed with 10 – 12 tons of manure and 120 – 150 bushels of lime per acre. If only working on a spreading rate of 120 bushels of lime, Greenwood would have applied at least 24,000 horse loads on his 600 acres, with 240 – 260 bushels per acre after two years. This equates to at least another 48,000 horse loads in all.

This is surprising for Joseph Gould would have been applying only half of Greenwood's lime per acre after two years. He would have applied 10,800 horse loads on each occasion. It is likely that carts were being used to carry the lime at c.15 horseloads per cart.

Not all the land was sown with oats. Some of it was sown with seeds instead. These were clover, trefoil, rye grass and hay seed (grass). Greenwood also planted '*Scotch and Swede Cabbage*'. Cabbages could be picked in winter when frozen ground stopped the supply of turnips.

Hay started being cut in mid-July and was finished by mid-August. When cut it was spread across the field, then turned with rakes into rows. It was then spread again and turned yet again into rows and so on until dry. It was finally raked into rows before being pitched into carts for removal to a haystack (usually given a thatched span roof with a ridge like a house) or pitched into a barn. Gould obtained 30 cwt per acre on his river meadows, whereas Greenwood got 20 – 30 cwt per acre (46). Gould was also growing potatoes. Commonplace you may think, but there is not much evidence of this in the dales around Hartington at that time. It seems to be yet another pointer to a resourceful man.

References

1 Dev. Coll., AS/1819, copy of the Inclosure Act, 1772

2 Dev. Coll., AS/1353, p. 402; Cotterell's address was given as South Head 'in Kinder'. It is south-east of Hayfield. The conveyance is dated 28/7/1570. It consisted of 'the Chapel and the Chapel Yard, Bathcroft, the pece beyond the water joining to the west, (believed to be land beyond the adjacent confluence of the River Wye and a stream), house occupied by Roger Cotterell and all the bathes, springes, waters and watercourses ronnying and being in the said parcilles and premises; see Dev. Coll., H/245/37; Lovell, M S., *Bess of Hardwick*, 2005, pp 238–39

3 Langham, M., & Wells, C., *The Baths at Buxton Spa*, 2005, pp. 26-27

4 *The Illustrated Journeys of Celia Fiennes*, 1685 – c.1712, edit., C. Morris, 1982, p.108; *A Tour through England & Wales*, D. Defoe, Vol.2., pp 166-68, Everyman Library, c.1927

5 Langham, M., *Buxton A People's History*, 2001, p10

6 Langham, M., & Wells, C., ibid, p 28-29

7 Dev. Coll., AS/1008,1126 & 1371

8 Young, A., *The Farmer's Tour through the East of England*, 1771, pp 208–14

9 Dev. Coll., AS/1394

10 For the benefit of Buxton local historians, Dorothy Bentley Smith in *A Georgian Gent, the Life & Times of Charles Roe*, 2005, p. 212, assumes that Brian Hodgson Junior took this lease in 1746 having stated that the son took the Hall Inn over in 1850–51. My reference to the father taking the 1746 lease is from G. Heathcote's 1773 letter to the Duke (Dev. Coll., AS/1394)

11 Dev. Coll., AS/98; the fourth payment was £400

12 Dev. Coll., AS/1509, P. Heacock's letter book, 1809, 28/10/1809

13 Ward., Rev. R., *A Guide to the Peak of Derbyshire etc.*, 1827, pp 169-70

14 Dev. Coll. 5th Duke's letters Nos. 765, 776, 778, 820, the Duchess to Countess Spencer

15 Dev. Coll., T-Series, Bundles 1–7

16 Ward, ibid., p 181-82

17 Dev. Coll., P. Heacock's letters, AS/1510, 4/3/1811, 10/3/1811

18 Langham, M., *Buxton A People's History*, 2001,

p 110; Dev. Coll., AS/901, John Heaton's Accounts

19 Hot Baths: see Dev. Coll., AS/1511, P Heacock's letter book, 26/12/1812; Water closets were first introduced in London in c. 1770 by Alexander Cummings

20 In 1828 the arrears stood at £7,123 (Hall Inn £233; Great Hotel £1,239; St. Ann's Hotel £2,954; Centre Hotel £2,697); Dev. Coll. T. Series, Bundles 1– 7; Langham, M., ibid. p.20

21 Dev. Coll., AS/901

22 Dev. Coll., AS/1511, Letterbook, P. Heacock to J. Heaton, 24/9/11812 and others

23 Dev. Coll. AS/1819, ibid., 28/10/1809. See note further down, about the church roof timbers also coming from Canada

24 For detail on Buxton profits, see Langham, ibid, p226; for piling at the church, see Ward, ibid., p 182

25 Dev. Coll. AS/1819 ibid. 13th May , 11th July, 25th August, 25th October, 4th November, 1809

26 Dev. Coll., P. Heacock's letters. AS/1509, 1/1/1810, 18/4/1810, 9/10/1810, 17/11/1810, 31/8/1811; AS1510, 21/2/1812.

27 Langham & Wells, ibid. pp 47-52. This book is recommended for a good history of the development of the baths

28 Langham, M., ibid, pp 19–12; Langham, M., & Wells, C., The Baths at Buxton Spa, 2005; Church Accounts from Dev. Coll., T-Series, Bundles 1 – 7

29 Endeavouring to continue Heathcote's need for 'delicacy', one reduced the smell from the toilet by adding a layer of earth (? Fuller's earth) after use. Hence the name for the toilet: earth closet. Presumably this was not happening at the bath.

30 Chatsworth Estate Accounts, 1745

31 Chatsworth Estate Account, 1804

31/1 Dev. Col., AS/351

32 Hanson, M., Wm. Gould's Diary, Pilsbury Area Entries, 1783 – 88, 2001, printed by Derbyshire Record Soc.

33 Dev. Coll., AS/1353

34 These were holders of land which was not as 'good' as freehold land as it was subject to payments to the Lord of the Manor when certain events happened, such as change of occupier, death etc

35 Dev. Coll., T-Series, T.14, Hartington Accounts 1830

36 Glover, S., Directory of Derbyshire, 1829, p 72

37 The Manor did have a rent charge against it. In 1758 it was paid to the Hon. Mrs. Southwell, being £97. 17s. 6d. per annum, although it was paid net of tax, which amounted to £19. 12s. 0d., a tax rate of 20%

38 Dev. Coll., L/114/18 & 19; Youlgreave tithe barn: AS/364

39 Impropriation was the application of ecclesiastical property to lay purposes. On the suppression of the abbeys in 1539, their income from great tithes was appropriated by Henry VIII. These were then distributed amongst his courtiers and their successors were called Lay Impropriators

40 Farey, J 1815, ibid, p 79. Land allotment provided for a stone wall around the allotted area. Creating smaller fields within it was at the cost of the new owner

41 Dev. Coll., L/114/13

42 Young wrote this about land rentals: 'about Matlock, land lets dear, many grass fields at 40s 0d (£2) an acre and down to 25s 0d and not a little arable so high as 30s 0d … I took the road to Chatsworth, none lets lower than 15s 0d except the new inclosed hills, much land rise to 20s 0d to 35s 0d.' It could be argued that using a figure of 25s 0d on 'new inclosed hills' as Young puts it could apply to Hartington manor, and indeed it may well have done in parts. However, it is hard to find a reason for suggesting that the bigger farms were returning profits low enough to justify this, especially with Farey suggesting how good and profitable the Gould and Greenwood lands were. Much of the inclosures must have been of land capable of matching the latter fields. Young, A, ibid, pp 208–14

43 Dev. Coll., P. Heacock's letters, AS/1510, 27/9/1810, 10/11/1810

44 Farey, J., 1815, ibid. pp 43, 94-95

44 see p. 67; Farey, Vol. 2, ibid. p 403 –5

46 Farey, ibid, pp 199, 142–3, 145, 179, 183, 189

4. JOHN HEATON AND LAND INVESTMENTS

Early Days

Heaton ran the Duke's legal affairs and had a growing interest in running the estates. He had a house rent-free in London at 6 Old Burlington Street, one of a small group of houses owned in London by the Duke. He was initially the auditor of the 4th Duke's Paternal and Maternal Estates. His work in 1774 included the procurement of an Act of Parliament to enable the Duke to grant leases of mines at Grassington; the opposing of Royal Assent to the Irish Fishing Bill, concerns relating to the Duke's marriage settlement; the Knaresborough election and of course much more. (1) His expenses for the year were £1,863.

Chapter 3 above, covers in detail the development work in Buxton. This chapter puts this within the context of estate revenue generation as a whole. Following his appointment as auditor in 1773, the first major capital expense of his appointment, indeed perhaps the first capital expense at all by the 5th Duke, was the construction of The Edensor Inn during 1775–77. Now the Estate Office and staff social club, it was built as a comfortable hotel for visitors to Chatsworth and those travelling through the area. There were very few other land purchases or other property development before the 1780s.

Heaton seems to have cut his teeth in estate management with the purchase in 1778 of Mrs. Dickenson's interests in the Goit (sic) Moss Colliery, Moss House near the colliery and the four-kiln lime works on Grin Hill south-west of Buxton in Hartington Upper Quarter. This was offered some years earlier to the estate but legal difficulties arose over mineral rights. The estate held other land on Grin Hill, which had been let to the Brock family since the 17th century and they had their own lime works there with eight kilns. The output from these two concerns was considerable. In 1766 it was reported that the Brock's concern at Grin and Peak Forest was alone producing 174,720 horse loads (11,235 tons) of lime annually. (2)

Heaton's purchase of the Dickenson lime works and colliery allowed a series of land improvement schemes to proceed on Hartington Manor farms south of Buxton. Nearly 20,000 tons of lime was spread by 1791 and it is likely that the work continued over a much longer period. The effect was to turn valueless heather-clad moorland into valuable pasture land.

On 1st April 1780, Heaton took control of the copper and lead sales from Ecton Mine. For the previous five years John Dawes had been responsible for this. He was a shareholder in Parys Mountain Copper Mine on Anglesey and a competitor. Heaton also became responsible for the profitability of Kingsley Colliery that he had just purchased for £21,500.

Legal Issues

John Heaton was also the Duke's lawyer and a lot of his time seems to have been spent dealing with often spurious issues testing his acumen for reasons of financial gain at the estate's expense. Shortly after the 6th Duke succeeded he found himself with several all at the same time.

In 1812, copyholders were in negotiation regarding enfranchisement of Hartington copyhold lands to freehold, which the Duke objected to. He also did not agree to a claim that the Hartington Liberty, governing lead mining customs and rights, was within the Derbyshire King's Field and therefore subject to (presumably the less onerous) jurisdiction of that Mineral District and the Court of the Soke and Wapentake of Wirksworth. This still meets under the *Derbyshire Mining Customs & Mineral Courts Act, 1852*. The Duke's mineral interests had been acquired *'by Grant'*, presumably as part of the purchase of the manor from the Duke of Buckingham.

Nearby, Sir Henry Crewe was *'demanding tithes from tenants at Alstonfield and Elkstones'* and John Heaton was *'looking to find a way of getting rid of the question without a suit'*. This was no doubt linked to the Crewe estate refusal to exchange land at Ecton where more room was needed to dump waste. This followed on in 1811 from a boundary dispute at Elkstones situated about 5 miles west of Hartington (where the Duke was Lord of the Manor, having acquired the estate in 1789) although the other party is not known. This irritation with the Crewe estate continued into 1813 when there was a proposal (not initiated by the Duke) for an Inclosure Act at Elkstones and *'an attempt to incorporate the district of Elkstones within the extensive Township of Alstonfield'*,. Presumably thereby landowners would be subject to the tithes of the Crewe's manor there. This was also resisted.

Elsewhere on the estate, someone with a grievance sent in news (it was called *'intelligence'*) to the *Sheffield Morning Post* in 1812 advising that Chatsworth had been burnt down by Luddites. It is not clear if attempts to discover the perpetrator were successful. Although an obvious irritation, there was a deeper issue here – maintaining the confidence of the many people from whom the Duke had loans. In 1814, threatening letters were being made to the Duke, and John Heaton was having to placate mortgagees etc. re. their securities *'to prevent calling in principal monies'*.

Under Chapter 3 is highlighted yet another difficulty, again in Hartington concerning Sir Hugh Bateman and his refusal to pay settlement costs of the Inclosure Award to the Duke. This was after a long struggle to resist opposition to the Act in the first place. It wasn't because of opposition to the Act in principle, it was the understandable result of many of those most likely to gain wanting to maximise their own interests.

Going for Growth

At some point in the late 1770s, it is fairly clear that Heaton and the Duke agreed on a capital expenditure programme aimed at significantly increasing revenue generation. There are some indicators of when this probably occurred. In 1777 liming commenced in Hartington Manor on Devonshire freehold land south of Buxton, at Cronxton, Clementseat and Coatsfield Farms. In 1778 the scheme was extended to include Harley, How Tor and other places. Some 4,218 tons of lime was spread in the years 1777–80 in fact. This was as a result of the purchase of the Dickenson's Colliery and lime burning interests.

However, where was the money going to come from? Activity at Ecton Copper Mine has seen the exploitation of an ever increasing deposit which was growing larger with depth. In 1775, Heaton had appointed a sales agent in London, John Dawes (mentioned above) who soon started to find an important demand for the metal. It was being smelted at Whiston Copper Works, to the south of the mine and on the edge of the Cheadle Coalfield.

With the knowledge that the mine had significant reserves of copper ore and more importantly, rich copper ore, here potentially was the dream ticket. Moreover, the ore produced copper metal which was more malleable and was highly valued for use in boilers

Right: The former Bull's Head, near Biggin. Built to offer accommodation next to the cross roads of Cardlemere Lane/Ashbourne-Buxton A515 road

Below: Under John Heaton much land improvement occurred: liming, drainage, new buildings and meres, like this one above Pilsbury

and domestic utensil manufacture. In order to release the assets lying below ground, more of it had to be wrought and brought to the surface. It also had to be smelted and additional hearths were needed. This latter happened in 1780. Therefore the capital expenditure programme would appear to have been agreed between c. 1778 and 1780.

Once the fires were lit in the new hearths in 1780, profits leaped up. The ore output started to lift in 1778 when it reached just over 1,000 tons. In 1781 it had more than doubled that. In 1777, 1779 and 1780 the profit was £8,700 to £9,000. In 1781 it was £27,500. During the next seven years, profits averaged £22,650 per annum. Here was the source of funding required. In 1790 the mine failed, having yielded a profit of £195,250 in a decade. What would have been achieved, one wonders, if that income stream had continued for another decade?

On 12th June 1790, *The Times* reported in a leg pull: *'The Devonshire copper mines have failed*

– *the party must now make up the deficiency from their inexhaustible store of brass*'!

The confidence that significant extra profits were to become available is breathtaking. In 1780, work commenced on The Crescent and its Stables. As is shown below, it was to cost over £60,000. However, it was the success overall across the Devonshire estates of increasing rental income which was the key to sustained capital expenditure. Langham states of Phillip Heacock, appointed as the Buxton agent in 1805: *'within two years he had completed a full assessment of rentals resulting in a considerable increase payable by tenants'*. (3) The same occurred in Hartington Manor and it is certain this area was not unique in the Devonshire estates.

Between 1777 and 1791, just short of 20,000 tons of lime is known to have been spread on Hartington lands alone. Sooner or later, the rental value of the improved land saw an increase in rental incomes.

Urban Development at Buxton

This increase in revenue financed the purchase in 1782 of the estate of Sir John Edensor Heathcote at Buxton for £8,000. (Although Heaton describes the purchase of the Staveley Estate as being in the sum of £35,346 in 1779, this was paid for over several years, the payments being completed in 1779). Two years before the Heathcote purchase, work commenced on the construction of The Crescent at Buxton. Including The Stables to the rear, the total cost of *'new buildings to 1790'* amounted to a massive £63,212. Additionally, the architect John Carr's commission to 1790 amounted to £3.858. Work was to continue for some years. From the schedule of known capital expenditure in the Buxton and Hartington parishes between 1776 and 1812, the Duke spent £213,925 in all. (see Appendix 2)

This list includes expenses from the Hartington accounts not included in Heaton's own calculation. If this was happening on other estates, Heaton may have spent quite a lot more than is realised. For example, the cost of the capital expenditure at Ecton Mine, on smelters, other buildings, one shaft over 600 feet deep and another twice that depth, all were funded from the mine's income before the profit was struck.

From these figures, it will be clear that Heaton must have devoted much of this time to developments in Buxton and Hartington Manor. The failure of Ecton Mine in 1790 both freed time from copper and lead sales, but focussed attention on the need to replace as much as possible the pronounced loss of revenue from the mine. However, before turning to that, mention needs to be made that purchases of land in the years 1787–1790 amounted to £19,627 in the Hartington and adjacent Staffordshire Moorlands areas. This was not just for land either. It included the purchase of tithes in Wetton for £2,563. Tithes not only brought in income, they attracted rights in themselves on allotment of land on Inclosure. Clearly Heaton was busy acquiring land in the Manor from this time with an eye to the future.

Developments after 1790

Continuing commercial activity in the Hartington Manor and Buxton area (other than urban development in Buxton, e.g. The Square and Hall Bank for instance) started with the Newhaven House Inn, completed c. 1792–93 (at least paid for in 1793). This was later followed by the purchase of the Bull's Head at Newhaven in 1801 for the carriers and less well-off travellers who would not have stopped at the Newhaven House. This was then closed when a replacement inn was built with less expensive accommodation than at Newhaven House. It was not only on the Ashbourne–Buxton turnpike road but adjacent to a crossing

The Old Vicarage, Hartington, built in 1789 and later the home of Cornelius Flint, the Ecton Mine manager, appointed by John Heaton in 1779

The ss. Ecton, which took Ecton copper metal to London, probably looked like this, a Yorkshire billyboy, although the sail plan may have differed. Painting by the late Edward Paget-Tomlinson

of the latter with Cardlemere Lane, an important Drovers' road coming from Cheshire. By 1846, it had closed, then known as Ivy House.

Land purchases continued with £29,941 spent chiefly at Buxton, Hartington Manor and Chesterfield. The latter consisted of the purchase from Sir Richard Kaye Bt., and his trustees of a lease, for the longer of three lives, of The Rectory and Tithes of Chesterfield amounting to £21,500. At least some of the money for this purchase came from payments for Ecton copper. (At the end of 1790, £16,679. 14s. 10d. for copper metal sales was due from Factor Agents or debtors for metal sold. There had been something of a set back in 1787 when some £40,000 worth of copper had arrived from Spain for sale, which the Duchess, probably correctly, guessed would lower the price of copper. She added poignantly: *'I hope it will be ye last importation'*. (4) Of the other land transactions, the major purchase in 1791 was from Edward Wheeldon. His lands at Upper Foxlowe in Hartington parish, Sterndale and Fairfield cost £6,094.

Heaton was inhibited in restoring the lost Ecton revenues by long agricultural leases of 21 years. The last review on Hartington Manor was in 1788, with the next due in 1809. He was able to report an increase in rental income in Hartington Manor alone in 1788 of £553 (for farm rents only) representing 33 per cent. By 1790 expenditure across all estates on land and improvements had resulted in mortgages, bonds etc. amounting to £310,298. The interest and rent charges on purchases amounted to £20,502 per annum. Although substantial, the total estate rental income in 1790 covered it well, at £69,936. (excluding Ecton revenues). However, the average loss per annum of £15,700 (over the previous $11^3/_4$ years) from Ecton would have bitten deep. (5)

Cavendish income did allow, however, for a strategy of massive capital investment that not only restored the lost Ecton revenues but which also financed the majority of the outlay. It is a story long forgotten and recalled below for the first time.

Heaton as a Manager

Before considering this, however, just what was Heaton's role other than possibly being one of the country's leading land purchasers and developers? William Gould's diaries give a reasonably good idea. To the 5th Duke, Heaton was the *'auditor'*. Today we would call him the managing director. He was very much a 'hands on' boss too, with a good eye for details. In the appointment of a new Superintendent of Husbandry at Hardwick in November 1783, responsibility included the buying and selling of cattle, i.e. the opportunity to maximise profitability *'and be under no control except from Mr. Heaton'*. The latter (Heaton) also suspected Mr. Longden, the contractor for the liming contract at Frith Pasture, south of Buxton, was not giving his all, having seen his work *'with the conduct and improvement of Sticcow etc.'* He was keeping himself well informed and acting upon the advice when it was not in the interests of the Duke.

The reference to Sticcow turned out to be ironic. He meant what was then known as Sticker Hill, a large ridge of land to the south of Harpur Hill, which butted up to Frith Pasture that lay to the west and is now the Harpur Hill Industrial Estate (at least at the northern end). At the southern end of the hill was Hillhead Farm, which still survives adjacent to Hillhead quarry that has taken an enormous chunk out of what was Sticker Hill and is now Staker Hill. Here was the 28 acres of land that Farey wrote about, declaring that the heath was replaced with *'a sweet and good herbage'* (see 'liming'). Longden was in partnership with Wheeldon, and Heaton was displeased with the general behaviour of the Wheeldons according to William Gould. Longden and Wheeldon accepted that they had laid *'bad lime'* and had offered to lay another 3,000 loads of lime, so the problem was real and not insignificant. (6) It does show as an example the extent to which Heaton was prepared to delve into daily activity on the estate.

A problem for Heaton was the inflation of prices to reflect the 'Devonshire factor'. A willing buyer always has a problem on striking a fair bargain when his pockets are deep and his shopping list a long one. In 1785, on instruction, William Gould let a farm in Fairfield at the previous rent, to help keep down the price of land around Buxton *'as they wished to purchase every conveniency about that place'*. With purchase prices at 25 times the net rent, the reasoning is clear.

The Outcome of Investment

Figures in John Heaton's own hand show that between 1773–1810 the Duke spent £670,199 on purchases of landed property and improvements to his estates. In the period 1790–1810, purchases and improvements cost £363,000, but the increase in total borrowings only went up by £66,342.

Table 1 How Expenditure on Property Purchases Grew

	Mortgages/bonds	Interest/rent charges
1782	246677	16907
1790	310298	20502
1810	376640	26742

The Devonshire accounting system failed to separate some capital costs paid out of gross income. Thus the cost of improvements such as the extension of the Newhaven House Inn, the cost of farm buildings being erected (houses as well as barns) and the considerable cost of building new stone walls following the Inclosure Award (called fencing in the accounts) are all on the Hartington Manor account, i.e. paid for out of Hartington rental monies. These latter costs are listed in Appendix 2. This may have been a convenient way for Heaton to extend his range of activities, with the costs 'lost' in the accounts and the monies paid for out of the manor revenues and not borrowed. He knew that there was no independent check on his working practices and the Duke admitted that *'I do not look enough into my own affairs'*. Nonetheless, there can be no assumption; the practice may have been cleared by the Duke. (7)

In 1810, Heaton summarised the income available to the Duke. It was the amount due from rentals, allowing for repairs, tax and interest and also deducting for the running costs of the three main houses in which the Duke lived, the cost of the others presumably being deducted from the local estate account. It amounted to £122,500, less £20,000 for repairs and taxes, i.e. £102,528. Interest and rent charges brought this down to £79,660 with expenses of London, Chiswick and Chatsworth amounting to £54,000 (see below).

The Duke's Financial Situation, 1810

Rental Income			£108,820
Ancillary income (royalties, tithes etc)		£ 13,708	
			£122,528
Less Repairs		10,000	
Property tax		10,000	
Interest (@ 5%)	18,832		
Rent charges		7,910 £ 46,742	
			£ 75,786 ★
Running costs, London, Chiswick, Chatsworth			£ 54,000
Profit available for Duke's expenditure			£ 21,786
			=======

Other details:

Amount spent on landed property 1770 – 1810	£670,199 +
Mortgages and Loans	£376,640
	£293,559
Other funds available (loans, Irish rents etc & the half years rent from estates to Michaelmas 1810)	£133,000 x
Rental Income (gross) 1773	£ 61,713
1810	£122,528

★   There is an error in Heaton's figures here. He has £79,660.

+   Spent in Buxton and Hartington £208,435 (of which Buxton was £181,111).

x   This excludes the value of furniture, paintings, stock and stores etc.

It is a pity that Heaton's calculations and details show only a snapshot of 1810. Although this shows the annual profit running at £21,786, the cash position is different viz:

Profit on year	£ 21,786
Less monies retained by Collectors & Agents for Improvements to properties	£ 7,149
Cash available for the Duke	£14,637

This shows the ducal purse getting decidedly smaller and must account for the lack of investment noted a few years earlier and the reason why the 6th Duke cancelled it altogether. Although cancellation of improvement work saw the cash available to the Duke running at c. £22,000 per annum, expenditure in Buxton was unavoidable, for the final account for St. John's Church in 1812 reveals that another £3,627 still had to be paid. This also begs the question of where the money had come from to reduce the borrowings on the investments by nearly £300,000. Much of it could have been the additional monies flowing from Ecton Mine. The profit from 1780–89 totalled £195,000. Some will also be 'lost' in local area accounts.

For example, Hartington Inclosure costs of over £23,000 are included in purchases (over 13,000 acres of freehold land came to the estate on Inclosure) and yet the cash was paid out of the area rental income and was not borrowed. The only problem with this is that the Ecton revenues crashed in 1790 and as shown above, purchases in 1790 – 1810 cost £363,000 with borrowing rising only £66,000. The issue is far from being clear. (8)

Neither is it clear if annuities to family members are included in the figures. If the Duke was running out of cash, his capital wealth remained rock solid. Heaton worked on a multiplier of x25 rental values (i.e. @ 4%) to calculate capital values. Working

The George Hotel, built in 1773 and purchased by Heaton in 1804 for the estate. It cost £6,000

on £75,000 net rental value per annum, multiplied by 25 gives £1.875 million, plus the properties at Devonshire House, Burlington House, Chiswick, Chatsworth, Hardwick, Londesborough and Lismore plus (as highlighted above) the value of furniture, paintings, investments, stock and stores.

The financial statement of 1810 (9) must have been prepared by Heaton to show how the investment of £670,000 was supported by a return probably above interest rates, let alone improved values following liming, drainage schemes etc. It also was to show that the Duke was running out of cash.

'The Auditor' was not too concerned to voice his views on his perception of rash spending by the Cavendish family. William Gould confided to his diary in April 1787 that Mr. Heaton 'complains much of the expenditure of the Duke of Portland respecting his income [he was the Duke's brother-in-law] and says he is living too fast. He also says the Duchess of Devonshire lost at play last year £30,000 to £40,000, which he (Heaton) is now borrowing to pay the same'. Heaton clearly took a dim view of the 5th Duchess's extravagance and the effect on Cavendish finances.

This particular problem had come to light some months before and by early 1787 the Duchess had agreed not only to stop gambling [she was soon in substantial debt again to the tune of £6,000] but had agreed to Heaton's suggestion that she cut her household expenditure. Two of her staff plus two footmen 'and some of the horses' went. Interestingly, she wrote to her mother describing a little of Heaton's character:

'I must tell you that I am vastly pleased with Heaton – his appearance at first is against him – tiresome on ordinary subjects – with some degree of insolence – but he has a comprehensive laborious, active mind and a spirit of order and regularity in the arrangement of business very pleasing – he has just finished extricating the Duke of Portland from distress and even by useful speculations gives him the prospect of affluence – I hope and think he will be as successful with us as our case is not so desperate as theirs was.' (10)

Nonetheless, one wonders whether the expenditure of £54,000 in a year on only three of the Duke's houses seems profligate, following the death of the 5th Duke's spendthrift wife. The Duke also did not bother to collect over £6,000 per annum rent for the Burlington estate having 'lost interest in it' as Heaton put it in 1810. Presumably this was to permit his brother-in-law, the 3rd Duke of Portland and his sister Dorothy to receive the benefit of it and fund their life at Burlington House. However, the Duke lost his sister in June 1794, aged 43 years having been married when she was 16 years old. The Duke of Portland died on 30th October 1809. It is not clear why rental income was not restored. Portland was Prime Minister twice: 2nd April 1783 to 19th December 1783 and 31st March 1807 to 4th October 1809.

The tightening of cash must have been behind the lack of investment at times seen in the Hartington estate between 1795–99 (as well as the Duke's indifference to his late wife's gambling creditors). Expenditure picked up in 1799 with the initial inclosures of Hartington Common and the first payment to the Inclosure Commissioners of £3,462 for land allocated to the Duke. As indicated above, the total cost of unencumbered land acquisition and stone walling etc. expenses under the Hartington Inclosure Act was £23,763. Several farms saw capital expenditure – Newhaven Farm, Coatsfield Farm, Pilsbury Farm, Handale Farm, Brierly Farm (now Brierlow) plus the new Bull's Head Inn at Biggin and Hartington Mill, which had a new drying house. Brierly Farm and the Inn were the last two substantial projects, started in 1807 and 1808 respectively and both completed in 1810.

Following the Duke's death in 1811, only work in hand was completed – fencing on the common at £366 and which may well have been for work completed beforehand – being the main item. The total of other work spent in 1811–12 amounted to only £102. In 1813, the amount spent was nil. Very little was spent on the Hartington estate and in Buxton in the next decade. The only notable exception being the Hot Baths at The Crescent in 1818. However under the 6th Duke, the policy of active revenue growth through capital purchases seems to have ended. The 6th Duke being known now for excessive expenditure on fine art (including statuary) and his building schemes such as the north wing extension at Chatsworth. It all came to a head with much debt reduction through estate sales, unpicking the wealth created by his father and John Heaton.

Today the 6th Duke is remembered as a hugely successful collector and indeed he was. It was at the expense of much of the hard work undertaken by Heaton on a treadmill trying to keep revenues matching expenditure. Today the 5th Duke is not recognised as being one of the greatest investors in landed property in the country in the period 1770–1810. Nor is Heaton's contribution to it, despite being so critical to its success. Moreover, the amount spent after 1790 was devoid of borrowings but for the £66,000 as indicated above.

This is of course at odds with the comments by Lees-Milne: (11) *Realising that his estates had been shockingly mismanaged and neglected towards the end of his father's reign – the old family solicitor, John Heaton, though loyal had become imbecile'.*

Just prior to the 5th Duke's death he (Heaton) had concluded the acquisition of over 13,000 acres of freehold land in Hartington and converted it to quality farmland with two tenants soon to be heralded by writer John Farey (see pp. 74-76) as amongst the best in the county; with two of the best farms on land that had been part of the common and previously of very little value. Hardly the work of an imbecile manager. His continuing work as the family lawyer has also been reviewed above. Moreover there are plenty of records to show his ongoing hard work under the 6th Duke.

Cannadine states that the 6th Duke inherited without the estate being settled upon him in trust for the benefit of future generations. The effect was to enable him (the 6th Duke) to do as he pleased with his inheritance. With only a short period between his coming-of-age and his inheritance, it may well be true. What is not explained is why an entailed estate needed to be confirmed between father and son. However, if it needed to be it also needs to be seen

The Duke had an apartment under his coat of arms in The Crescent. The rooms later formed part of a further hotel, The Central. The Duke and Duchess found the rooms better than they had expected

in the context that the 5th Duke did not buy all of his acquisitions under settled terms. Out of the £670,000 spent on acquisitions and improvements, some £205,000 of acquisitions were unsettled. It could well have been his intention to pass these on as an unsettled estate, having nothing to do with his death. In fact only the Cumberland estate and purchases after 1804 were unsettled. (12)

When Heaton retired in 1817, the Duke gave him a gratuity of £2,000. It had been well earned. He might have felt ready for his retirement but he died in 1818. He died with two mortgages for £10,000 each and a third for £4,000 on his property from Snow & Co. His account with the Duke on his retirement in 1817 showed £3,910. 15s. 8d. due to the Duke, which eventually was paid by £1,600 in 1819 and a final commutted payment (by Charles Heaton, grandson and executor) of £1,500 in 1832. The Duke waived the right to interest when he learnt that Charles Heaton did not have the resources to pay it.

From surviving correspondence it would appear that John Heaton had not kept his own personal affairs in order. It appears that it was felt by the grandson that John Heaton ought to have had a *graduated addition between 1764 and 1811 which it was considered he might properly have recommended to the late Duke of Devonshire and which recommendation His Grace might have prudently adopted – the difference to my grandfather from this long period of nearly half a century – would have been no less a sum than £25,945'*.

If Heaton had asked for a rise and the Duke had agreed, the increment would of course have begun after Heaton started work for the Duke as his agent in 1773, (this was when Heaton commenced taking instructions on legal work). (13)

Heaton was succeeded by James Abercrombie who went on to become an MP and Speaker of the House of Commons in 1835.

See Appendix 2 for a list of the acquisitions in Hartington and Buxton.

Mrs Heaton

By contrast with William Gould, John Heaton travelled by coach, often with his wife and with a servant. The Heatons enjoyed a higher social life than they may have anticipated. There are a couple of references to this in the 5th Duchess's correspondence and are not entirely complimentary in the comments about Mrs. Heaton. It does point to them possibly living a life beyond their means:

'Some orange ribbon large or small
Why Mrs. Groves has it all
Nay this is scarlet – coarse as tape
T'wch bind poor Mrs. Heatons shape
And make for vigoureux a cape'

This same note continues with another poem:

'Oh do not think I want for nouse
Or question my behaviour
Dreams of an orange favour
Poor Madam Heaton trims her gown
For tho' short legd and sallow
The little body loves the ton
And wch be, rarely yellow' (14)

The clamour for orange ribbon in November 1788 was because the ladies wished to wear the colour in celebration of the centenary of the abdication of James II on 16th December 1688, partly orchestrated by the Earl of Devonshire who was raised to the Dukedom as a result. James II was succeeded by King William of Orange and Queen Mary. The ton was the highest social circle in the land and its two leaders were the Duke and Duchess of Devonshire.

The centenary of the arrival of William of Orange at Brixham on 5th November 1688 was celebrated by the Duke and Duchess and, also it seems, on the estate. The Ecton Mine accounts record the expenses (nearly £22) of *'a feast to the workmen in the memorable 5th of November 1788'.* Although there is no mention of any celebration in the Hartington area, it is likely that such a celebration took place, although the men working at Ecton would have been missing.

In June 1809, Philip Heacock, the manager of the Buxton & Hartington estate, noted in a letter that Mrs. Heaton was *'dangerously ill; recovery doubtful'.* (15)

References

1 Dev. Coll., AS/1717

2 Leach, J. T., *Derbys. Arch. Journal*, Vol. 116, 1996, Grin Hill, Buxton, A Major Derbyshire Limestone Quarry, p 107

3 Langham, ibid, p19

4 Dev. Coll., 5th Duke's letters, No. 820, Duchess to Countess Spencer

5 Dev. Coll., L/60/20

6 William Gould's Diary, ibid, 5/5/1785 and 1/12/1785

7 5th Dukes letters, No 533, 15/9/1783, Duchess to Countess Spencer

8 There is also a difference in the total expense for the Hartington Inclosure. In the Expenditure list from 1773-1810 it is shown as £23,763. The accounts at the time show £14,255. This probably means some figures are missing

9 It is not catalogued at the Muniment Room

10 Dev. Coll., 5th Duke's letters. No. 795, 14/1/1787, Duchess to Countess Spencer

11 Lees-Milne., J., *The Batchelor Duke, 6th Duke of Devonshire 1790 – 1858*, c. 1990, p18

12 Cannadine, D., *Aspects of Aristocracy*, 1994, p168 Dev. Coll,. L/114/27/4

13 Dev. Coll., AS/337

14 Dev. Coll., 5th Duke's letters, No. 923, 4/11/1788; This reference to vigoureux presumably relates to the mother of Louise Vigoureaux, born in 1790, who was left £500 in the 6th Duke's will. She died 6 years before the Duke and was the same age as he was

15 Dev. Coll., AS/1819, Letterbook, 1809, 10th June 1809

5. LIVING OFF THE LAND

Farming for a Living

The map of Hartington parish of 1614 drawn by William Heyward (1) gives a lot of detail on the area at that time. The land area consisted of 23,230 acres/9,401 ha. The seven largest farms covered 3,328 acres/1,347 ha of this. Dowall Farm, including High Edge (231 acres/93 ha) and Great Chrome (33 acres/13 ha) totalled 461 acres/87 ha. Harly (sic), including Hindlowe (112 acres/45 ha); Hardhirste (34 acres/14 ha); Houghstone (32 acres/13 ha) totalled 488 acres. Glutton, including Harley Edge (162 acres/66 ha); Glutton Hill (28 acres/11 ha); Hitterell (24 acres/10 ha), totalled 302 acres/156 ha. Poolhall extended to 413 acres/167 ha; Burbage, 385 acres/156 ha, and Glutton, 302 acres/122 ha. The seventh and largest holding was Earls Booth at 977 acres/395 ha. All of these were in the north of the parish.

The amount of commons and waste was huge at 11,400 acres/4,614 ha. Fuel was scarce with relatively little wood, a problem which plagued the Ecton Mine near Hartington between 1770 − 1790. Axe Edge, south-west of Buxton, described as *'The Great Common Moore'*, consisted of 4,000 acres/1,619 ha of *'moarish and mossie grounds wherein they digge peats for their firinge and more on lower common land'*. There was pressure on the common from neighbouring parishes which claimed (successfully) that they had rights of turbary, giving them access to Hartington lands to dig for peat and to carry it out of the parish.

It was fortunate that coal was found on Axe Edge. Its quality could have been better, but it kept home fires burning (hence the Hartington Coal Road) as well as supplying furnaces at the Grin Hill lime works south-west of Buxton, let alone many small limekilns which were built across the parish by enterprising farmers. Some of the large holdings began to be reduced in size by the Georgian period but many good sized productive farm holdings were to emerge as a result of the 1808 Inclosure.

A main feature of community life in the parish was an echo of its medieval past. Around Hartington itself were three fields divided into strips of differing occupiers. Although larger enclosures and amalgamation had occurred giving reasonable sized fields in one ownership − or at least one occupation − the furlong length strips still existed, with many shown on Heyward's map of 1614.

Perhaps the field between the village and the River Dove was the most important and valuable of the three. It was flat and crossed by the water of the River Harding which flowed down what is now Factory Lane and on towards the Dove. It probably had deeper and richer soils too. It was of course more sheltered and harvested produce was nearer to village barns (locally called shippons).

The other two fields were higher on the plateau above the village, one north and one south of Hartington Dale, known together as the High Field. Ploughing would have been by heavy horses or perhaps oxen, which were quite prevalent in the 17th century. Their use in this area is preserved in place name evidence, viz: Oxbatch, north of the former Mermaid Inn on Morridge, and Oxensitch at Axe Edge plus Oxdale, north of Alsop-en-le-Dale. In 1728, rent was being paid at Butterton for an Oxgang. (2) Perhaps an indicator of a widespread population of oxen is a reference of 1686. In this year, Tristham Drable, a smith (and therefore by inference of large stature), spent time between 1st June and 21st September throwing oxen. He didn't pick them up of course, but he did bring them to the ground. (3) This means he was shoeing them.

The period of time involved (nearly 4 months) would seem to indicate more than an occasional beast. (4) Having brought the animal to the ground, he would have brought the head down so that a horn went into the earth, effectively anchoring the animal while metal plates (shoes) were applied to each clove of the hoof. (Hartington had its own smith in 1614: Richard Milnes). Oxen were expensive to buy, costing between £7 and £10. 10s. 0d. in 1757. (5) Although Drable was paid on the Chatsworth account, one wonders if he went out onto the Derbyshire estate, dealing with local tenant farmers' needs. In 1798 Mathew Halksworth is recorded as being paid 11s. 0d. a week (he was paid every quarter) for working the ox team on the Chatsworth Estate. This was quite a lot of money at that time. (6)

As the land was being ploughed, what was it ploughed for? Cereal crops are the likely answer. In the eighteenth century turnips were grown also as animal feed although it is likely that it provided cheap domestic food too. The seed was purchased in Bakewell by Chatsworth tenants from Wetton and a similar source must have been used throughout the neighbourhood. Cereals would have been ground at both of the two manor mills, Hartington and Crowdecote, presumably for both domestic use and animal feed. In 1719, Wetton had a pinner, or hayward, for *'Wetton Hill and the Wheatlands'* – Joseph Birch – indicating the growing of wheat there on neighbouring Devonshire land. (7) He would have been responsible for rounding up stray animals (as the pinner) and responsible for maintaining fences to stop the animals from straying (as the hayward). Hartington Mill provided bran for the underground horses at Ecton Mine from 1780. (8) The Mine must have been a good customer, for Samuel Bonsall took his cart to the Mill once a week.

Barley would also have been grown and there is a Barley Dale marked on Hayward's 1614 map, off Biggin Dale (to the west of Biggin Grange). In 1746, there was a Barley Yard at Crowdecote. (9) Barley Lands is a river meadow just above Pilsley mentioned in the Inclosure Award. Purchasers would have included local inn-keepers who made their own beer, with malt and hops brought in by packhorse and later by cart. Ashbourne had several malt houses and was well known for its beer – at least by the latter half of the seventeenth century, if Charles Cotton is to be believed. (10)

Farey noted in 1809 that the harvest at Newhaven for both hay and corn was a fortnight later on average than it was in the Derby area. He also recorded that he had seen oats standing in the shock and covered by snow on 25th November 1808, between Buxton and Hartington. (11) In the 1970s, in some fields adjacent to the west side of the A515 just north of the Bull I'th Thorn Inn, the hay was always cut very late in the year and sometimes lay with snow on it before it was carried. By contrast, wheat was not as hardy and in sustained poor weather could fail.

A letter from Godfrey Heathcote to John Heaton in 1773 states that lands [at Buxton] in general underwent a rotation of arable meadow and pasture. So in the second year the grass was cut and in the third year the land was left for grazing and of course, manuring by the animals doing the grazing. (12)

In the 1780s there may not have been too much spare hay production. The Ecton Mine needed it for the underground mine horses but often could not buy it locally, buying hayricks wherever they could and on one occasion going as far as Winster in order to do so.

Butter and cheese production presumably occurred on a domestic basis with any excess being sold on. The establishment of a butter market in Bakewell in 1710 would have given a further outlet. (13) Hartington of course, had its own weekly market. In fact it is the oldest in the Peak District, dating from 1203. Strangely, very little information survives on it. In 1829, it was held on a Wednesday *'chiefly for butter, poultry and butcher's meat.'* (14)

Cheese and wool were other revenue earners. In 1783 William Gould obtained £2 per hundredweight for his cheese. His lambs' wool sold at $5^1/_2$d per lb and sheep's wool at 6s. 9d. per stone (just under 6d. per lb) delivered to Chapel-en-le-Frith free and with credit until midsummer (six months). In 1786, the wool from his sheep, which had reached three years in age, amounted to 576 stone or 3 tons 12 cwt. Had he received 6s. 9d. per stone for it, the value would have been £194. 8s. 0d. By 1798, the price for fleeces had risen substantially to 9s. 6d. a stone. (15)

There is not much documentary evidence to show that the area supported root crops in the late 18th century and especially in Hartington parish. However, indirect evidence is available from the nearby Devonshire Estate at Wetton. Seed was purchased in Bakewell. In 1787 a crop of turnips was produced from part of Wetton Hill Pasture, which was sold to Daniel Cantrell for £10. 0s. 0d. A crop of oats from the same pasture was sold for £135. 11s. 0d. and was no doubt despatched to Wetton Mill to be ground. These crops were, incidentally, grown by the Estate. The following year, oats and turnips were grown and a consignment of sheep sold. (16) Turnips were used to fatten animals in the spring for market, especially sheep. It is highly likely that turnips were being grown by Hartington tenants of the Estate, but records do not survive to tell us what the farming activities of the various tenants were. In 1757, both *'wethers and sheep'* were being kept on turnips at Chatsworth (see below). (17) A wether was a castrated lamb.

The commons provided game for those able to snare or shoot it. As early as 1686, ten brace of *'moure poultry'* was taken first to Chatsworth and then on to Hardwick before being despatched to London. As it was divided into four deliveries between 12th December and 2nd January 1687, presumably on this occasion they were bound for the Earl's table, rather than kitchens at Hardwick etc. (18) Moor poultry is likely to refer to grouse or black cock. If game was consumed by the estate in general and by the Duke in particular, other produce once despatched was sold on: sheepskins at 1st. 0d each in 1757. (19) Some outlets also reduced animal fats to tallow for sale to candle manufacturers such as Mr. Cresswell in Ashford, Mr. Roberts in Winster and Mr. Armstrong in Ashbourne. In 1757 tallow was fetching 4s. 0d. per stone (14lbs). There were occasional deliveries of it to Hartington Mill, in addition to candles.

Farming in the late 17th century

In the 1680s, the manor kept a large estate in hand – at Glutton and at what was called 'Harrison's farm' – land at Harley, Booth and perhaps Crookhill, (where £23. 16s. 8d. a half year's rent was paid to the Queen Dowager for herbage). In fact Glutton Farm was probably included from 1685 when William Harrison's lease had terminated with distraint against his stock. The accounts give some indication of the farm management practices carried out there by the estate. Cattle and sheep were bought and sold through various local fairs. In 1686 these were Hope, Leek, Tideswell, Macclesfield, Bakewell, Chesterfield, and Chapel-en-le-Frith, where beasts were bought, and Ashbourne Fair, where sales were made of horses as well as cattle and sheep.

Perhaps of more interest was the purchase in 1687 of 16 cows at 'Barnsly'. (20) A second purchase, at Penestone probably gives a clue as to the route taken to the manor farm. Penistone is on the direct route from Barnsley which would be taken if the animals were

Glutton Farm, dated 1675

driven over the Woodhead Pass and on to Glossop. Here they would go south to Hayfield and then to Buxton. (21) It seems likely that the Barnsley animals had been driven south to that market, possibly from Scotland, for the animals from there were much in demand. Over 100 years later, the Chatsworth estate account for 1801 shows that Scottish beasts were still being purchased. Additionally, in the same year $104^{1}/_{2}$ yards of Scottish carpet was also bought at 3s. 10d. per yard and a year later, Scotch sheets costing £51. 4s. 0d. was purchased from Radley & Hewitt. Other, later, purchases show that Scottish goods were favoured. These imports of Scottish produce did not completely overshadow the produce of Wales however, with 17 Welsh sheets being purchased by the estate in December 1809.

Farey states that Scotsmen drove animals south to the Peak District, where they were presumably sold. Although a much later reference, this may give an idea as to the provenance of the animals bought at Barnsley and Penistone. The purchase shows not only that the manor was prepared to conduct operations over a wide area, but was probably trying to introduce better quality stock onto the farm. The purchase from Hope, Chesterfield and Macclesfield, may have been other examples of this and indeed of animals, which may also have been from the north.

A year later (1688), 22 cows were purchased at Barnsley (abbreviated to 'Beny', which fits if pronounced 'Baernsley') and costs charged for three days and nights for two men (12s. 0d.) and hay purchased for '21 beats'. Presumably one cow had a follower still suckling. The distance from Barnsley to Glutton is over 40 miles and if this means that the animals reached Glutton in three days, they were being moved fairly quickly.

At the annual accounting in 1688 for what were termed the *Harrison's farms*, in the Upper Dove valley, 199 sheep were in hand. Costs included mowing and haymaking – 31 acres (presumably at Glutton) and a further 12 acres at Booth. A total of 120 sheep were bought that year, plus 38 *'beasts'*, chiefly cattle, which were fattened and sold on, making a useful profit of nearly £32 on an outlay of £100. Fencing and ditching was also done plus thatching at Glutton. Washing and shearing 100 ewes and 80 lambs contributed wool, which was subject to a tithe payment in favour of a Mr. Milnes for *'wool and lamb'*. For looking after the cattle at Glutton, John Redfern was paid a wage of £5 per annum. This does not seem a lot and may indicate that his board and lodging was also found.

The running of these upland holdings by the Estate contrasts with the age-old practice of letting out land to others upon payment of rent. This was still being practiced in the manor at Pilsbury Grange (where there were two tenants – and two houses to this day); plus Cronxton and Callinglow. Also in the accounts are payments for *'pitch, tar, tobacco and mercury 7s. 11d.'* and in 1685, 100 sheep *'for Christmas'* were valued at £5.

By 1680, when Plot visited Staffordshire (23) most of the common arable land had been enclosed, but some seems to have survived at Hartington, just across the River Dove. However, enclosure of some of the common land would appear to have been underway at about that time. In 1684 men were paid for *'fensing'* at Madgedale, just north of the village of Hartington. It is at the top of Hide Lane, where a shallow dale drops towards Long Dale. The strip fields extended this far, but ended in the vicinity of Madgedale, so it could be that inclosure of common pasture land rather than arable, strip-farmed land, was also taking place. Fencing was also a feature of work at Glutton in 1688, when four men were paid 18s. 8d. (8d. each per day) for seven days' work. It will have been noted above that similar activity happened at Glutton in 1686, so there was regular carving of land out of the common by the estate. (24) Of course, many fields are noted on Heyward's map of 1614, so enclosure was nothing new here.

Agricultural practice in Staffordshire in the late 17th century and 18th century saw the replacement of copyhold tenures by a leasehold system and control of farming practices by restrictive covenants. (25) The former does not appear to have happened on the Devonshire estate in the Hartington manor. Moreover in Staffordshire there appeared to be a continuing rise in rental income. This was not the case in Hartington manor either in the late 17th century and early 18th century. Here, land was let for 21 year terms without revision. The year 1757 was a lease renewal year across the Derbyshire Estate for instance.

Weston. (26) states that Hartington Manor was purchased in 1663 but had previously been leased off the Duke of Buckingham, whose father had acquired it from the King in 1616. The Estate did own land in Hartington parish prior to 1663 and leased out Pilsbury Grange for instance. As early as 1628 and 1629, it was yielding £120 per annum, split equally between Richard Bateman and Nicholas Hurt of Castern. (27)

During the eighteenth century, attention was focussed on improving efficiency and profitability from agriculture. There were probably two main motives behind this: improved profitability of lands worked in-hand and increased rents from tenanted lands. Phillips has shown that this happened on the North Staffordshire estate of the Leveson-Gower family. This consisted of land chiefly south of Newcastle-under-Lyme, together with the Wall Grange estate south west of Leek. Drawing on previous work by Mingay and Wordie, Phillips looked how the estate had changed between 1714-1809. (28) Development initially worked around amalgamation of farms into larger units and later consolidation, with a reduction in the distance between the farmstead and the fields. It was the latter that particularly introduced efficiency savings. Of course, the estate had a further dimension to resolve. This was the amount of limestone heath land, especially once the solution to it (liming) was appreciated. The value of spreading manure was already known in the late 17th century as shown in the Devonshire accounts but was clearly widely practised, according to Plot. What is surprising is that he also mentions the value of improving heath land by liming, so why did it take so long for this to be adopted on Devonshire estates?

At the time of the 1614 Hartington survey, the desmesne land was reported to consist of 45 messauges, 80 tenements and 2 watermills, plus *'standing and decayed 4,960 acres of land of all sorts'*. There was clearly a lot of land needing improvement. Although this could not be done on the common (nobody paid rent for the use of it), it could on the tenanted land, but this did not happen until John Heaton did it.

Improving the land; initial attempts

Plot clearly recognised that the Staffordshire moorland area had poor soils and states that the area was not sown with much wheat because the soil quality was not good enough. He goes on to state that on the heath land, it was seldom inclosed, or fenced, but where it was done, it was never for above five years, when it was abandoned. He described the manner in which such land was treated: Initially it was stocked with mattocks (? animals) and then laid fallow through the winter. The following summer it was dressed with manure and lime, allowing four loads to the statute acre. It was ploughed in mid–September and sown at the end of the month with rye at a rate of 2 strikes per acre. This crop was rotated over the next two years with barley and white peas, followed by two years of oats. (29)

Sometimes the heath land was limed for three or four years before ploughing. Another method was to plough the vegetation in and let it rot, harrowing and sowing the upturned sods for two years before re–ploughing. As an example of the latter practice, Plot quotes the Ipstones area, south west of Hartington. Better than these two alternatives however, was to dig the turf and burn it in the field during May. Lime was then mixed with the turf ash and the field ploughed before Michaelmas (September 29th). The land was then sowed the following spring with barley and in succeeding years with a rotation of oats, rye and oats again. It was then left fallow for four years before being ploughed again just once for *'any grain'*. If this was better, it is not clear why it was not universally adopted.

Plot wrote that the fields were fenced with 'quicksets' (hawthorn), half cut and the top half laid on the ground and earth covered to cause additional sprouting. Alternatively, wooden pales were used for fencing. (30)

Writing nearly a century later in 1771, Arthur Young wrote that around Tideswell *'for many miles there has been worked as great improvements as in any part of England. All this country* [i.e this part of Derbyshire] *was black ling* [heather] *but a few years ago and common land. It is all now inclosed* [but not at Hartington Manor, however, where a group of local people prevented the inclosure of the common until 1808. *The first work was the inclosure which was done at the landlord's expense, but no more than a ring-fence, the sub divisions were made by the tenants: it is all done by dry walling. Landlords, as soon as the ring-fence is done raise the rent to 12s. 0d. an acre'*.

He described the method used to eradicate the heather and inferior grasses: The lime was laid in spring and early summer. *'On the better sort of land, the ling all dies away (burnt by the lime) at Michaelmas and nothing more is ever seen of it, but natural grasses with plenty of white clover comes up instead of it.'* This reclamation process took up to three years to complete. (31)

Following a poor summer, the farmers experienced a poor winter with stocks of fodder sometimes insufficient to feed the animals. There is to us now an obvious answer, which was not practiced in this area and which is now taken for granted. Land used for the hay crop was not improved [as it is now] but simply left. The land became increasingly poorer, more acidic and in places started to revert towards heath land. Grass became poorer and coarser

The Hartington Coal Road at Harley Farm, north of Earl Sterndale

and yields remained low. The grass became 'mossy'. Some land was given over to the poor production of cereals *'from a fear that they won't, after a proper course of husbandry lay down to profitable pasture'*. You would think that if the limed land produced better crops, it would produce better grass, but local farmers did not believe that.

A George Wood of Buxton took up the gauntlet and in 1809 ploughed 37 acres and reseeded it. The Manchester Agricultural Society awarded him a *'seven-guinea silver cup as a reward and encouragement to others'*. (32) This had followed the example of Thomas Pickford at Kings Sterndale, Buxton, in 1805, who ploughed *'heathy limestone land'*, limed it and sowed white clover, trefoil and hayseed on the west side of the village for his tenant. Farey described it as good pasture when he saw it in 1808. This was also done by ploughing to a depth of only 3 inches. It not only proved that it was possible to improve grass yields but that it was also possible to get away with it on thin soils which local farmers also believed could not be achieved.

Given the difficulties in maintaining supplies of fodder through winter months, it comes as no surprise that the Ecton Mine had difficulty buying surplus hay for the mine horses. It is strange that these old practices persisted on lands close to the Devonshire estate which had been liming poor quality soils for half a century.

It is reasonable to suppose that one of the methods mentioned above for improving the land, was used as Devonshire heath land was inclosed. For instance, if an inclosed area was abandoned after five years, then new fields were continually being brought into cultivation. This may well explain the week or so spent annually fencing and in one year ditching (which probably happened each year). This probably reflects the work of inclosing a new field on an annual basis to replace another one which was being abandoned. To date, the earliest Devonshire record located which details wholesale land improvement was in 1757–59 at Blakelow Pasture, Hassop, when 3,000 tons of lime was used on perhaps 60 acres of land (see below for more detail on this and the Hartington estate improvements also mentioned below).

A limekiln was working at Crowdecote Bank in 1778 (33) and bringing in 10s. 0d. per annum in rent. A limekiln was operating at Ecton Mine in 1783 (using stone from the mine); another commenced in 1786 at Wetton Hill and Biggin Moor had one in 1789 (34). These however were small affairs, the bulk of the lime was being made at Grin, south-west of Buxton and at Peak Forest. None the less, there would appear to have been nearly 100 small limekilns eventually across the parish, especially allowing for the transient nature of some of them.

At the time of harvest, the moorland farmers did not cut the barley and oat crop with scythes (which they called mowing) but reaped with *'hooks'* (billhooks). They reasoned that the land was too 'grassy' and that they would lose half of the corn should they mow it, especially in a wet season. Cereals and rye, when cut, were bound in sheaves or shocks and nine of these were gathered together and set on end and covered with three more sheaves. These were then left to stand for 10–12 days before being carried. (35)

Oats were used as winter feed for stock in the event of the hay running out. In 1808, the stable horses at Chatsworth were being fed on oats during the winter. (36) In really bad times, farmers would resort to unusual alternatives such as ash and holly leaves (the latter cut from the upper branches) (37) or gorse (see below).

Problems with rats

Corn was kept in barns or in ricks resting on stone saddles (which looked like a mushroom) to deter rats. Plot noted that bird droppings seemed to be disliked by rats, especially if they found it on their fur. Ricks built on saddles had a timber base covered with furze (gorse) which was an efficient deterrent. One farmer he met used bird droppings, but he was not a moorland farmer. A mat of gorse seems likely to have been a better bet! This may account for the sowing of furze seed on Grin Hill in 1820 at a cost of £7. 17s. 6d. (38), unless it was being used in the limekilns as kindling or to be used as fodder, cut up and mixed with straw. (this was quite common). (39) Another use for gorse, albeit noted in Cumbria, was for fencing material, being cheaper than fleaks – interwoven panels of hazel branches – (40). Unfortunately the surviving records of Hartington Manor give no further clues). The amount of seed purchased for Grin Hill seems to indicate quite a large quantity at nearly £8, so it was probably a cash crop which could have had a variety of customers and uses. Farey records that a tenant of the Duke of Devonshire, on the Staffordshire border of the county, fed his horses on *'chopt* (sic) *and bruised gorse that had been passed between the rollers used at Ecton Copper Mine'.* (41)

New and Improved Machinery

The Hartington accounts do not indicate any detail on the embracing of new agricultural technology. One would perhaps expect the tenants to do that. There were only a handful with a holding large enough to justify the investment until after the inclosures. However there is some indication that half way through the 18th century a change in practice may have occurred at Chatsworth. In 1757, the Rabbit Warren was removed. Part of the Warren was ploughed in the old style by oxen with a mare drawing ahead of them. This suggests that they were still ploughing with cumbersome, heavy wooden ploughs, [with an iron share] in the traditional way. That year, the Warren yielded 356 quarters of oats. At this time,

Calton Plantation was ploughed *'with the great Plough'* which suggests this might have been something different. Perhaps it was something like the Rotherham plough, with a swing head, which had been introduced a quarter of a century or so previously. This lighter, iron plough, did not require oxen to pull it and had the advantage of causing less compacting of the land as a result. It was also quicker. (42) Calton Pasture is east of Bakewell above the Wye Valley.

The ploughed portion of the Warren was sown with oats, barley and turnips – a four year rotation (part would be fallow). The area of turnips was 26 acres. Some 27 *'Scots'* (cows) and 61 wethers (sheep) were purchased *'for the turnips in ye Warren'* in October 1758. The oxen came from Scotland too (*'Scots oxen'*). The turnips were hoed, indicating that a seed drill for planting the seeds in rows was probably in use.

Young (43) wrote in 1771 that in the Matlock area and between Chatsworth and Chesterfield, the Rotherham plough was in common use, so maybe the *'great plough'* marked its local introduction. He also stated that in the Matlock area, *'they here plough with oxen in stiff work, 6 or 8 in a plough, but they sometimes plough with 2 oxen and one horse. With only 2 oxen they do an acre a day'*. The thought of 6 to 8 large oxen used together for one plough does make you wonder if the *'great Plough'* was really large, old and cumbersome after all! This number of animals put to one plough was a practice going back centuries.

Although the strip system at Hartington precluded anything but the continuance of ancient practices (controlled by the Manor Court), Heyward's 1614 map of the parish shows that quite a few enclosed fields existed and the granges were also free of the strip system. Therefore practices at Chatsworth in the 1750s would be no different to those on the Hartington Manor estate. Each year would see the spreading of dung (and ? lime), planting of seeds, killing of moles and rats, cutting the oats, barley, hay and any wheat. The cereals would be then thrashed and winnowed to prepare them for milling. Hay would be set in stooks in the fields to dry before being carried and stored in haystacks. The latter would be given a pitched top (like a house) so that the surface could be thatched to keep out the rain.

In the 1780s, Ecton Mine bought thatch from Pikehall to the east of Hartington Manor. Farmers on a tighter budget probably used rushes. A field north of Heathcote Mere is called Rush Mere (GR141605) As necessary, land would be trenched (soughed) and stone laid therein to improve drainage. The stone, lime and dung would be carried to the fields in carts using oxen or heavy horses to pull them. Hoed turnips suggest that the crop would be carried, or at least pulled from the ground. Cabbages were also grown because they could be cut when turnips were frozen In the ground. Animals would need to be separated from other areas of cultivated ground. Fleaks were often used for this.

In fact, the work of today's farmer bears a good resemblance to the work 250 years ago; only the effects of mechanisation, fertilisers etc impinging on the work today compared to then.

Today we read about drovers' roads and packhorse ways but the movement of animals by foot must have been taken for granted, although today many people will never have witnessed it. It has been mentioned elsewhere herein of the movement of cattle in the 1680s from as far away as Barnsley to the Upper Dove Valley. In 1810, 100 sheep from Ferrybridge, Yorkshire, were driven to Chatsworth. Three cart horses and a bull were also brought to the estate from Booth Ferry in Yorkshire. In the same year 31 Spanish sheep (6 rams and 25 ewes) were purchased for Chatsworth at Col. Downies' sale at Islington in London. It is clear that although the movement of animals to and from local fairs was as common as one would expect, long distance movement must also have been common. It was not just the province of the Welsh and Scottish drovers. However although the nation had witnessed significant improvements in the transportation of goods, the large scale movement of animals and/or shortened delivery times had to await the arrival of the railways.

Making the Countryside Green

The Hartington Common and waste lands were said to extend to 12,000 acres by Godfrey Heathcote, the Duke's Agent prior to the appointment of John Heaton. (44) Pilkington records that it was *'susceptible of very great improvement. The soil in most places seems to be good and is covered with a fine turf'*. (45) The problem for the estate was that land improvement though liming wasn't possible on the common because all the commoners had the right to use it, rent free. Efforts were therefore undertaken on freehold land either let to tenants or in hand e.g. Frith Pasture, a large area of poor land north of the far reaches of the River Dove. The estate had to await inclosure before improvement on its apportioned part of the former common lands could be improved. Unfortunately, objections raised by commoners wanting to maximise their personal holdings as a result of inclosure delayed the process for 50 years no less.

Cultivated land outside the common extended from the river meadows into much of the area around Hartington and over to Heathcote and Biggin. Proceeding north, the desmesne lands of Pilsbury Grange and Cotesfield were cultivated together with Cronxton Grange, Clement Seats, the area around Hurdlow, Wheildon Trees (the name in 1614) and the area of Earls Sterndale. Higher up the River Dove were farms at Glutton, Parkhouse Farm, Dowal Farm and the Earls Booth (adjacent to Dowal). The remainder was common pasture from south of Biggin up to Dow Low Moor, with a further extension up the side of the Roman Road (High Street).

Beyond this area the land bounded by the Rivers Dove and Dane over to the north west of the parish was poor land, with the exception of some other small fields around Burbage and Harpur Hill. An area of very large enclosures north of Dowal Farm. including Harley Edge, High Edge, Thirklow and even the Earls Frith (later called Frith Pasture) was of more doubtful quality.

Consequently, much of the land between the Leek − Buxton road and the Buxton − Ashbourne road south of Buxton was moorland, especially the western half of that area. Heyward's map of 1614 describes it as moor, heath, rough and *'for most part for peats and firing'*, the latter being Leap Edge. This area is now green fields (or quarried away or the industrial estate). The difference John Heaton's liming programme made is most noticeable either side of the Leek − Buxton road as it descends to Buxton from Cisterns Clough. On the left (west) side of the road is Axe Edge, poor moorland whilst on the right are green fields.

The liming of fields was well known in the 17th century and lime burning was well established in that century at Grin (the hill on which Soloman's Temple was later built). There were two concerns there: Mr. Brock with eight kilns and the Dickensons at the east end of the hill with four.

There does not appear to have been much attempt on the Devonshire estate to lime the limestone heath lands in the first half of the 18th century. A major improvement scheme occurred at Blakelow Pasture at Hassop in 1757-59, following its inclosure. It was limed with 28,966 loads of lime and lime ash. This was presumably delivered by packhorse involving an

A Black Clough Colliery shaft. The wall in the background ends at the northern tip of Staffordshire This scene shows unimproved ex-common land.

incredible 58,000 journeys to the kilns and back, probably to Grin Hill (46). A letter dated 24th November 1766 survives from Godfrey Heathcote to Thomas Brock at Grin about an extension to the latter's lease for quarrying and burning limestone to lime. This letter refers to lime ash being collected by farmers to improve their lands (47). In 1773, John Heaton took on the job of Duke's Auditor, but he was in effect, managing the Derbyshire estate. In 1778, the Duke purchased Goits Moss Colliery, Moss House and lands for £2,350 from Messrs. Dickenson and others on Axe Edge (48).

Mrs. Dickenson had endeavoured to sell the coal mine and their four lime kilns to the Duke in 1764, but this was declined owing to a dispute over the mineral rights. Godfrey Heathcote, in a letter of advice to the 5th Duke in 1773 was of the opinion that Robert Longden (of Countess Cliff Farm, south of Harpur Hill). and Richard Wheeldon (of Cronxton Grange) had purchased the Dickenson coal mine at Goits Moss in about 1767. Moreover, the mine was then (1773) currently for sale. Heathcote's advice was that the mine be purchased by the Duke. He did in fact own the adjacent mines, which were let to the Brock family and had been since the 17th century. The Duke was to buy the mine in 1778, but from the Dickensons. Were Longden and Wheeldon trying to sell a leasehold interest, or were they the cause of the dispute over mineral rights?

By 1790, both of the Grin Works was in hand and the profit going to the Duke. The Brock lease had also recently expired and either a renewal was not granted, or not sought. However the lease and kilns had been sub-let between 1767–72 by the Brocks. Leach has pointed out that the kilns were taken in hand by the estate from 1790 – 92 and managed by

Thomas Wild who had rented them in 1789 – 90. Direct management continued until 1799 when they were rented at £300 per annum by a James Clowes, returning after that to estate control until 1818, when Robert Bagshawe (then the manager) became the tenant. However lucrative sales into Lancashire had reduced to nil and the lime trade was badly hit by outlets on the Peak Forest Canal, despite demand for lime on the estate, post-inclosure, at Hartington Common (49). However surviving documents for 1807 – 13 indicate that although nearly 62,000 tons was sold in that period, the profit was only £1,800, little different than the Clowes rental per year. Working in hand by the estate did however stop anyone running it in competition to, or in a way that would prejudice, Devonshire interests. After the Hartington Inclosure there were thousands of acres of acidic soil which needed lime applied for at least two or three years in succession. This was of course additional to ongoing lime requirements on the rest of the Hartington estate and the other Devonshire lands in the Peak.

Presumably a resolution of the dispute mentioned above paved the way for the Dickenson purchase. This then enabled the Duke to produce his own lime and use his own coal to fire the kilns. Leach states that the colliery was at Goits Moss, Taxal, where John Dickenson was Lord of the Manor. However this was nowhere near Taxal village for the parish extended to Goits Moss. The mine held the rights in an area of Axe Edge covered by the 1759 Buxton – Macclesfield turnpike in the north and Tinkerspit Gutter in the south, other boundaries being fences etc. (50) The Moss House included in the purchase was situated on the turnpike road at about GR 013715, south-west of Derbyshire Bridge at the head of the Goyt Valley.

John Heaton must have been encouraged by the purchase of Goits Moss Colliery for two years later he purchased Kingsley Colliery at Hazles Cross, near Kingsley on the Cheadle Coalfield to supply the Whiston Copper Works and the Ecton Mine with coal. In this instance the purchase price was a considerable £21,500 and had returned a profit of just £8,874 in the ten years to 1790 when the mine failed (51). It was something of a paper profit only, for the colliery supplied the smelter with 10,000 tons of coal a year.

In 1780, the Duke leased the rights to the Goits Moss Colliery again to Wheeldon and Longden on behalf of themselves and Isaac and Edmund Wheeldon, described as inn holders of Buxton. The rent was to consist of 13,000 horse loads of good and well burnt lime, consisting of 12 pecks per horse load (i.e. 3 bushels per horse load). The lime was to be delivered and dropped in *'proper heaps'* for spreading on land within the Parish of Hartington, but no further distant than Cronxton Grange. Lime kilns were to be built at the Duke's expense. The term was for 19 years (52)

The work at Hindlow Farm and Sticker Hill (known locally as Sticcow) was not without an unforeseen problem. The laying of lime was not done properly. William Gould referred to this is his diary in 1785, two years after John Heaton had expressed dissatisfaction on the workmanship employed. Messrs. Longden and Wheeldon proposed to lay 3,000 loads of lime *'in lieu of bad lime heretofore laid on, otherwise they was (sic) willing to give up there lease to the Duke of Devonshire'.* (53) It is likely that instead of using lime (as contracted) they had thought that they could get away with poor quality lime ash, full of impurities.

Heaton's displeasure with the Wheeldons may have been linked to Isaac Wheeldon's decision to give up the tenancy of Buxton Hall at about that time. See also under Frith Pasture at the end of this chapter for more shoddy work being suspected on liming.

It is not readily appreciated that limestone soils can be acidic. It is caused by leaching of minerals in the soil as water percolates down into cracks and joints in the underlying limestone. The acidic soils then support bilberry, heather and coarse grasses. Today limestone heath land in the area still exists, but is rare. Examples are at Alsop Moor Plantation (GR 165574) and at a field still called the Heather Moor at GR 173580 on the road to Parwich from the A515.

The year 1778 also saw John Wheeldon's neighbours agreeing to spread lime. Thomas Melland at Harley Farm was to receive 6,000 loads and a similar quantity in 1779. Ralph Needham agreed to spread 3,600 loads on How Torr in 1778 and 2,000 loads in 1779. John Wheeldon also occupied Dowal Farm and High Edge to the north west, but no lime agreement appears to have been struck for these farms at that time and no subsequent record has been found. High Edge was not limed until 1790 and 1791, and was then divided amongst three tenants yielding £65 in rent. (54)

The details for Dowal Farm also have yet to be located. Further liming took place at The Frith in 1787 – 91 on some of the poorest soils to be improved. Harley Farm followed in 1791. All of these, i.e. The Frith, High Edge and Harley, were serviced by limekilns built on the land, with both limestone and slack (coal) carried to the site. A further kiln was built at Sherbrook in 1789. This might have been located where Sherbrook Lodge was built (later the youth hostel) on the corner of the Ashbourne Road and Harpur Hill Road. A structure existed in the garden, which might well have been a limekiln. It had a stone arched roof in the manner of a kiln, although the possibility remains that it was a limekiln erected later for the purpose of providing lime for the house!

A deal was struck through William Smith to pay the keeper of the Ladmanlow Toll Bar for the carriers of slack from Goit (sic) and Black Clough Collieries. He was paid fifteen guineas (£15. 15s. 0d.) which represented a 'bulk-rate'. The same year, 1790, William Tunnicliffe was paid 13s. 9d. for *'composition'* (i.e. the bulk-rate) for carriers' horses with slack passing through the Flash Toll Bar and William Brunt paid £1. 9s. 8d. for the same reason. This was for slack heading for High Edge. (55)

The paucity of surviving agreements between the Estate and its tenants clouds the issue of whether the latter were under any obligation to improve the land. However William Gould's tenancy arrangements with the Estate were not confined to Pilsbury. He also tenanted Park House and Ludwall Farms (in addition to occupying the off-estate Lowend Farm between Sheen and Hulme End). The last two estate farms were sub-let to William Poyser from Lady Day 1784 at £185 per annum, on a full repairing lease. The agreement included a requirement of the tenant to plough about six acres of land at each of the two farms; to lay and spread upon Park House 20 cart loads of lime (c. 20 tons) and ten cart loads at Ludwall, both annually. Additionally, he was *'to lay out yearly £5 in draining properly with stone and £10 in lime at the kiln, including the 30 cart loads. I am to repair the Park House barns and build him one bay there for a labourer to live in, also to build him a cow-house at Ludwall for 20 calves or stirks'.* (56)

The requirement to do draining work suggests that this may have been also in the head lease from the Estate and perhaps the liming too. The mention of *'the kiln'* probably relates to the Pilsbury limekiln, built later in 1785. The Crowdecote Bank kiln was still in use in 1791. (57) Draining became a priority for further land improvement in 1810, with much work being undertaken in the Buxton area particularly.

Coal for Lime

West of the Leek – Buxton road rises Axe Edge Moor. Its principal feature consists of a (roughly) north–south ridge supporting boggy moorland and exposed to the worst aspects of our weather. Running down this ridge is the outcrop of a coal seam suitable for household

William Wainwrights Account for the Lime Kilns on Grin.

1810

From 31 Decr 1809 to 31st Decr 1810

Dr.

£ s d

To Arrears returned on the last Account ending 31st Decr 1809 — — 47 12 9

To Lime sold into Cheshire, Derbyshire & Staffordshire
No 1 Potts 514,770
No 2 Do 3308
No 3 Do 32,084 loads sold
90,270 44,813. 10 1625 15 4

To Extra Price of 9 per Load, see No 23 — 13 1 9

To omitted crediting this Extra 1 per Load upon the Arrears in the last Account ending 31st Decr 1809 — 5 9

£1691 18 3

Cr.

31 Decr 1810

£ s d

By Arrears unpaid for Lime sold to 31st Decr 1809, see No 20 — 144. 19. 3
Do — Do to 31st Decr 1810, see No 21 — 28. 6. 2 } 173 5 5

By Labourers for Burning 44,813 loads 10 loads of Lime, see No 16 — 1046 11 7

By Repairing Kilns and Road, for Coals Carriage &c into other Material used at the Works, see No 17 — 157 15 3½

By the Accountants Wages for one year, ending 31st Decr 1810 — 40

By Balance of his Account, passed to Mr. Heacock — 314 5 11½

£1691 18 3

Accounts for Grin Quarry, 1810 (above) and Thatch Marsh Colliery, 1810 (opposite-page) Chatsworth, Devonshire Collection, T-Series Bundle 3

use, known as the House Coal. To the west is another, poorer, seam which was better suited for burning lime. In fact it had little other use in this area. Being poorer and less valuable it was at least nearer the surface. Roberts and Leach (58) indicate that the deepest part of the seam was only 75 ft/25m. below the surface. They conclude that there are at least 100 shafts, which worked this coal over the extraction area.

On the House Coal seam there are even more – 130 shafts. There appears to have been three different mines working this seam at different times. Ravens Colliery in the north, Thatch Marsh in the middle and Black Clough Colliery at the southern end. These were drained by the Duke's level to Burbage, the total length being c.2.5 miles/4km. Coal was exploited southwards beyond the Duke's boundary (also the county boundary). It was also exploited westwards, both in the River Goyt in Cheshire (in the Manor of Taxal) and at Dane Bower Colliery particularly.

Seventeenth century maps mark the mines as does a map relating to a county boundary dispute of c. 1599. (59) According to James Brock, writing in 1774, his family had been tenants of *'coal mines and limestone quarries lying in Hartington [parish] and in the neighbourhood of Buxton'* for over a century. (60)

The Estate accountant of 1685 recorded rental income at that time including some of the coal mines on Axe Edge. In that year, William Brock and Francis Norton paid £12. 0s. 0d. for *'the lime kilns and cole mines'*. Additionally, Francis Norton, Henry Jackson and William Brusell paid £8 *'for the Cole Myne att Thatch Marsh'*; Norton also paid £3 for *'the Cole Myne att Black Clough'*; Andrew and Francis [Norton] paid £2 for The Orchard and Andrew Norton £10 for Otterhole Mill. Although under a list of farm rents at Burbage, one wonders whether the reference to Orchard is for the farm or nearby shafts. Confusingly, the Black Clough Colliery is in Orchard Clough and not adjacent to Black Clough Farm, which is further to the west. In 1698, the record is:

'Mr. William Brock for ye Lime Pitts and Cole Mines	£12. 0s. 0d
For another Cole Mine	£ 7. 0s. 0d.
For another Cole Mine	£ 8. 0s. 0d'*.

The Nortons appear in the account, including for Otterhole Mill, but are not shown as being linked to the mines, which must have been taken over by the Brocks. The rental records in the 18th century show the Brocks paying rent for three lots of coal mines, although the names are not always given. (An example of this is the rental for 1706 when Mr. Wm. Brock was paying three amounts as in 1697 but there is not even a reference to *'cole mines'*, let alone which ones. (61) In 1718, a further entry appears for Mr. Brock of £7. Was this for another mine or for Otterhole Mill, which usually appeared after the three Brock rentals? (62)

A case before the Hartington Manor Court in April 1746 would appear to offer a solution as to which mines were covered by the Brock rentals. other than Thatch March and Black Clough. In 1746, Mrs. Brock was fined (amerced) 10s. 0d. if she did not fill in or fence off the unoccupied coal mines at Guilt Head (sic) [Goyt Head], Thatch Marsh and Ravens. This is the only known reference to shafts at Ravens seen in the Devonshire records. This is the relatively flat area of land north of the current Macclesfield – Buxton road and immediately east of the headwaters of the River Goyt – an area now known as Ravens Low and Ravens Low Flatt – bounded to the east by Berry Clough. Mrs. Brock was given 6 weeks to complete the work. (63)

Thirty years later, the Brocks were paying rent for Thatch Marsh, Black Clough and Goit (sic) Moss. Goyt Moss is to the north west of the Ravens area and clearly the same letting. The latter reference in 1773 (64) is in a recommendation made by Godfrey Heathcote, the Duke's accountant, relating to various issues in the Buxton area. This is the same document referred to above under liming (Making the Countryside Green). He confirms that the Brocks were also leasing lime kilns nearby [at Grin]. The rent for the three collieries was £50 per annum, until 1767, when a new 21 years lease was agreed at £200 per annum expiring in 1788. (65) The tenant was James Brock of Stockport. The 1767 lease was entered in the document in the names of Thomas and Bridget Brock, the names subsequently deleted and replaced by 'Mrs'. The lease included Coal Mines, lime pits, 2 dwellings [Moss House and Moss Hall] plus 51 acres /20.6ha of land.

In c. 1750, the Brocks had driven a drainage sough from the Goyt Valley to drain the Goyts Moss area. Roberts & Leach mark a level as having an entrance near GR 018721, close to Derbyshire Bridge. However this drains the Ravens Colliery workings in the House Coal seam, whereas James Brock is very specific: *'a drain or sough brought up at very considerable expense to lay dry the kiln coals at Goyts Moss'*. The location of this level is not known unless it is in fact The Ravens Level draining Ravens and Goits Moss Mines.

In 1754, another sough was driven at a cost of over £300 *'to lay dry the coals for the house use … at Thatchmarsh, at which colliery [I] have been sinking money for these last seven years'* (i.e. since 1767). Some £400 was still needed to be expended to *'put the mine in a proper working condition'*. James Brock contended in a petition to the Duke, that at about the time that he had taken on a further 21 years lease in March 1767 it was realised that this extra expenditure was necessary.

However there was a covenant in the lease that it be renewed when the Duke reached the age of 21 years (1769) if requested by Brock. He was now requesting that renewal, to remove restrictions in the lease. These prevented the House Coal being sold at more than 5d. a horse load, whereas the general price was 6d. Likewise, the kiln coal (for burning limestone) was restricted to 2s. 9d.(about 13.5p.) per score whereas the price at the Peak Forest Quarry was over 4s. 0d. (20p) per score. The latter (a score) was the equivalent to about 2 tons in weight, according to James Brock. This is important for Roberts & Leach assume it was equivalent to 1 ton, although stating that their estimate could be wide of the mark. (66) It affects their calculation of the tonnages raised by 100%.

The above raises the question about the location of the 1754 drainage, or sough, level. Two levels were driven from Burbage (to the east of the House Coal seam) into Thatch Marsh. Farey (1811) stated that a new tunnel at Thatch Marsh Colliery was being made to take a railway. It had started *'lately'* under the control of George Dickens. In 1807, Dickens had spent *'driving the level at the collieries near Buxton, for one year to 31st December 1807, £478'*. This must relate to this later level, known as the Goyt New Tunnel. (67) It was completed in October 1813, when Dickens suggested that the price charged for coal be increased by 10d per score. There had been a previous price increase in 1808, both probably to help cover the cost of driving the tunnel. However full production was being delayed because of the need for a ventilation shaft at the inner end, which was expected to take a further three months to sink. Therefore the earlier level, known as the Duke's Level, must have been started in 1754. Roberts & Leach suggest a start date of c. 1770, but assumes continual working to reach a particular shaft by a known date. (68)

As we have seen above, work had stopped at the level by James Brock as £400 was needed to obtain *'a proper working condition'*. Although he had been working on the level between 1767 and 1774, it may not have been continuous. His expenditure between 1754 and 1767 of only £300 suggests that this may be the case. What is known is that by 1790 this level was being used as an underground canal to boat coal to the surface at Burbage and that, according to Farey, the level was to reach 2 miles in length. Its entrance is located in Level Lane, but is now buried.

There was also an underground canal at Black Clough, which could have been independent, or connected to the end of the Duke's Level and of course, there was another one nearby opened at the Duke's Mine at Ecton in the 34 fathoms level in 1766. The main drainage level or sough at the Duke's Hazles Cross Colliery (at Kingsley, serving his copper smelter at Whiston) was also called Duke's Level. It was $1^1/_4$ miles in length and was commenced prior to 1770. It was not a canal, however. (69) It would appear that having gained control of the mines, John Heaton recommenced work on the Brock level to drain the mine southerly to exploit further reserves to a considerable depth. No doubt the name Duke's Level was introduced at this time (c. 1790).

Heathcote, in his 1773 statement to the 5th Duke, advised that a Mr. Dickenson, one of the Duke's tenants on Grin Hill, with a lime works there also had coal mining interests adjacent to the Duke's interests on Axe Edge, but in the parish of Taxal. It would have been the source of the coal for the Dickenson lime works. A disagreement over the boundary between the two interests resulted in a boundary perambulation on behalf of the Duke. Although the Heyward 1614 plan had not been produced at the time, the result had confirmed the 1614 boundary. However two of the Duke's employees had subsequently reached *'an agreement'* with Mr. Dickenson, (according to the latter) without authority and which was not ratified in writing. Clearly Mr. Dickenson played on this *'agreement'* to try and obtain personal advantage. Godfrey Heathcote recommended the purchase of the Dickenson lands/mines and the merger of the coal interests.

In 1778, the Dickenson interest in *'Goyts Moss Colliery, Moss House and lands'* was purchased by the Duke for £2,350 and presumably leased to James Brock, hence the much increased rent from 1778. Heathcote, in his letter of 1773 to the Duke confirmed that the coal obtained here was a poor quality, fit only for lime burning. The acquisition seems to suggest that the Goyts Moss area was being worked by two companies – the Brock and Dickenson concerns with James Brock being confined until then to land held by the Duke.

Having been associated with the Axe Edge mines since at least 1685, the 1767 lease was to be the last for the Brock family. It is not clear whether a renewal in 1788 was declined or whether the family withdrew. It needs to be seen however in the context of the drive for income growth being undertaken by John Heaton and Brock's interests in the lime works at Peak Forest. However it has to be said that this drive for growth was stimulated in 1790, when Ecton Copper Mine failed, which was after the lease ended.

However, in that year, 1790, Heaton reported that the lime works and collieries were in hand and were then receiving considerable improvement. In a separate note, Heaton went on to record that Goyts Moss Colliery was also in hand, and the produce of it (profit) for two or three years would go *'towards perfecting the improvements of the other collieries and lime works near Buxton'*. (70)

The improvements ongoing in 1790 fortunately gave work to some of the redundant miners from Ecton, employed in sinking a new shaft – The New Rise Shaft – at Goyts Moss Colliery. The domestic arrangements relating to the men's accommodation etc. is unknown.

Given the paternalistic nature of the 5th Duke, whether this shaft was vital or simply useful is also not known. Four shafts were sunk in 1790, the New Rise Shaft the deepest, reaching a depth of 32 fathoms (192 feet). The mine records have a satisfying reference of *'liquor given to the Ecton Miners and mason 14s.'* (71) Fourteen shillings would have bought about 84 pints of beer. An extension of workings at Goyts Moss Colliery was clearly what Heaton referred to.

The results of the capital expenditure on Axe Edge are unclear as they have not yet been located. Certainly by 1790, the collieries were under the managerial control of Thomas Wild. He may have been related to George Wild, described as being of Goyts Moss, prior to moving to Ecton Lea, to a house built for him as an Ecton manager, a short while before his death in 1791. The mines continued to be run by the estate until 1824, when they were taken on lease by Thomas Boothman at £800 per annum. If John Heaton was looking for a similar return on Axe Edge as at Kingsley, he need not have worried. Although accounts are missing until 1807 (relating to the year before i.e. 1806), thereafter until 1817 (except for 1811, which are also missing) the average profit was £934 per annum.

Boothman was known to the estate for it bought coal from him at Digler Colliery in 1810 for the Duke's kilns at Peak Forest. At that time Philip Heacock felt the need to advise him that the quality of his coal needed to be improved. Boothman was mixing fresh coal with older coal which had deteriorated from lying on the bank for a considerable time. (72)

Much of the coal was used for lime burning. The accounts show that a lot of it was sold to farmers from Cheshire and Derbyshire. It seems that they had to buy their own coal for the lime they were intent on purchasing. In 1815, 49,208 loads of lime were given by Peak Forest lime works (owned by the Brock family) in exchange for coal valued at £1,538. The coal was valued at 7½d. per load which conveniently equates with the number of loads swapped. Consequently, the trade off meant 1 load of coal being given for 1 load of lime. (73)

Heaton's determination to work the mines in hand saw a steady output amounting to 153,450 tons in the seven years 1806–12. With a profit of just under £1,000 per annum on average, it would appear that this sort of level continued until 1824 when Boardman was prepared to take the mines at £800 per annum. However Black Clough Colliery was apparently abandoned in 1809. Output in 1806-09 (four years) was only 3,532 tons, yielding a total profit of only £122 in the four years. The sale price per ton was slightly above that received for coal from Thatch Marsh and Goyts Moss combined, so perhaps the seam (s) being worked were worked out. Incidentally, in 1806–12 the two main mines between them purchased 5.6 tons of candles over that period. (74) Black Clough is known to have been worked later than 1809, so it is likely that it was let out.

With the coals from Goyts Moss clearly of a poor quality – but ideal for lime burning – and those of Thatch Marsh Colliery not much better (75), it is hardly surprising that another use would have been for lead ore reduction. Ore hearths were widely spread across the Peak, but in the third decade of the 18th century were supplanted by a smaller number of cupola furnaces. In these, the hearth had a low arched roof which reflected the heat to give higher operating temperatures. Many were in the east of the Peak, but there were cupolas at Hope, Bradwell, Hucklow, Bonsall and at Ecton Mine, the only one near to Hartington. However, details of proceedings of the Hartington Barmote Court refer to smelters and ore burners as early as 1730. (76) On the rear of a document recording the Court proceedings for 1730, is a reference to *'8/8/1730 Due to James Warrington for forty four l'ds [loads] of coulks to the smelting men 2s. 0d.'* and in 1734 is a reference to a fine levied on ore burners who did not appear at the Court when charged to do so. It is possible that these men would be using Axe Edge

A impressive limekiln close to Bostern Grange, just south of Hartington parish. It must be one of the finest farm limekilns in the Peak. Over 100 limekilns were built on Hartington parish farmland

The limekiln north of Earl Sterndale

coal, especially with the early existence of the Hartington coal road. (77) The list of burners attached to the Barmote Court Suit Rolls also occur throughout the Derbyshire orefield and do not mean that the smelting sites operated by these men were located within the Hartington liberty [or mining area]. The loads of *'coulks'* delivered in 1730 were probably destined for an unknown slag hearth, where lead slags were reworked to extract more lead from them.

Timber and Timber Products

In a drive to improve revenue, tree planting was embraced with enthusiasm. In part, this may have been because of the demand for timber by the Duke's copper mine at Ecton. It was a prodigious user of timber. Whole woods were robbed at Castern in the Manifold Valley, where £400 was paid to Nicholas Hurt. A wood close to Biggin Grange is another example. Timber was being bought off the Shawe Estate north of Cheadle in Staffordshire and from Barleyford Wood north of Rushton (on the Leek–Macclesfield road). Getting the timber from the latter took three days and nights to deliver to the mine.

An early reference to the timber planting programme is in 1782–83 *'the expense of the Nursery and Plantation at Buxton £157. 8s. 11d'*. Langham is mistaken in thinking that the plantations were for aesthetic reasons but that was a pleasant and secondary benefit for visitors. Not just visitors to Buxton either, for timber was planted on various estates. For instance, much timber was being grown on the Chatsworth estate. In 1809, 7,625 trees were planted on Eyam Common adjoining Fallcliffe Wood and 13,000 more at Birch Hills adjoining the Hassop Brook. (78)

Over at Buxton, The Crescent was not opened for business until the middle of the 1780s and it is shown above that the planting programme was well underway by then. Langham has shown that in the two decades 1820–40, an average expenditure of c. £500 on plantations was being made. (79)

As early as 1805 significant timber sales were to be seen. The mill at Hartington bought nearly 600 ft/200m. of oak which brought in £59. Nearly 1,000 ft/330m. of oak was despatched (both shipments from Chatsworth sawmill) to Cronkston Farm. (£92), Much smaller consignments went to Thatch Marsh Colliery, Axe Edge; Newhaven House Inn and Pilsbury.

In Buxton, the Nithen End public house was purchased along with its land at Curbar, which was planted with timber – presumably Curbar Wood originated in this way. Much land on the Chatsworth estate was turned over to woodland, including Yarncliffe [Wood]. Soon, timber supplies were being made to many of the larger Devonshire farms in Hartington, as houses and farm buildings were refurbished or extended. Thatch Marsh Colliery was a regular purchaser. The irony was that the main ore-body at Ecton Mine failed in 1790 before significant sales got underway.

In 1809, the Chatsworth woods alone yielded £2,000 gross with £250 coming from both the new Bulls Head Inn at Newhaven and buildings at Buxton. This consisted of oak, fir and chestnut. Other timber sold included ash and a very small quantity of elm. The sales were augmented in 1809 by *'sales for His Grace's use'* (i.e. on the Devonshire estate). This accounted for another £1,911 being put through the books.

In addition firewood and faggots (branches) were cut and charcoal created. In 1808, 100 quarters of the latter were made along with a hearth (at 10s. 0d.) at a cost of £6. 6s. 8d. If there were four quarters to 1cwt., then this represents $1^1/_4$ tons of charcoal. It was available for sale but none of this is recorded in John Heaton's revenue projections. Bark would also have been sold on for tanning. The baffling complexity of measurement is seen with a reference to the selling of bark at Curbar Wood, Buxton in the year to Lady Day 1803. The estate received from Mr. Holmes £20. 4s. 0d. for 2 loads, 8 roods and 6 yards of it. A load is a measurement by volume and a rood and yard a measurement by area and length respectively! Charcoal was also being made for use (at least) in the kitchens at Chatsworth. (80)

Also in 1809 a further 5,000 trees were planted at Buxton to create mixed woodland, including 1,000 'broadleaved elms'. Philip Heacock, the Collector for the Buxton and Hartington estate, was also seeking advice about a further plantation on the Peak Forest Estate. A couple of years later, Heacock ordered 10,000 trees from Chatsworth's nursery for 'use in this place' i.e. Buxton and 40,000 in 1812. (81) In that year he expressed the desire to plant 100,000 seedlings at Newhaven in the Spring. However there appear to have been plantations of timber existing there already. A visitor wrote in 1812: 'Many extensive and thriving plantations which have been made near the inn will occasion a change in the appearance of this tract'. The Newhaven House Inn is described as being 'a large handsome and commodious inn, where travellers may meet with excellent accommodation'. (82)

Pilsbury Grange

Pilsbury Grange farms sit adjacent the road from Hartington running up the valley bottom. In fact at Pilsbury it continues unmetalled, the road going to Crowdecote on an old packhorse road coming over from Cheshire. Immediately to the north of the farms are the remains of Pilsbury Castle, which may have been the original settlement of Hartington village. The holding here was always let as two farms and two farmhouses exist today adjacent to each other. It was formerly abbey land, the holding belonging to Merevale Abbey as was Cronkston Grange and Needham Grange. A document of 1614 (83) relates to this farm and states that William Gould held it on lease and had done so far about nine years. One of the farms was on a rent of £85 per annum and the other (Bateman's Farm) at £100 per annum. Pilsbury Grange was formerly called by the name of Rogersley Farms (see below, Rogers being a tenant).

At the end of this lease, the Grange was let (c. 1626-27) to Nicholas Hurt of Castern Hall at a rental of £225 per annum and by Richard Bateman at £240 per annum. Both rents were paid 'by bonde' either to London or Chatsworth. Could this be the rent for one year, for the rent in 1629-30 was £120 per annum (£60 for each holding)? This rent was unchanged in 1665. The rents were paid to the estate of the Dowager Countess. Richard Bateman had been succeeded by Hugh Bateman. He was the tenant of Pilsbury Grange in 1663–64. The other farm here was then occupied by Thomas Rogers. The latter was succeeded by John Rogers who was the tenant until 1684. On 29th March of that year, the tenancy passed to William Goode. (84)

His tenancy details survive. He took it for one year at £93 rent. The agreement included a covenant providing an increase in the rent at the rate of £5 per acre for any land ploughed in excess of the acreage ploughed by John Rogers. All dung produced had to be applied back onto the land and the buildings had to be kept in good repair. This indicates that part of the tenancy here was given over to arable land, although the acreage is not known. In 1696,

William Goode was still in occupation *'yet out of lease'* and paying a rent of £185. Either he had extended a lot of arable land or seen a rent rise per acre. Perhaps both was the answer.

Although it is clear that Pilsbury Grange was held in two occupations, were there two dwellings from an early date? In 1742, a new house was built for Richard Gould at a cost of £100, but the accounts do not make it clear if this was a replacement. In 1788, Richard Gould (having taken the occupation at Pilsbury Grange of William Gould) persuaded the estate to pay an advance for a meagre dwelling there at a cost of £5. We therefore appear to have the construction date of the two houses there. It is probable that this Richard is different from the other earlier house builder with the same name. The matter is even more complicated for the other half of Pilsbury Grange was occupied by William Gould, the estate administrator for Hartington until his death in 1795. However his successor was his son, Joseph.

Prior to the time of the new house being built in 1742 (in 1737 to be precise), Joseph and William Gould paid £110 rent per annum each. Joseph Gould was also renting Crowdecote Mill in 1737 at £3 per annum. In the five years from 1737 to 1742, Richard Gould would appear to have taken over one of the occupations and the new house seems to have followed as a result of that. (85) A little later, in 1748–49, a further house was built, this time at Cronxton Grange, the cost being £40. Elsewhere, occasional capital expense by the estate continued: e.g. in 1765. *'paid cash to John Wheeldon being the charge of building a large barn on the farm at Dowall in Hartington Manor £125'*. John Heaton was to increase the level of capital expense a couple of decades later (see Chapter 4). Early in 1785, William Gould (The Collector of Rents) agreed to build a lime kiln at Pilsbury Farm *'on the common, near the upperground'*. Following the Inclosure, work started in 1799 on enclosing fields, but it was a year later that payments 'of fencing' were made for Pilsbury Farm and also Pilsbury Dale. In 1801, deliveries of slate were being made to *'Newhaven House Buildings'* and a note in the accounts states that some of the slates were used at Cotesfield and Pilsbury Farms. The same set of accounts records the construction of farm buildings at *'Coatsfield'*. (86)

A recent article on Pilsbury Castle, situated a little to the north of Pilsbury Grange, speculates on whether the timber-built castle was succeeded by a stone-built hall and whether this might have been at Pilsbury itself. In possible support of this, mention is made of a traditional story that the Manor Court was still held at Pilsbury, possibly until the 19th century. The latter is certainly not true. In 1685 the Manor Court was being held in Buxton and would probably have done so at least from 1663, when the Earl of Devonshire acquired the Manor. Although the venue is not stated, it was likely to have been at the Buxton House (or Hall) Inn (now The Old Hall Hotel). In 1710, the two Courts were being held at Hartington and this was still continuing in 1718 so this could offer an approximate date for the construction of the original inn at Newhaven. It is possible that the Court moved there, once built, although the Great Court Baron records do not record the venue prior to 1756 when it met at Newhaven House. (87)

The Buxton Court paid for two rooms – presumably for the freeholders' and the copyholders' courts. They would meet in an inn, as lunch was found for the Court officials and the jury (a minimum of 12 men in each Court plus the officials). It is unlikely that they would meet in an unlicensed building with no provision for food and beverage. The Court Baron must have met at the same time as the Court Leet as there are no recorded costs other than those which occur in the manor accounts. These, somewhat frustratingly, simply refer to *'court expense'* and sometimes how many meals were purchased.

In 1725, surviving records show that the Hartington Liberty Barmote Court also met at Newhaven with its jury of 24 men, who had their lunch provided. It seems a logical point to make that the Mining Court would meet at the same place as the Manor Court, a practice which certainly happened later in the 18th century.

Frith Pasture

The area south-west of Harpur Hill is now known as The Frith and is partly covered by an industrial estate. It was previously Frith Pasture and at the beginning of the 17th century, it was The Earl's Frith.

It was generally pretty poor in terms of quality and use as pasture. It comes as a little surprising therefore to find that one of the earliest records relating to it concerns a dispute. Ralph Heathcot, of Middlecliff (which sits above the junction of Hartington, Long and Hand Dales, east of Hartington village) wrote to the Earl on August 25th, 1679, complaining that a Thomas Needham of Ferneybotham (sic) put cattle onto the Frith between Michaelmas and Lady Day and two beasts on it each summer as well as digging 30 loads of soil annually (presumably peat for fuel). Henry Lomas *'of Haslinghouses'* being a tenant of the Eyres of Hassop seems to have been acting similarly. Ferneybottom is south west of Longnor, south of Frith Pasture. (88)

A hundred years later, a record details what The Frith consisted of. In 1783, William Gould recorded in his diary that Frith Pasture contained some 400 acres of very poor land. He reckoned that it had about 170 acres of *'white dry land, 130 acres of ling* (heather) *inclining to peat moss, neither wet or dry; and 100 acres very wet and strong peat moss'*. He described it as being *'exceedingly cold and high and is of but little value, and when improved will answer very little other purpose than a sheep farm to some better land'*. In fact in 1783, the Frith was let to a summer tenant and had 223 sheep on it. He also recorded that the neighbouring rents for summer pasture, where the land had been limed, was 17s. 0d. for a twinter; 13s. 0d. a stirk, £1. 15s. a year old horse and £2. 5s. 0d. for a 2 year old. (89)

In August 1783, William Gould was back at Frith Pasture and recorded that the cattle there looked well upon it but *'the land being so very poor they grow but little'*. There appears to have been some dissatisfaction on the part of John Heaton about the conduct of the liming being undertaken by Mr. Longden and he asked if William Gould's son, Joseph, would take the tenancy of the Frith Farm so that a watch could be maintained on the liming. Although this was in January 1783, the practical aspect was that most of the lime burners had been hired for the summer by April and the job was left over until the following year. This would seem to suggest that the ex-Dickenson kilns at Grin had not been expanded to cope with extra demand. In fact the estate seemed to be content to build lime kilns as and where needed. In the event, the liming of Frith Pasture did not take place until the summer of 1787. William Gould recorded that 'there is only one kiln, which draws about 100 horse loads every day and they appear to lay on early 300 loads of lime on every acre'. Opportunity was taken to drain some of the boggy ground too. (90)

An account survives for Frith Pasture for 1787-88. This confirms that the management was under the control of William and Joseph Gould. Grazing had been let to 22 farmers and the stock taken onto the Frith consisted of 2 horses, 28 twinters, 19 stirks, 98 ewes and 50 lambs. The chief expense was the keeper's wage £4. 10s. 0d. and taxation – poor assessments,

5. LIVING OFF THE LAND

Headborough's Levy, land tax and access via turnpikes and private roads. The profit was just short of £30 – not much for 400 acres. It isn't clear what benefit the Goulds received – certainly nothing financial was carried in the account. Maybe they had the benefit of free grazing. (91)

Excessive Weather

The effect of excessive swings in the weather – wet in winter and drought in summer – seems to have been more frequent in the late 18th century. Some effects of winter severity are recalled under the section herein on 'The Poor'. However, there were also effects on the farms. William Gould's diary reveals some of these. In May 1783, he wrote that the *'country is much in want of rain … they have a poor prospect of good crops'*. A few weeks later, he was being proved right for *'the crops of corn [are] short, poor and late throughout the neighbourhood upon the stubble land, but better upon the leys'*. Matters were somewhat better on pasture land, which were *'good and full of grass, the meadowland light'*. Matters were alleviated to some extent in late September at the stock sales. Ewes fetched 14s.0d. per head *'which is a great price, lean from the common'*. Mutton was selling *'remarkably well'* and is *'very scarce'*. If mutton was scarce in September 1783, lambs were also scarce too. Gould rode to Longnor Fair in the August of that year. The Fair usually produced a number of lambs to be sold, but there were very few that year and those that were fetched high prices. A couple of years later in 1785, the *'hay crop [was] light, scarce a ton off an acre'*, following a very dry season. The corn crop was no better at the September harvest, Gould describing the Pilsbury yield as *'very unkind'*.

In 1799, there was significant flooding with riverbanks washed away at Chatsworth and sand left in the park there. It must have been significant for it took 81 days to clear it away. There was another big flood at Chatsworth in 1806, when just short of £20 was paid in June for clearing away rubbish left in the Park by the water, a substantial sum of money. Other major floods occurred in 1756 when the footbridge at Birchinlee Ford near Derwent was lost and in 1809. There are likely to have been others which went unrecorded in the Devonshire Records. In January 1757, snow fell for almost the whole of a week. Glover records details of floods in Derby, especially in 1736, 1740, 1770, 1795 and in 1842, when some streets were under 6ft/2m of water. In 1673, a flood was so great that part of St Werburgh's church was washed away and the steeple fell. (92) These storms must also have impacted on the Dove Valley too.

Sheep Washing

The washing or dipping of sheep involved the immersion in water to drown any ticks etc. in the fleece or on the skin. A photograph survives showing this being carried out at the site of the Dovedale stepping stones, in the River Dove. (93)

Sheep washes survive at Hayfield, Ashford-in-the-Water and Bakewell for instance, although nothing survives of the Dovedale site. Pilsbury Farm washed its sheep in June and this probably also took place in the River Dove, possibly where the old drovers' road forded the river near to the farm. The sheep wash also included the sheep of Richard Gould of the adjacent additional Pilsbury Farm let from the estate. The sheep were described as being *'tolerable well wooled and in good condition'*. Presumably in better condition from their immersion than several people who were thrown into the river *'according to custom'*! (94)

References and Notes

1 Dev. Coll., Map No 20621

2 Dev. Coll., AS/426. An oxgang was 20 acres

3 Dev. Coll., AS/401

4 For more information on the shoeing of cattle – in this case prior to driving them to English markets – see Moore-Colyer, R., *Welsh Cattle Drovers*, 2002, pp 83–87

5 Dev. Coll., AS/1062

6 Dev. Coll., Chatsworth Account Book, 1798, p. 28

7 Dev. Coll., AS/937, 13th Nov. 1719

8 Porter, L., *Ecton Copper Mines under the Dukes of Devonshire*, 2004, p 26

9 Dev. Coll., Records of the Small Court Baron, 1st July 1746, Brooke Taylor, Box 7–8, Book 8

10 Walton, I., & Cotton, C., *The Compleat Angler*, 5th edit., reprinted 1971 by Scholar Press, Pt. 2, Ch. 1, p11

11 Farey, J., *General View of the Agriculture of Derbyshire*, Vol. 1, 1811, p 96

12 Dev. Coll., AS/11353, copy letters from Godfrey Heathcote, p. 402, 28/1/1773. The location is given in a subsequent letter on p. 403

13 Dev. Coll., AS/1008. It was established by Anthony Buxton and others with a £100 bond (loan?) from the Duke of Devonshire

14 Glover, S., *Directory of Derbyshire*, 1829, p 72

15 Dev. Coll., Chatsworth Account, 1798, p 25

16 Dev. Coll., Wetton Accounts, T-series, Box Nos. 1–7, Records for 1787-88

17 The four year rotation system incorporating turnips had been used in Norfolk since the late 17th century, Plumb, J.H., *Econ. Hist. Review*, 2nd Series, Vol. 1, pp 86-89, but the date of its introduction to Derbyshire is not known

18 Dev. Coll., AS/402

19 Dev. Coll., AS/1062

20 The Barnsley cows cost £46. 11s – just under £3 each. Charges for this purchase – presumably driving them to Glutton – cost 14s. 0d. The second purchase was of 11 cows for £26. 15s. 0d. and 2 oxen for £10. 10s. 0d. at Penistone – referred to as Phene in the accounts – many of the market town names being abbreviated

21 This building is of course much later, dating from c. 1830, but the former inn is a relevant reminder of the drovers of earlier times,

22 Dev. Coll., Hardwick Papers, 450

23 Plot, R., *Natural History of Staffordshire*, 1686; his book was published 6 years later

24 Dev. Coll., Hardwick Papers, 450

25 Yates, M.E., *N. Staffs. Journal of Field Studies*, Vol. 15, 1975

26 Weston, R., *Hartington, A Landscape History etc.'*, 2000, p 40

27 It was part of the estate of Countess Christian, Dowager Duchess of Devonshire, Dev. Coll., AS/1009. However the documents accounting for rental income exist from 1664 amounting to £1,228, plus a fee farm rent of £98 (probably a ground rent or similar rent charge. Dev. Coll., AS/182, *'Rental Income from the lately purchased manor of Hartington'*. The gross amount of rental income was the same in 1683. Dev. Coll., AS/95

This would appear to be a half-yearly figure, for in 1697-8 *'due at Mich'mas 1697 and Lady Day 1698'* was the sum of £1,319. This excluded an additional £176. 10s. 0d. for desmesne tithes of the High Peak and for Buxton Hall (£60) which was included in the Hartington Manor figures. The sum of £1,319 was for the farm rents. It did not include cottage and copyhold income, but did include Hartington Mill at £10. 10s. 0d., Otterhole Mill (west of Buxton) at £10 and Mr. Wm. Brock *'for ye lime kilns and colemines'* £12 plus £15 for two other coal mines. No figure was included for Crowdecote Mill (unlet) and for lot and cope income for lead ore. (Lot and Cope were payments made by lead miners. Lot was a duty payable to the Lord of the Field or Lord of the Soil (mine owner) for the miner's privilege of free access to the mine and to wood and water. Cope was duty paid to the owners or lessees of mineral duties for the selling of lead ore to a buyer of choice rather than the King. (Rieuwerts, J.H., *Glossary of Derbyshire Lead Mining Terms*, 1998, pp 48, 102). Thus it was with a rental income at this level, or thereabouts, that the Hartington Manor gross rental income went into the 18th century

28 Phillips, A.D.M., 'A Note on Farm Size and Efficiency on the North Staffordshire Estate of the Leveson-Gowers, 1714–1809. *North Staffordshire Journal of Field Studies,* Vol.10, 1979, pp 330–338; Mingay, G.E. 'The Size of Farms in the Eighteenth Century' *Econ. Hist. Review*, Vol.14, 1962, pp 469-88; Wordie, J.R., 'Social Change on the Leveson-Gower Estates', 1714–1832, *Econ. Hist. Review*, Vol. 27, 1974, pp 593-609

29 Plot, R., ibid, pp 341 & 343

30 Plot, R., ibid, pp 357 & 382

31 Young, A., *The Farmer's tour through the East of England*, 1771, p 214-15

32 Farey, J., ibid. p 201

33 Dev. Coll., AS/1005

34 Porter, L., *Ecton Copper Mines under the Dukes of Devonshire, 1760-1790,* 2004, p 189; Dev. Coll., AS/1054

35 Plot, R., ibid, pp 353-355

36 Dev. Coll., Chatsworth Estate Account, p 81

37 Spray, M., *Agricultural History Review*, 1981, Vol. XXIX, 'Holly as Fodder in England', pp 97–110

38 Dev. Coll., T-series, Box 1–7, Buxton Accounts

39 e.g. see Geraint, J., *Life and Tradition in Rural*

Wales, p 50

40 Winchester, A.L., *The Harvest of the Hills*, p 138

41 Farey, J., Vol. 2, ibid, p 356

42 Dev. Coll., Chatsworth Estate Accounts 1757-58, AS/1062

43 Young, A., The Farmer's Tour Through the East of England, 1771, pp 196–98

44 Dev. Coll., AS/1394, letter dated 16/8/1773

45 Pilkington, ibid., Vol. 2, p 301

46 Dev. Coll., AS/1062

47 Dev. Coll., AS/1353

48 Dev. Coll., L/60/20

49 Leach, J.T., Derbyshire Arch. Jnl., 1996, Vol. 116, *Grin Hill, Buxton, a Major Limestone Quarry*, pp 101-136

50 Dev. Coll., L/76/20

51 Dev. Coll., L/60/20

52 Dev. Coll., L/76/20). 13,000 loads equates to 900 tons approximately

Farey refered to this lease a decade later, (Farey, J., *The Agriculture of Derbyshire*, 1811, Vol. 2, pp. 436-37) stating that the work was under the direction of the Duke's agents, Mr. Robert Longsdon and Mr. George Brassington. Farey states that in 1783, the lime was spread on 28 acres of land at Hind Low, Sticker Hill and others near to Hill Head Farm. The cost was £350 to the Duke including spreading which indicates that the original lease had been amended. The results, although slow in coming, were apparently striking with the heath being exterminated by the lime and replaced by *'a sweet and good herbage'*.

On the basis described by Farey (i.e. 28 acres was covered by 900 tons [13,000 horse loads] of lime), the 1,862 tons of lime sent to Blakelow Pasture – now known at Bleaklow – would have been used on 58 acres if the same dressing rate was applied. (Farey states 14,000 horse loads, but the lease records 13,000 loads. At 6d. per load, the cost of £350 equates to 14,000 loads. If Farey's date of 1783 is correct, the 13,000 loads under the 1780 agreement, was still being laid down in 1783. Farey's *'sweet and good herbage'* was changing the landscape to the south of Buxton.The purchase of the Dickenson's lime works was definitely linked to a programme of liming, for on 13th December 1777 (i.e. prior to the purchase of the colliery and lime works), it had been agreed that the Wheeldon's farms would be limed. These were Cronxton, Clement Seat, Coatfield, Dowal and High Edge farms. (His rents from Lady Day 1778 were to be:

Cronxton	£ 84
Clement Seat	£ 28
Coatfield	£ 58
Dowal	£ 150
High Edge	£ 30
	£350

Wheeldon had also agreed to lime three of the farms within three years with the following quantities of lime:

Cronxton	9,000 loads	(578.7 tons)
Clement Seat	6,000 loads	(385.8 tons)
Coatfield	12,000 loads	(771.6 tons)

If the lime was laid by the estate, an additional rent of 50 guineas (£52. 10s. 0d.) would be payable. Wheeldon agreed to lay it himself. The cost (6d. a load) was £675, or £32 for each year of a 21-year lease. This was clearly cheaper than an extra £52 a year if the Duke bore the cost. Farey states that the common form of weight of lime in Derbyshire was the load and this weighed three bushels (Farey, J., ibid, Vol. III, 1817, pp 473–74). A bushel equates to 40lb and Leach uses this weight in his article on Grin Quarry. Consequently, a horse load was 144lb and 100 loads weighted 6.43 tons (Leach, J., ibid., p.107). John Wheeldon had therefore agreed to spread 1,736 tons of lime. If this was moved by cart, nearly 3,500 journeys would have been involved (outwards and then back to the farm). If packhorses were used, 54,000 journeys would have been made. It is noted that different documents refer to both John and Richard Wheeldon at this time for the same tenancy.

53 Wm. Gould's diary, 6/4/1783 and 5/5/1783

54 Dev. Coll., AS/1406 and T-Series, Bundle 3, 1798

55 The figures for limestone and slack in the 1787–91 period indicate an average burning rate of 1 load of slack to produce 2.58 loads of lime. The quantity of limestone required is not stated. [However, Williams (*Williams, R., Limekilns and Lime Burning*) states that 100 units of limestone yields 56 units of quicklime. Assuming 90% purity, the ratio of 2 : 1 is usually adopted. This has been used in Appendix 3}. The limekilns appear to have been built, or repaired, annually. Three kilns were built in 1789 on Frith Pasture and two kilns were built at High Edge. At a burning rate of 2.58 loads of lime to 1 load of slack, 111,971 loads of slack were used. (Dev. Coll., AS/1300).

Appendix 3 summarises the known use of limestone, coal (or slack) and lime production used on the heath land in Hartington Manor south of Buxton, together with the poorer soils in use for pasture. It is likely that the materials were moved by a one-ton cart, despite lime still being measured by the horse load. The figures for lime (300,081 loads/19,204 tons) indicate that on a 2:1 ratio, 38,400 tons of limestone was used. (Probably from Grin Quarry), Peak Forest Canal Proprietors started quarrying in 1819, taking stone by tramway to Bugsworth (now Buxworth) Wharf. Between 1819–24, 317,223 tons of limestone and 17,004 tons of roadstones was obtained, with a royalty of £2,718 paid to the Duke. This would have surprised John Heaton had he still been alive. In 1809 he would not agree to sell limestone from the Peak Forest estate until the canal proprietors agreed to a clause in their proposed Canal Act. Lord George was the 5th Duke's brother and Beard Hall is south-east of New Mills, north of Buxton. Development work at this mine started in 1817. Negotiations with the Peak Forest Canal company regarding limestone seem to have resulted in limestone extraction at Peak Dale not starting until a similar date. It does seem that the estate was prepared to wait go get what it wanted; matters being wrapped up, maybe coincidentally, at about the time John Heaton retired in 1818. (Dev. Coll., AS/1509, P. Heathcock's Letterbook for 1809, 15/4/09 and Heathcote, C., *Mining History*, Bull, P.D. M.H.S. 'The Formation and Early History of Beard Colliery etc'. 2008, Vol. 17, No. 2, pp 47-55).

The rent for Goits Moss Colliery was struck in an amount of lime to be delivered and spread on designated fields. The quantity was 13,000 loads in a year. It is known that this quantity was laid in 1780 and this volume was laid across Hindlow, Sticker Hill and Hill Head in 1783. It is reasonable to assume that this volume was laid in 1781–82)

56 Wm. Gould's diary, 29/12/1783

57 Dev. Coll., Hartington Accounts 1795, T-Series, Bundle 3

58 Roberts, A. E, and Leach, J. R., *The Coal Mines of Buxton*, 1985, p 29–21

59 National Archives, MPC 274 (1)

60 Dev. Coll., AS/1395, dated 15/8/1774

61 Dev. Coll., AS/1225

62 Dev. Coll., AS/199

63 Dev. Coll., Brooke Taylor Docs., Nos. 7-8

64 Dev. Coll., AS/1394

65 Dev. Coll., AS/1053

66 Dev. Coll., AS/1395, 15/8/1774, letter from James Brock to the Duke

67 Dev. Coll., T-Series, Bundle 1–7, 1807

68 Dev. Coll., AS/1511, Heacock's Letter book, 26/10/1813; Roberts & Leach, ibid, p 57

69 Porter, L., ibid, 2004 pp. 86-91; also p 198 re Hazles Cross

70 Dev. Coll., AS L/60/20 pp 3 & 5; AS/1053

71 Roberts & Leach, ibid., p 39

72 Dev. Coll., P. Heacock's letters, AS/1519, 26/9/1810

73 Dev. Coll., T-Series Box 1–7

74 For a recent appraisal of coal mining and limestone burning in the Axe Edge and adjacent areas, see Wood, E., *The South-West Peak : History of the Landscape'*, 2001, pp 110-137

75 Farey describes the latter as being 'brassy' i.e. including lumps of iron pyrites – Farey, J., *The Agriculture of Derbyshire*, 1811, Vol. 1, p 212

76 Dev. Coll., AS/619

77 For more on this see Willies, L., Bull Peak District Mines Hist., Soc., Vol 4, No 1, 1969, relating to cupola sites in Derbyshire. I am grateful to Dr JH Rieuwerts for his assistance at this point.

78 Dev. Coll., Chatsworth Account Book, 1809, p 7

79 Langham, ibid., p 227

80 Dev. Coll., T-Series, Bundle 1–7 (re Curbar Wood bark); Chatsworth Account Book, 1808, p 72 (re charcoal)

81 Dev. Coll., AS/1509, ibid, 26/2/1809, and AS/1510, 27/3/1811, 5/1/1812

82 Davies, D.P., '*A New History & Descriptive View of Derbyshire*, 1811, Vol. vii, p 499

83 Dev. Coll., AS/600

84 Dev. Coll., AS/162; 189; 1010

85 Dev. Coll., AS/1227/1

86 Wm. Gould's diary 1783–88. 13/3/1785; Dev. Coll., T-Series, Bundle 3

87 Landon, N., et all., *Derbyshire Archaeological Journal*, 2006, Vol. 126, 'Pilsbury : A Forgotten Castle' pp 82–102; Dev. Coll., AS/437

88 Dev. Coll., AS/40

89 William Gould's diary, ibid, 1783–88 (a twinter was probably a cow having wintered for two years, a stirk a younger cow); Dev. Coll., AS/421 for 1713 reference

90 Wm. Gould's diary, ibid, 13/6/1787

The horse loads of lime spread is to be found in the Hartington accounts (Dev. Coll., AS/1300) and amounts to 150 acres at a spreading rate of 500 loads per acre for the area, noted by Farey (see under Making the Countryside Greener). A total of 125,000 loads were laid and if Gould was correct that an initial 300 loads per acre was laid, then the spreading rate in subsequent years was less, at perhaps 100 loads per acre in years 2 and 3. However, a substantially larger quantity of lime was laid in years 2 and 3 (see Appendix 3 for details) and it is not clear what Farey had in mind

91 Dev. Coll. AS/1433

92 Glover, S., *The History and Directory of the Borough of Derby*, 1843, pp 84–85

93 Porter, L., *Bygone Days in Dovedale and the Manifold Valley*, 1997, p 9

94 Wm. Gould's diary, ibid, 14/6/1785

6. THE DUKE'S MINE : ECTON

Situated just over the manor boundary (the River Dove) is the rounded form of Ecton Hill. It is of limestone, harder than the softer shales of the valley upstream. The hill rises over 300 ft/100m. above the adjacent River Manifold. This river has occupied a wide and shallow valley, which changes to a deep and incised form on reaching the limestone. Deep within this hill was a large deposit of copper ore. Workings in more recent times pre-date the Civil War and a prehistoric antler pick recovered from an ancient working a few years ago makes Ecton one of the oldest mines in the country. However it was c. 1752 before it was realised that the form of the near vertical deposit being worked was widening. At this time, the mine was being worked by speculators under a 21years lease from the Duke signed in 1739.

Ore production had risen to five to six hundred tons annually until 1759 when the extraction rate was increased in a mad dash to remove as much as possible before the lease expired. Hopes of lease renewal were premature for the Duke decided to work the mine for himself. From 1760 to 1790 when the main deposit failed, production increased and up to 2,500 tons per annum was raised throughout the 1780s having slowly risen prior to that date. Notably, the mine was profitable from the Duke's commencement, earning a total of £294,000 between 1760 and the end of 1791. It was a huge tax-free sum.

For purists of accountancy, it was actually more than this as the costs of development at the mine, the building of the smelter in 1770 and its extension in 1780 etc. were all capital costs included in the mine accounts. Here at Ecton in the 1780s was the deepest mine in the country, with probably the first shaft to exceed 1,000 ft./300m. in depth. Once Boulton & Watt had mastered rotative motion driven by a steam engine, the first of their new generation of steam engines for hauling erected in the Midlands came to Ecton, only the fourth to be erected anywhere.

The tonnages were small compared to the vast open working at Parys Mine on Anglesey. However there, the profits were swallowed up by huge bank borrowings, which totalled £500,000. At Ecton, no borrowings, not even from within the Cavendish monies, let alone a bank, was necessary. Although tonnages were comparatively small, what was being brought up was far richer than at Anglesey, reaching a recovery rate from copper ore of over 20% to smelt to metal (i.e. 10 tons of ore produced 2 tons of metal). Today, a rate well under 5% may be considered economic. In the 1780s, the mine was producing a profit of £25,000 per annum; a huge sum even for the deep pockets of the 5th Duke.

The impact the mine had on the local community was clearly great, both from the management point of view and the movement of materials and employees. One readily thinks of men toiling in the mine, women breaking the ore down and 'washing' it to separate the ore from rock and spar. Clearly, there was a larger picture: men cutting timber many miles away and hauling it up valley sides; candle makers making over 10,000 a year to keep the mine going (no candles, no ore); carriers moving ore and coal in a continual stream by pack mule and cart with others producing hundreds of tons of fodder to sustain the animals; brick makers; providers of sand, stone, iron implements, ropes, feed for the mine's underground horses, clay and nail makers making huge quantities to satisfy the mine's requirements and keeping yet more carters in employment, some working full time fetching and carrying the needs of the mine. More men took away copper metal from Whiston and lead metal from Ecton. In the 1780s, the copper metal was shipped down the River Trent from south of Derby to Gainsborough. Here

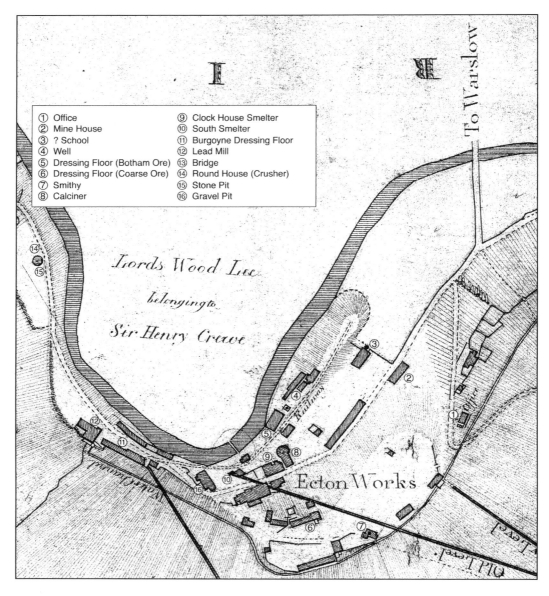

① Office
② Mine House
③ ? School
④ Well
⑤ Dressing Floor (Botham Ore)
⑥ Dressing Floor (Coarse Ore)
⑦ Smithy
⑧ Calciner
⑨ Clock House Smelter
⑩ South Smelter
⑪ Burgoyne Dressing Floor
⑫ Lead Mill
⑬ Bridge
⑭ Round House (Crusher)
⑮ Stone Pit
⑯ Gravel Pit

Lords Wood Lee

belonging to

Sir Henry Crewe

To Warslow

Ecton Works

Above: Potter's plan of Ecton Mine in 1809, Chatsworth, Devonshire Collection

Right: This is believed to show the Ectom packmules train used for taking ore to the Whiston Smelter. The engine house detail is a fanciful artist's creation. From *The Mine*, by Rev. Isaac Taylor

it was loaded onto a ship, *The Ecton*, and taken down the North Sea and up the River Thames to the centre of London to a warehouse where it was sold. This was later demolished to make way for the original Billingsgate Fish Market.

All this activity created a considerable organisation with a significant influence on the local economy and in the movement of materials. Not least was the copper ore bound for the Duke's smelter at Whiston, some 8 or 9 miles to the south of the mine on the edge of the Cheadle Coalfield. In the period 1760–89 nearly 42,000 tons of copper ore was raised. Whilst some of this (the poorer quality ore) was reduced by roasting at the mine, most of this quantity left the mine by horse/mule, with 10 animals to the ton. Of this 9,000 tons went to smelters at Denby near Derby, Cheadle, Macclesfield and possibly to Warrington. From 1780, the ore went to Whiston, with the mules returning daily, doubling up on the number of journeys. On top of this were at least the 2,000 tons of lead metal taken through Hartington to Derbyshire merchants.

Coal was brought as back carriage from Whiston (and also from the Duke's other colliery at Foxt Wood, just north of the smelter) to the Ecton calciner (where some poorer ores were reduced to drive off impurities, including sulphur). The mine smelter then roasted the same ore before it was taken to Whiston. From 1786, coal was also required for the newly built brick kiln at Newhaven. Fireclay was needed for the Ecton furnaces and was dug at Newhaven. When the furnaces needed to be replaced, the stone was brought from Revidge, north west of Warslow. The furnaces also needed bricks – in fact the mine seems to have been a prodigious consumer of them.

Initially both burnt bricks and unburnt bricks, i.e. red clay in the form of bricks to be fired in the Ecton furnaces, were sent to the mine plus white bricks made from silica sand at Newhaven. From 1782, Whiston also had its own brickworks. The furnaces also needed large quantities of sand, with stone at Revidge (west of the mine) being reduced to sand to provide it. Lime ash, the residue from turning limestone into lime, was used during the reduction process and this was sent as required. To aid the smelting of the lead ore, pigs of lead were purchased from the Shacklow lead mill of Barker & Wilkinson. It was situated at the bottom of Taddington Dale on the A6 north west of Bakewell.

At Whiston, large quantities of coal were needed (at the rate of 3 tons, possibly more, to one ton of ore). It came from Ross & Shaw Collieries (initially) and later Hazles Cross (also known as Kingsley) and Foxt Wood Collieries which were owned by the Duke. Fireclay for the eight Whiston furnaces came from Cauldon Lowe and Milkhill Gate Green, east of Cauldon Lowe village. The stone and sand came from nearby Whiston Common. Wood ash was purchased for the refineries while lime ash was used at Ecton as noted above. (1) Additionally there was the running and development of the Ecton Mine itself plus the two coal mines, and the opening of a coke works at Hazles Cross in 1788. The manager, Cornelius Flint, was clearly a resourceful man.

The mine itself consumed lots of timber. Initially it came from the slopes of the Manifold Valley, down river at Castern, and Biggin Grange Wood south east of Hartington. Later, timber was brought from Barleyford in the Dane Valley, north of Rushton on the Leek – Macclesfield road, and from the woods around Whiston and on the Shaw Estate of Mr. Beech, near Cheadle. Cut timber (called deales or dales), were also purchased in Stoke-on-Trent and taken to Etruria to be shipped down the Caldon Canal to Froghall, bound for the mine, probably via the turnpike road to Warslow. The purchases each month of timber has to have been significant, if only because of the huge quantities of nails, which were bought:

from August 1779 to December 1780, for instance, 185,500 nails of different sorts were purchased. An additional 27,200 were also purchased, but these may have been bound for the new buildings at Whiston.

Regular shipments of iron were sent from various forges to both Ecton and Whiston. The Alderwasley Forge of Francis Hurt (of Alderwasley Hall) sent bar iron, brewers' squares, ladles, ladle moulds, hoop iron (for strengthening barrels etc.) to both works. The materials for Whiston were sent to Ashbourne where they were collected. Other works were the Ashbourne foundry of Robert Longden; the Basset Foundry at Mayfield and George Critchlow's works at Pethills on the River Hamps, between Ford and Winkhill in the Staffordshire Moorlands. Mr. Bird (perhaps of Chesterfield) and the Chesterfield Foundry also sent supplies. Specialist castings were also ordered from other manufacturers, such as Smith & Knifton of Oakamoor and initially from Walkers Foundry at Rotherham.

Gunpowder chiefly came from Wilkinsons at Chesterfield in barrels and half barrels. These were returnable, with a deposit payable on each purchase. Candles were sold on to the miners at cost. Most came from Mr. George Cresswell, of Ashford, near Bakewell; others from Anthony Bradley of Ashbourne and Richard Roberts of Winster. In the seven weeks Reckoning of November 1780, 1,321 candles and 742 lbs of powder were delivered to the mine. More candles were used at Whiston. Annual deliveries were regularly of over 10,000 candles and $3^{1}/_{2}$ tons of gunpowder.

Sieves (sometimes called riddles), barrels, spades, hammers etc. were needed as replacements or for extended production. The sieves mainly came from Hathersage, although some 'sieve bottoms' came from Alderwasley Forge on occasions. Ropes were continually in demand, wear and tear clearly being a major factor, although the damp conditions must have taken a toll too. Fires were kept burning near the underground capstan to try and keep the ropes in the main haulage shaft as dry as possible. The ropes seem to have been purchased from several suppliers, but Calab Willock of Winster regularly provided many. At one point he requested more time to make them in the winter (if possible) so that he could ensure the best quality by making them only when it was dry. Later, wire ropes were to be used, brought from long distances. On occasions, even hemp ropes came from as far away as Manchester and Liverpool.

Provisions for the mine horses: hay, oats and bran, had to be brought in too, although the carriers to and from Whiston paid for the feed for their own animals except when fodder rose drastically in price. The mine carriers must have been substantial purchasers of fodder.

Additionally there were the office materials, including paper, which chiefly survives in the Chatsworth Muniment Room. It was used for most suppliers to create their invoices, some clearly being prepared for them, and for the accounts of labourers and smelters' wages etc. Oil for machinery ('train oyle') was regularly bought, together with soap. In the ten months from November 1779 to August 1780, the mine purchased 44lb of 'sope'. In the same ten month period, 42 quarts (10. 5 gallons) of oil, 2 pints of ink, a stone (14lb) of 'tarr' and 5 stones of pitch, were sent to the mine, plus many more items. Other 'domestic' items included pack thread for sewing the ore bags, materials for the mine house and even rum for hospitality. Today it is, rightly, not appreciated just how much was being carried by pack horse, pack mule or by cart and the occasional wagon. Only through the actual invoices has the detail come to light. It is incredible that so many (perhaps at least 4,000 to 1790) have survived.

Additional to the everyday activity described above were two other areas of activity. The lesser of the two were the exceptional purchases. The Christmas/New Year party of 1780 is an example. This saw local ale house brewers sending over 150 gallons of ale, and other suppliers sending over 100lbs. of beef and cheese and over 250 bread cobs to keep everyone happy. One hundred clay pipes for the smokers (most of the men, one supposes) were provided to round off the event. In contrast, a 'scale beam' of over three tons in weight must have taken a huge effort to transport to the mine in 1780, especially if the roads were as bad as Pilkington reported in 1789 (see Chapter 9). Other examples were the chains (nearly 2 tons) which were ordered to lower horses into the mine. Most carts at this period would carry a ton, perhaps exceptionally up to one and a half tons.

Another unusual order was for the construction of the Fishpond at Back Ecton to feed water to the blast furnace waterwheel. This order was for about a mile of gritstone blocks with a channel cut through one side to convey the water when laid end to end. These came from a quarry at Sheen, possibly the one where Belle Engineering Ltd. is situated. The largest item sent to the mine would have been the component parts of the steam engine provided by Boulton & Watt from their Soho Works in Birmingham and also from John Wilkinson of Bersham near Wrexham. It was a small affair compared to those of a century later, but for the time, they would have been unusual and cumbersome items to have to transport.

The second area of daily activity around the mine would, of course, be the workers, details of which are discussed below. From the management point of view, Cornelius Flint, the mine manager had to keep production on track, using his experience and that of his miners, to exploit ore reserves to the full and in a safe and expedient manner. He also had to arrange for all the external activities to run smoothly. It was a time when deliveries could take weeks, cash had to be fetched on horseback from Chesterfield in large quantities with the ever-present risk of robbery, either between Chesterfield and Ecton, or between Ecton and Whiston.

Even ordering simple items often meant sending the shopping list by hand. On 12th December 1786, William Salt was sent to Ashbourne to pick up some 'lether' together with the mail, which cost 2s. 0d. During the construction of the steam engine in 1788, plans from Messrs. Boulton & Watt were despatched to the Blackamoor's Head Inn in Ashbourne (now Wigleys Shoe Shop, St. John Street) which someone had to go and collect. This random activity went on all the time. All this, in a business which was one of the largest in the country running one of the deepest mines in the world, with little technology, in a simplistic but clearly efficient manner. It was a great achievement.

The unique nature of the mine deposit and its geology resulted in interest in the mine from the curious to the cognoscente. Some were no doubt industrial spies but they would have learnt little as the mine had no secret processes, indeed very little of technical interest of value to a competitor, from here or abroad.

However, the sheer size of the place created demands, which were certainly unusual. One of the earliest ropes for the mine's Boulton & Watt steam engine, supplied in 1789, came from Samuel Goodwin of Leek. He was a grocer whose shop was on the corner of The Market Place and Derby Street. He was also a rope supplier to the mine and needed to make a rope probably 1,350 ft/ 405 m. in length costing the mine £100. He supplied it in two lengths, the two weighing a total of 33cwt, over $1^1/_2$ tons, to be spliced together at the mine. It must have been one of the longest and largest ropes ever made (at least for industrial purposes) at the time. It had to be the longest Goodwin had ever made. It probably had a circumference of 7 inches/ 18 cm at the top and 5inches/ 12..7 cm at the bottom.

The mine operated a canal, called the Boat Level, at the 34 fathoms level. The mine carpenter, unlikely to have ever seen the sea, was called upon to make the boats. In the 1780s some of the timber needed to be of such a size that it was not readily available in this

The top of the Ecton pipe working, the main ore body of the mine, with the engine house (now altered) beyond

country and was imported from Eastern Europe *('Danzig Baulks')*. Danzig is now Gadansk. They are likely to have been taken to Gloucester or Runcorn and delivered to Froghall via the canal system.

Employees at the Mine

Out of the 300 employees working in the 1760s, 50 were women who beat the ore down to the size of a nutmeg or less, at tables, with children keeping the women busy and removing the beaten ore for bagging and sale. The rest would be the ore getters, others driving levels and other development work, labourers, water pumpers (called watermen); drawers of ore and stone up the shafts in barrels etc. (all of the underground men being called miners). Boys pushed wagons until replaced by horses but female labour underground of any kind was not practiced.

The miners' way down into the lower reaches of the mine, where the ore was being extracted, was by ladderways described as being in poor condition, with a constant danger of falling into an abyss below. In 1784 a new pumping engine was installed at river level in the mine's main shaft. It was necessary to maintain the pumping pipe and a ladderway was installed, the shaft being divided into two parts by a vertical wooden wall several hundred feet high. The miners would no doubt have used this ladderway to get to and from work as well.

The women and labourers worked a ten hour day. Prior to the regular employment found at the mine, the concept of working weekly for another person was unusual (it was practised on the farms and at the Grin Hill lime kilns at Buxton, although only there for 30 weeks a year each summer). However there was no regular practice of it on any scale in many rural areas. Although some textile mills had existed from the early 18th century, the concept of a widespread pool of labour used to working full time each week was still in the future in 1760. To have 300 employees working at the mine by the mid-1760s was something new in rural Derbyshire and indeed over a larger rural area.

Even working deep underground was a new concept. In 1773 the mine reached 1,000 ft deep. It was probably the first in the country to do so and there would not be many, if any, others that deep anywhere. Access at river level reduced the descent necessary by some 450 ft., but the daily descent of 500 ft/ 150m, or more each working day was no joke.

For the women, working in open-sided sheds, beating (it was known as bucking) the ore down was no joke either. There was the dust created, although much of the ore delivered to them would be damp or even wet from mine water, or rain from being stacked on the surface. Additionally, adjacent furnaces would have been producing significant sulphurous smoke and fumes. There is no evidence of assistance for women suffering from repetitive strain injuries. It seems likely that the condition was not appreciated at the time.

A six-hour shift for the men allowed some time for agricultural activity for those with a smallholding or animals on the common and perhaps several strips of land in the communal fields around their village. However all of the employees had to get to work which meant a daily walk unless an enterprising carter ran the equivalent of a bus, which seems unlikely. It would be relatively easy for Hartington employees to walk down the turnpike road (they were not charged any toll) but those from Wetton, Alstonfield and Butterton faced a walk (longer for most) across fields in all weathers. The women would have their children with them, although few girls appear to have taken up permanent weekly work. Having arrived wet, they presumably stayed wet all day unless they could get clothes dry in one of the furnace buildings. There is no mention of a canteen or anywhere for mothers to prepare food for themselves or their children although a 'school' existed for the under 6s. Those above that age were found work.

Employees from Warslow had the easiest journey, the mine being visible from the village, maybe fifteen minutes or so away. However Warslow became an impediment for those heading for the mine and wanting to cross Warslow Common, such as those from Butterton. The Alstonfield Manor Court banned such practice upon a fine of five shillings, about the weekly wage for many of the women. Potentially this could have affected some of the Manor tenants and no reason is known for this. One just wonders if there was some bad blood between the Harpur (later Harpur-Crewe) estate, who controlled Alstonfield Manor, and the Devonshires. It cropped up in the Devonshire Accounts from time to time. There was a case in Chancery brought by the Devonshire estate against Sir Harry Harpur in 1785. (2) It spilled over into the 19th century when the mine was desperate for more land on which to tip waste stone, and the Harpurs failed to oblige. This Alstonfield Manor court decision forced the Butterton workforce to find alternative ways to work, one of which involved using the Onecote–Warslow turnpike road and walking to Warslow before dropping down The Dale to Dale Bridge, adjacent to the mine. The only bridges down river from here were the now removed Lees Bridge between Swainsley and Wetton Mill, or Wetton Mill Bridge (assuming it existed prior to 1769, when the Ecton – Wetton Mill road was built). It is likely that some older crossing existed here to reach the Mill. Whichever way was used would have been longer than crossing Warslow Common.

For the women who had their own household, a 10 hour shift, plus 2 hours spent walking to and from the mine, left them with a busy life in the remaining 12 hours of the day, unless a parent or somebody similar was at home to do at least some of the domestic work. This was a weekly routine for everyday (except Sundays, Christmas Day, Easter Monday and possibly a half day on Shrove Tuesday) no matter how well or unwell a woman was feeling.

This may explain, at least in part, why many girls did not work every week or even a six day week. Perhaps they were needed at home, although their wage would equally be valued. Alternatively it may have been the arduous nature of the work taking its toll of young girls. Many young, able-bodied women however were earning an adult's wage where they clearly could compete with an older adult. Unfortunately for them, they were paid (i.e. women) at only 75% or less of the labourer's rate for a man.

The Miners

Other than the labourers in the mine – those looking after the pumps, mine machinery, horses living underground, removing ore and stone etc. were the contractors. They were the men with a contract to do a specific job of work – driving a level from A to B; sinking a shaft a certain distance etc. Some of these men were on prestigious work such as sinking the main shaft from the large underground chamber at river level where the pumping engine and winding engine were later erected.

It was 600 feet deep and in 1773, when nearly finished, took the total mine depth past 1,000 feet from the shaft top high above on the hillside. Ecton was then the deepest mine in the country and possibly very few, if any, were deeper beyond our shores. In 1784, another shaft, this time starting near the top of the shaft mentioned above, was commenced. It is situated adjacent to the barn seen on the skyline from the Manifold Valley. The first ropes for this shaft (it was used for winding ore) were in excess of 1,212 ft/ 364m. long. The shaft had taken four years to sink.

Other work undertaken by the contractors was to drive levels to gain access to a new area or 'for wind' i.e. ventilation. The men were paid by the fathom (6ft/2m.) and payment was made to the leader of the team. As a result, the number of men employed on contract work is not known specifically.

Another group of men were those who worked on ore extraction. Their job was to create the mine's wealth working in copper ore. They were paid by the tonnage of ore hauled up the shaft. In poor veins, ore had to be extracted from veins along with adjacent spar and rock if necessary. It was then ground down and the ore, which was heaviest, separated in water from the lighter waste. Much of this was left untouched initially, at Ecton.

This was because the ore was concentrated in large masses or ore bodies as they were termed. Having worked one out, the ore contracted to a much narrower 'pipe' which was then followed downwards to another ore body. There were eight of these and they became bigger with depth. It was described as a whole as being like a bell, getting wider as it went lower. Unfortunately a bell has a flat bottom and so did the mine, a feature which saw the mine fail in 1790. Thereafter, output continued, but at a much reduced volume, picking out the earlier ignored poorer veins.

It is easy to imagine the men working in a huge cavern with large rock faces of yellowish ore (brass coloured is perhaps more accurate). Sometimes it was darker, even green or blue in colour. Men would work off long ladders to bring the ore down. Such a great concentration of ore would mean it was easier to extract free of rock, spar, etc., reducing dressing costs. It was also rich in metal content, an added bonus.

Adjacent to the Ecton Mine – only a few hundred yards to the south – was another branch of this deposit, the Clayton Mine. The Duke did not own it, but had shares in it. It too had a similar form, but was not as big in cross-section. Here the men in the early years of the 19th century worked in hammocks bringing the ore down. So rich was the deposit that there is another traditional story, handed down orally from generation to generation, that the men involved were only allowed to work three days a week as they were earning too much money compared to the rest of the workforce.

When the Clayton Mine was being drained prior to reworking, in 1884, the manager reported in the *Mining Journal* that they were draining one particular large opening or chamber. They were pumping 24 hours a day to lower the water level one inch and the

The mine house of 1780

pumpmen could not see the sides of the chamber to the north or the west. (3)

Normally, the only light available to the miner was a candle which was held by a lump of sticky clay to the front of his helmet. The latter was made from strengthened *papier mache* with a brim which supported the candle and protected the wearer's neck from seeping water.

The highest of the eight deposits in the Ecton Mine occurred at the 34 fathoms level (204 ft/61m.) below the river and Ecton Sough, the main level into the mine. At the 34 fathoms level, the height of the deposit was 45 ft/13.5m. As stated above, the deposits became larger with depth with the main one said to be some 450 x 300 ft/135m x 90m. in extent across its floor. A good stone thrower could not hit the sides or the roof of this chamber, called the Great Opening.

The Labourers

These men and boys fell into two categories, those employed on the surface and those underground. Some of the surface hands did both, bringing out the horse-drawn ore wagons, for instance. They did a variety of jobs: dealing with waste rock that wasn't dumped underground, maintaining roads around the mine, clearing snow in winter, breaking ore and rock before it was crushed by the women and later by a crushing wheel etc.

Others initially worked capstans drawing water up shafts. There were no less than 37 of them before most were replaced by a simple water-powered pumping engine in 1784. Even then ore and waste rock had to be removed in large 80 gallon barrels. Horses living permanently underground lifted water, ore and rock to the 34 fathom level. The ore was sent straight up to the Ecton Sough level (at river level) and drawn out of the mine by more horses. On the other hand, the water coursed along the 34 fathom Boat Level to Apes Tor Shaft, situated by the riverside at the north end of Ecton Hill. Here it was lifted by the barrel and tipped into a channel running under the road to the river. Rock was loaded into the boats and also raised up the same shaft. Much of it was used in an adjacent limekiln.

All the 'little jobs' about the workings would be done by the lesser-paid labourers, earning around 1s.0d (5p.) a day. Another job, often relegated to boys, was manually providing ventilation into the blind workings being driven by the contractors. There always seemed to be one job after another to keep them busy. Sometimes available men found themselves confined to the mine for days on end in the case of an emergency, such as a sudden ingress of water. The mine kept them both busy, fed and watered, with plenty of meat and ale during such times. More ale was available upon the conclusion of exceptional pieces of work such as in 1783 *'when the Great Beam was got into the Mine'*. It was at John Marsden's (a publican) so the men found the ale on the house at the end of a difficult job getting the water powered pumping engine installed.

The labourers working underground had their candles found by the mine. The contractors had their candle costs deducted from their payments.

Work at the Mine: Ore Dressing

The method of treatment of ores was primitive, although the process was done in a building, which was unusual. Dressing was principally the occupation of women and children – 'washerwomen' as the accounts put it at one point. The early Devonshire accounts record that there were two teams of women (and children) at work: washers under Ann Parker, and knockers (later termed buckers) under Elizabeth Keeling. The washers earned 4s. 6d. per week, much more than the knockers, who were on 2s. 6d. per week. In March 1761 there were probably six employees washing and probably 17 knocking. There were also 22 pickers at 1s. 6d. per week under Thos. Wint, which may indicate that these were principally children at that wage rate.

Efford, (3) writing in 1769, states that:

'The ore is carried out by boys and thrown into a heap and two men with large hammers or sledges are employed to break it up into small pieces. Next, it is carried in small hand barrows by small boys to a place under a shed erected for the purpose, to be picked, sorted and laid in different parcels: best, second and worst. This operation is performed by little girls from 8 to 12 years old.

'Next the ore is carried to another large and convenient shed where about 50 women sit back to back on benches to buck or beat the ore with flat hammers still keeping each particular sort together. (The flat hammers were called 'buckers'). The ore is reduced to a fine sand: sometimes when the ore was very rich it was only broken into pieces the bigness of a nutmeg: But poor ore was broken small with flat hammers until hand driven stamping mills were erected and a convenient supply of water was laid at hand.

'The ore, now reduced to a small sand, it is again removed to the 'Buddles' for washing, where an old Cornishman has the sole superintendency of it, as a great deal of the finest ore would be lost if this operation was not properly performed. Here, then, it is correctly washed and cleansed and afterwards exposed for sale in the open air, in various heaps, 'ticketed' accordingly to the different qualities and quantities. "Ticketing the ore" is taking a couple of handfuls off any heap of ore and putting them into a canvas bag, by way of samples; then little labels are fixed to the bags, signifying the quantity of each parcel. When a load of ore was ready, notice was given to the smelting house whose proprietors or managers attend, and each bids what price he thinks proper (generally from £7 to £16 per ton) the highest bidder being the buyers; it is fetched away at the buyer's expenses.

'The refuse part of the ore, which is not fit for sale, is beat down small and carried to the smelting house on the premises erected by His Grace, and there run into large pigs or bars, and is then sold for around £70 to £90 per ton. Upon the whole nothing is left. The great advantage to the country around arises from the number of hands employed, and the circulation of between £3,000 and £4,000 cash annually, in a poor place and thinly inhabited before this place was discovered, but now quite improved, and more than 300 men, women and children employed winter and summer, who have proper overseers for every department, and where everything goes on with the utmost harmony and cheerfulness. The

miners, as before hinted, work at 2d. per hour, six hours at a time; women, by task, earn 4d. to 8d. per day, and are paid by measure according to the quantity of ore they can 'buck'; girls and boys from 2d. to 4d. a day, some more; thus there is constant employment for both sexes and all ages from 5 to 60 years of age.'

The carpenter's shop, the smith's forge, the cooperage, with neat dwelling-houses of the superintendents, little kitchen gardens and out-houses annexed, are all singular in mind, and happily adapted to make life agreeable in that solitary place which lies between two monstrous hills, separated at least two miles from other inhabitants. This copper mine, in the state above described, clears annually between £8,000 and £40,000 profit, and if worked with the spirit which accompanies large returns, double the sum might be made of it; but His Grace, it seems is content that it employs all the labouring poor who present themselves for work from the neighbouring parishes.'

Despite the use of the word 'washing', both by Efford and in the accounts, the expression was to indicate the need to clean or separate the ore from ground rock or spar. The ore was not dirty as such.

The need for care to ensure the volume of small particles of ore was not lost was important. The ground-up waste was dumped in the river, to such an extent that it was possible to walk across it from side to side. It was all carried away in times of bad weather especially in the winter. In 1836 two men were tasked at removing silt from the river just beyond the bend above Ecton Lea within a quarter of a mile downstream from the mine. This was then treated to extract the tiny particles of ore deposited where the current had slackened. Records show that 42 tons of copper ore was extracted in this way and sent to Whiston smelter that summer, all recovered from the river.

The timing of it is specifically recorded too, for on the day that the first batch was weighed (some 30 tons) there was an eclipse of the sun and it went dark. There was no total eclipse in this country between 1724 and 1927, but there was an annular eclipse on 15th May 1836, covering the area between north Cumbria and Perth. Its effect at Ecton would have produced at least a 90% eclipse, possibly more, turning daylight to almost night-time (4). The amount of ore recovered is staggering, given the care in trying to avoid this happening and the size of the particles – probably smaller than grains of sand.

The ore dressing account for August 1779 indicates that there were then 99 people dressing ore. This included 44 males (chiefly boys). The highest wages were paid to 4 men (6s. 0d. per week). The head women were 4s. 6d. per week. Most of the women employees were paid 3s. 0d. per week, some being paid 3s. 0d. for themselves and a child who was helping them.

The majority of the dressers earned 3s. 0d. or less – down to 1s. 6d. per week. Out of the 55 women, 51 are named. The most common name was Elizabeth and Mary (10 women with each name) and there were 7 each called Ann, Hannah and Sarah. Only 4 people did not sign for their wages with a 'X'. It would be easy to assume that those earning 3d. per day were children, but the rate could apply to the work undertaken. In August 1782, Hannah Fogg was paid for 24 days at 3d. per day and 7.5 days at 6d. per day, but if 4d. per day was to be taken as a child's wage rate, 24 of them were employed out of 125 dressers in all employed at the work at that date.

Almost 75% of female workers seem to have been able to work for more than 66% of working days per reckoning, which suggests that they were attuned to the new regime of regularity of employment offered by the mine. Wages were paid on the reckoning day, every

7 to 8 weeks. Flexibility of working was at the lower end of the scale, amongst children for instance, who may have been required at home and amongst girls who may have been less resilient to the work, as indicated above.

There is some evidence of children working with mothers but it would be nice to know if this was to assist the parent to get her work done or whether she was simply keeping a close watch on one of her brood.

The mine offered regular, daily work in a non-agricultural environment. The need to turn up daily and undertake regular hours of work, often repetitive work, would have been a new concept in the district. Even Sunday working was necessary for key employees such as the water drawers. However some of the workers took time off (two days) to go to Chesterfield Fair each year. This was possibly not unusual, for Chester records that suppliers of the Oakamoor forge were actually paid at Leek Fair in 1594 and 1607. (5)

There were fairs nearer too, for each of the local villages had, and still has, its wakes week. In 1900 *"bull, bear and badger baiting, cock fighting … are still talked of as having been among the old Wetton Wake amusements, held at the Windle Hollow Alehouse Bowling Green when 'old Seth of Ipstones' brought his bear and the cockpit was placed near the same spot"* (6) Windle Hollow is now better known as Hope Marsh between Wetton and Alstonfield.

The Visit by the 5th Duke

The 5th Duke appears to have visited the mine in the early autumn of 1783. Where he went underground is not known. His father descended to at least the 34 fathoms level (204 ft/ 62 m), if not lower, in 1763. Much more was available to be seen twenty years on.

The precise nature of the accounting indicates that five candles at 5¾d each were used during his visit. Elsewhere it is noted that malt and hops were purchased in September 1783 and more in November. The first consignment could have been to make beer for the Duke's visit for consumption by the workers. Whether he had a soft spot for bread and butter pudding has succumbed to the passage of time, but the ingredients seem to have been purchased from Robert Low, a grocer and provisions merchant of Warslow, prior to his visit. Low supplied virtually all the 'domestic items' to the mine for years. Amongst the ingredients were nutmeg (2d.) and 1oz. ginger (1d.)! Low also supplied green tea and 1oz. of what looks like Bohea Tea plus 1lb. of lump sugar (on September 23rd) no doubt for the Duke.

The Duke's wife, Georgiana, collected minerals and was encouraged by White Watson, the Bakewell geologist who ran the nearby Ashford Black Marble works. Her collection survives at Chatsworth and it includes several specimens of copper and spar from Ecton. The Grotto in the garden (not open to the public) is lined with spar from Ecton, but whether this was removed to Chatsworth at about this time is not known. The spar is sprinkled with tiny brass coloured crystals of copper ore.

Gratuities

It is known that the 4th Duke, like his son, went to visit the mine. It is recorded that he left the miners ten guineas to spend on drink and the accounts record on 1/10/1763 *'to Wetton Tenants and these Minors (sic) at His Grace's Order £12. 12s. 0d.'* So it would seem the tenants received two guineas to spend on drink and the miners (at 1/8d. a gallon, the price pertaining in 1780) something like 126 gallons or 1,000 pints in round terms!

In 1783 the expense accounts record *'[to] C. Flint [the mine manager] added to the Money*

Left: A silhouette of Cornelius Flint **Right:** The grave of Cornelius Flint in Hartington Churchyard

that His Grace the Duke of Devonshire left when he was at Ecton 12s. 6d.'. On this occasion, the 5th Duke left the miners £16. 5s. 0d. He went also to Hartington where he left the [bell] ringers £1. 1s. 0d. (7).

One could be forgiven for thinking that the payment for *'Expenses of a Feast to the workmen in the Memorable 5th of November 1788'* was a celebration of Guy Fawkes Night or the successful starting of the Boulton & Watt Engine (it was actually trialled three weeks later). The 5th November 1688 was the day that William of Orange stepped ashore at Brixham, Devon, an event partly orchestrated by the last Earl and first Duke of Devonshire. He came with his army to seize the throne, but the transition was peaceful and he reigned jointly with his wife, Mary, until her death on 28th December 1644 and then singly until his death in 1700. The Duke and Duchess celebrated the event in Chesterfield, possibly at Revolution House, its current name.

In August 1779 occur the first references in the mine accounts to gratuities (effectively a pension). Both Richard Naylor and William Shore received 4s. 0d. (20p) per week, along with *'Widow Baker'* (2s. 0d.) and *'Widow Sheldon'* (1s. 0d.) per week. Presumably these resulted from mine accidents, where there were dependant children. In February 1780, the *'Widdow Lovill'* began to receive 2s. 6d. per week, all the other amounts remaining the same. By the end of 1784 the numbers had declined to two people – Mrs. Baker and Mrs. Sheldon on the same pension as before.

The Christmas Party, 1780, seems to have been a good example of Cavendish largesse. It was held at the mine, as Sampson Stubb's invoice states that he delivered 20 gallons of ale from Warslow. In all, the party feasted on 136 gallons of ale at 1s. 8d. per gallon ($2^1/_2$d. per pint); 261lb of beef at 3d. a lb; 264 pieces of bread (22 dozen) which may have been one per employee, giving an otherwise unrecorded number of employees at that time; 44lb of cheese at $2^3/_4$d. per lb and a quantity (? 1lb) of best tobacco pipes. The total cost was £16. 7s. 0d. A further party was held a year later and it is reasonable to assume it was an annual event, although in one year at least it appears that it was held in January, with snow being the cause. The Reckoning for

November 1782 included for two deliveries of 2cwt of hops, which may indicate that the mine was making its own beer for consumption at the Christmas dinner! The same account (per C. Flint) also includes six bottles of rum at 3s. 6d. per bottle for use on pay days. The December 1784 account shows that the making of their own beer was still in favour!

Amongst miscellaneous expenses at Whiston in early Autumn, 1786 is the purchase of half a load of malt (18s. 6d.) and 2cwt of best hops (2s. 0d.), so maybe someone would soon have been preparing refreshments for the smelters' Christmas festivities too. Unusually, the mine not only paid for a '*Feast to the workmen on the memorable 5th November 1788, £31. 11s. 6d.*' (see above) but additionally, the hands seem to have had the day off, for 144 workmen were paid 2s. 0d. '*wages for the day*'.

In March 1770, Robert Shore, the mine manager, claimed his expenses of £2. 19s. 3d. '*for sundries on His Grace's birthday*'. He was celebrating the latter's 22nd birthday, having acceded when he was 16 years old (and apparently inherited an annual income of over £60,000). (8)

Health & Safety at Work

In 1769, Efford reported on the poor state of the ladderways which give access to the pipe workings. One can only think that this deterioration had occurred after the Duke's visit.

Towards the end of 1761, payments for a '*Bead*' (bed, spelt by a writer used to pronouncing it 'bayed') at £4. 18s. 4d. and a '*Blanket & Cas*' (casement) 9s. 2d. were probably for accident victims. The blanket etc. came from John Bestall and he was paid on 2nd January 1762 '*for sundry's attendg Thos Swindale Kild in ye Mine 6s. 6d.*' Later that year, in May, Mr. Doxey (presumably a local doctor) was paid '*for ye cure of Wm. Manifold Hurt in ye Mine £7. 19s. 6d.*' and on 31st December '*for the cure of Josh. Mycock hurt in ye mine £4. 6s. 6d.*' which, if nothing else, shows that the high costs of private medicine and health care are nothing new.

There are some high costs of providing '*flanil etc.*' and '*lining cloth etc*' during the decade, which perhaps had more to do with the provision of accommodation and corporate hospitality than health care. It should be noted however, that flannel was purchased later by the Hazels Cross Colliery to make waistcoats for men employed in wet parts of the mine. However the doctor was needed again in March 1766 when Elizabeth Sleigh attended on '*John Tompson Hurt in ye mine*' followed by Mr. Doxey's bill for attending him, paid in February 1767 (£1. 10s. 0d.). The Sleigh family were landowners at Hartington. The current Charles Cotton Hotel was previously the Sleigh Arms. More intriguing was the payment of £8. 13s. 6d. in November 1769 to Isaac Greenhough '*bill for Coventree Doctor*'. The nature of the injuries demanding a specialist from Coventry is not known, but must have been serious. This was at a time when even a broken leg was life-threatening and the treatment for infection was pretty basic, often lacking in effectiveness.

In August 1774 is the following reference: '*John Chadwick bill fetching the Crowner 10s. 6d.*' This was problematical until it was realised that it followed the death on 29th July 1774 of Solomon Barker at the mine, which is recorded in the Butterton Church Register. Grasping the spelling of Coroner was giving difficulties to the book-keeper. Presumably he had to come from Leek; permanent Coroners' Courts are a feature of modern times. It was common for him to head for the stable and his horse in the event of fatal accidents, his hearing often being held at a local inn to which the body seems to have been taken. In the case of the mine, it no doubt would lie in the mine house, after its construction in 1780. In 1779 Dr. Eli Cope was charging 5s. 0d. a journey to visit injured miners and 2s. 6d. extra for a night visit. In August 1779 he went to Holmend [Hulme End] in the night to see Will Chadwick, administrating *'applications to [his] head and side'*, treating him with 'apodeldoc' which cost 1s. 0d. extra. Opodeldoc is an external application, or soap liniment, which was *'extremely useful in bruises and sprains etc. The part affected is to be frequently bathed with this liniment and as far as possible, kept constantly covered with it. Two ounces of opodeldoc and two drachms of laudanum form the anodyne liniment, which is still more efficacious in sprains and contusions; in rheumatic pains and similar local affections'* Opodeldoc consists of soft soap (8%, camphor, oil of rosemary, water and alcohol). (9)

In June 1782, Martha Wheeldon was paid for *'ye cure of John Goodwin when he was Bruised and Burned by a shott in Ecton mine (10s. 6d.)'*, which had occurred in 1780. This was followed in 1781 by a more serious case when she attended on *'ye cure of John Hibert Bruised and Burned Boath Hands, Armes, Face and one legg by a shot in ye mine'*. These occurred when a fuse failed to ignite properly. The miners had a dilemma of hanging about not knowing whether it had gone out or was burning very slowly. In these two cases it seems likely that the men had approached the fuse as it had gone off.

One miner was paid to go to Sheffield to be fitted with a pair of glasses after his sight was affected by a shot in the mine. More distressing was the injury to one of James Watts' team installing the 1788 winding engine. He had part of two fingers of his left hand totally severed *'by the cogs of a wheel'*.

All these relate to accidents which involved the mine in cost. There must have been lots more which didn't get a separate entry in the account books and are therefore now unrecorded. Working in wet conditions, fumes or dust-filled rooms or levels must all have taken their toll. It was so damp in the area of the capstan at the top of the 600ft. main shaft in the mine that fires were kept burning to stop the rope from rotting. The rope would have also become wet from water issuing into the shaft, but it shows graphically one of the problems faced equally by employees as well as equipment.

Martha Wheeldon seems to have administered *'Salver'* to Thomas Brindley, also in 1781 when *'Burned with Coper'*. This is the first record of an accident at Ecton smelter. There were two men by that name (father and son) working at Ecton, both at the top of the pay scales for labourers at 9s. 0d. per week. In March 1781 the father was also paid for *'Attendance of*

A 19th century photograph of a delivery to the post office in Hartington, then opposite the Charles Cotton Hotel. This scene would not have been much different if it had been taken at the beginning of that century

Furnaces' and perhaps he was the one who had the accident.

Smelter accidents appear to have been rare, although there was a major one at Whiston in November 1780 when Dr. H. Moreton was treating *'Miles Finnecan at Oakamore'*. At least the patient recovered and the doctor charged £1. 11s. 6d. for *'journeys to Oakamore and the dressings and curing of an exceedingly bad burnt leg'*. Copper metal melts at 1,083°C. Miles Finnegan continued to receive his 9s. 0d. per week wages as a smelter (as distinct from a labourer) whilst he was off work. It is reasonable to assume that this was usual at the mine too. Unfortunately the accounts for the latter half of 1781 are missing and the details re. John Hibbard cannot be checked. The accounts of the collieries are meagre in the information they give, but additional to a fatal accident recorded for Hazels Cross in 1783, Dr. H. Moreton submitted his account. (Reckoning March 1787) for treating William Wettwood *'for airing a bad wound on yr. leg 5s. 0d.'*.

Payment of Wages and Expenses

Cash was obtained by the mine from Messrs. Wilkinson at Chesterfield. The agent (Robert Shore and then Cornelius Flint) fetched it from there. Flint later described the procedure as being accompanied by *'two stalwart miners'* and these were Ralph and Joseph Bonsall. All three went by horse-back and they also accompanied Flint to Whiston where payments were also made (and presumably also for the two collieries). There is no note indicating that they were ever robbed, nor any oral tradition of this. A statement of disbursements in 1777 indicates that there was no pattern to the days when money was collected; it appears to be purely at random. In January 1782, the mine purchased a *'pair of saddle pistols with bags and moulds'* for £1. 7s. 0d. They were purchased off Hervis and Redfern of Birmingham and cost 1s. 6d. to transport by coach to Derby, where they would have been collected by the mine from the Duke's Town House. A check of the gun collection at Chatsworth to see if these survive was unproductive.

All payments at the mine were receipted and paid two to three months in arrears. See also under Chapter 9 for details of arrangements for shipments to the mine, replicating a practicable and widespread way of handling such activity.

Refreshments were provided on the mine's pay days. In March 1781 Cornelius Flint claimed his expenses for providing 15 bottles of rum (they cost £2) for pay days since the previous June. He also claimed for six pay day expenses at £2. 14s. 0d. possibly for food etc.

References

1 Porter, L., *Ecton Copper Mines Under the Dukes of Devonshire 1760–1790*, 2004, pp 124-156

2 Dev Coll., AS/1717

3 Efford, W., *Gentleman's Magazine*, reprinted in Bull, PDMHS, Vol. 1, No. 5, pp 37 – 40. Efford records the 1763 visit of the 4th Duke to the mine but does not mention the 1766 Boat Level

4 *Mining Journal*, 27/10/1884; Porter, L., & Robey, J. A., *The Copper & Lead Mines around the Manifold Valley, North Staffordshire*, 2000, p. 226

5 Chester, H.A., *'Churnet Valley Iron: The Mills and The Mines'*, 2002, pp. 38 & 40 viz *'Pd to Collyers at Leek Fair £20'*. [in 1607]

Bromfield, P., op cit, Part 1, p 13

6 Roberts, J., *History of Wetton, Thor's Cave and Ecton Mines* 1900. Roberts was the Wetton School Master in 1900

7 Dev Coll., AS/1717

8 Forman, A., ibid, p 17

9 Tindal, J., *Companion to the Medicine Chest*, 7th Edit., 1817. Also pers. comm.. Arthur & Barbara Williams, both retired pharmacists who used to dispense opodeldoc early in their careers

7. THE MILLS: CEREALS, MALT, COTTON & EMPLOYMENT

Mobility of Labour

Chapman (1) suggested that Hartington (and Tideswell) may well have been places where villagers of ability did not know of the opportunities offered by the large towns and their textile mills. Surely though, this could not have been the case with Hartington. Situated some two miles from one of the deepest and most profitable mines in the world (Ecton Copper Mine) in the 1780s, there was a continual flow of goods to the mine, with much coming from the Leek, Cromford and Belper areas. It is inconceivable that gossip with the carriers did not take place. Indeed the carriers were the news vendors of their day. The building of new and large mills together with the working opportunities offered by them must have been a talking point both at the mine and in the neighbouring villages.

Chapman makes the point that the large factories had to compete for labour resources which were in short supply at a time when contraction of lead mining in the Peak had created a pool of labour. The failure of the Ecton Copper Mine in 1790 increased this. What is strange is that the Ecton workforce was used to the regime of a regular daily work ethic, set hours and the discipline of specific working practices for forty years. Why was it that quite a few so many of them clearly set their face against moving to the towns and their mills? Some certainly were prepared to move. Work for some of the miners was found at the Duke of Devonshire's Thatchmarsh Colliery on Axe Edge, and Bromfield (2) has shown that at least one man from Grindon went to Grassington in Yorkshire where the Duke had lead mines. It's not clear how many Hartington villagers worked at the mine but some surely did, especially as the mine manager lived in the village. One wonders whether Thomas Cantrell opened the (later) Brund Corn Mill in 1790 as a textile mill to take advantage of the displaced Ecton workforce or at least some of it. The apparent starvation of over 70 Wetton residents in 1796 – when the Duke paid for oatmeal and coal to be sent to the village by the cartload (3) – would seem to be the result of poverty induced by the closure of the mine.

However if this seems to show a resolution for residents to remain in the local village come what may, there is little evidence to sustain the thought. More work needs to be done on this, but it is beyond the scope of this book. However the point about Brund Mill above remains persuasive and presumably Cantrell would have taken advantage of such a determination in 1790.

There was some direction of labour however, which shows that the area was not so 'cut off' as Chapman seems to have believed. In 1806, Isaac Wilshaw, at the age of eight years, was bound as an apprentice by the Overseers of Fairfieldhead. Incidentally this parish borders the River Manifold at Brund Mill. Presumably he had been orphaned or was an illegitimate child being raised at the cost of the parish. His apprenticeship was to Daniel Hambleton of Ashford near Bakewell, a framework knitter. When he was aged fifteen he became chargeable to the parish of Bakewell, where he lived, and *'his Master agreed with Joshua Skidmore of Ashford, Framework Knitter, that he should serve him the remainder of this time'*, i.e. until he was 21 years' old. (4) This example would have been common practice as Overseers of the Poor strove to reduce the financial burden of the Poor on the Parish.

With over 500 people employed at Ecton Mine in the mid–1780s, and redundancy pay totalling £547, the total of people affected would have run into hundreds. In 1797 a further group of 57 men and 21 women were made redundant, the men receiving a guinea (£1. 1s. 0d./£1. 5p.) and the ore dressers half that amount each.

Textile Mills

There were some textile mills in the immediate neighbourhood. These included one in Hartington Market Place, built by Thomas Cantrell. It was opposite the cottages to the right of the colonnaded shop where the three terraced houses bear a date stone reading T & JC (Thomas & Jane Cantrell), 1777. This is likely to have been a hand-operated spinning works at that date and unlikely to have used the water of the River Harding flowing past the front door (and probably in a culvert). However it is unclear how many people were collectively employed by these concerns. If these three houses were 'workers' cottages', it is probable that they were for overseers rather than loom operators. Unfortunately, the works appears to have been burnt down in 1786 (when it was apparently worth £2,000). Pilkington visited it in 1783 and found 60 people at work, manufacturing cotton, thread, linen and 'check' (5). It is likely that home production of yarn and cloth would have been practised in the Hartington area, not just supplying local mills but other people as well. Perhaps some of the Ecton workers found employment in this manner where they were sufficiently industrious to do so. There is an interesting reference to this type of activity to support this, although the location of the workers is not given. In 1801 a Mrs. Gregory supplied tablecloths to Chatsworth made from huckaback, which was spun and woven by local people. (6) Huckaback was coarse linen or cotton used to make towelling.

On 28th August 1784 Thomas Bassett of Mayfield near Ashbourne went to Pilsbury to propose to William Gould (the Duke's local rent collector) the building of a cotton mill on the latter's estate at Lowend, between Sheen and Hulme End. Bassett suggested that Gould propose terms if he (Bassett) was to build the mill. If Gould built it, he suggested a rent of 10% of the cost. Nothing appears to have come of this proposal, although Brund Mill was built a little further upstream by Thomas Cantrell in 1790 (see above).

Although the Hartington and Ludwell Mills are known (the latter being just north of Hartington village, but not on the estate), it appears that a *'cotton works'* of Messrs. Oliver existed at Glutton Bridge. (7) William Gould was back at Glutton Bridge in May 1785 with a Mr. Smith of Mansfield. The latter *'approved of it very much and seemed to have a great inclination to purchase some frames'*. (8)

They were still at Glutton in 1789, when a Mr. Oliver paid *'2 years' acknowledgement for lowering the bed of the River Dove on account of his Cotton Mill near Glutton Bridge, due Lady Day 1789, 2s. 0d.'* A Thomas & James Oliver, plus a Thomas White, were declared bankrupt at a cotton mill in *'Alstonfield'*, early in 1800. (9) It is likely that this would relate to Glutton, the reference to Alstonefield indicating the parish not the village. The payment above to the manor relates to use of the riverbed. It was on the Staffordshire bank, immediately below the bridge. The use of water power at these riverside textile mills suggests that they would be used for carding and the first stages of preparing for spinning. unless they were using Arkwright's water frame (patented in 1769). However, these machines did not produce as fine a thread. This was overcome by using Crompton's 'mules' for spinning from 1779. (10) At the end of 1795, Thomas Taylor of Warslow was advertising for a partner or purchaser of a five-storey mill for *'a brewhouse and cotton business for mules and jennies'*. This is probably the

Thomas Cantrell's textile mill of 1777 opposite the colonnaded village stores when in use as a penny lodging house. In the foreground are the local Volunteer Force, possibly from Ashbourne, as they trained here

mill which existed on the Warslow Brook. Part of the leat is all that remains of this, visible on the right as you cross the road bridge on the B5053 heading for Warslow. (11)

There would not have been many other opportunities to soak up the labour pool produced by redundancy at Ecton Mine. The new farms carved out of the common upon the Inclosure would have created some demand, but that was nearly two decades later. It is inevitable that there must have been some upheaval as families left village communities for a new life in nearby towns and cities. Your author's maternal family of Goldstraws may well have been an example of this, albeit at Ipstones, south-west of Hartington, moving from the village to Leek in the 1840s.

The mills mentioned above would have given some chance of work but none of them appear to have worked for any prolonged period. The same could not be said for the growing, fashionable status of Buxton with an accompanying need for a hotel and guest house. Buxton itself was growing – no doubt a magnet for rural people much the same as the mill towns. This may have assisted those in search of work from the area of the mine who chose the hotel/inn service industry as an alternative to the rigour of mill life.

Corn Mills

Many parishes, providing they had access to a reliable stream, had a parish corn mill and Hartington was no exception. It had a good supply of water in the River Dove and a mill existed apparently in 1244. (12) There is a further reference to the mill dated 6th June 1434. The mill was then copyhold and Richard Laydman paid a fine of 7d./3p for admission to *'ground with a mill in Hartington, formerly held by John de Wetton for the benefit of Adam Newbyggyng, vicar of Hartington.'* (13) The mill was sited by the road to Hulme End where a bridge was later built.

Crowdecote Mill served the Hartington Middle Quarter parish. No mill is recorded for the Hartington parishes of Nether Quarter or for Upper Quarter, unless this was the Otterhole Mill (see below), which may well have been the case. It was west of the village of Buxton.

To the east of Buxton was the probable site of Fairfield Mill at the head of Ashford Dale. Crowdecote was also built on the River Dove, just below a strong spring which augmented the shallower waters of the river.

Whereas the cotton mills employed numerous workers, (Cantrell's Mill in Hartington Market Place employed c. 60, as seen above), the corn mill was just the opposite, with the bulk of the work being the responsibility of the miller himself. In the 17th century records of Hartington and Crowdecote Mills, when they were worked 'in hand' by the Devonshire estate, there was only one employee at each mill, or at least only one paid by the estate.

Hartington Mill

In 1614 the tenant was Henry Cavendish, who presumably sub-let it to a miller. The 1614 survey terrier (14) states that the rent to the estate was 33s. 4d. per annum, but that the mill was worth £25 [p.a.]. In 1666 the mill was repaired and William, the 1st Earl of Devonshire, endorsed a note *'I am content to allow Mr. Shalcross £25 towards the repairing of the mill at Hartington Sept 24 1666, W. Devonshire'*. (15) The allowance was made in the Lady Day Rent.

The late 17th Century

Although some wheat and barley was ground regularly in the 1680s at Hartington Mill and from 1686 at Crowdecote Mill (but not in 1684-5), and a small amount of malt produced at Hartington, the main output was ground oats and oatmeal. It was sold at Bakewell Market and to local people e.g. Mr. Rudiard (Rudyard) of Monyash.

Measurement was by the peck, although in 1685 there is a reference to oats from 1684 amounting to 64 strikes *'by ye old measure'*. The miller was paid by the kiln-full for handling oats.

At Crowdecote in 1684 the local smith provided a band for the mill shaft, which must have split. This probably did not resolve the problem sufficiently, for the mill was rebuilt over the winter of 1684-5. This included the purchase of a pair of new millstones at a cost of £5. The reconstruction cost was £46. 18s. 4d., but does not appear to have affected the existing waterwheel. Minor repairs affected both Crowdecote and Hartington Mills on an annual basis but in 1688, there must have been a lot of flood water, for repairs to the weir at both mills were necessary. Worthy of note is that Hartington Mill was *'repaired'* also in 1684 and Otterhole Mill near Buxton was rebuilt in the same year.

The Hartington miller in 1684 was William Mellor. Both mills were 'in hand' and not let to the miller. Repairs at Hartington must have been substantial. Edward Greensmith was paid for the carriage of *'5 wain load and 2 horse load'* of timber. Thomas Joule, a mason, was paid for erecting walls and thatch was purchased for the roof. The blacksmith was Thomas Malkin at Hartington and Joshua Greensmith at Crowdecote.

An interesting cost in 1684 in the Hartington Mill account was 5s. 0d. for three justice warrants and other charges *'in serving for stolen goods'*.

Otterhole Mill

Otterhole Mill, to the west of Buxton, off Gadley Lane was also rebuilt at a cost of £46. 5s. 8$\frac{1}{2}$d. in 1684. The mill accounts are not included with the two manor mills. A new mill shaft 14 ft long and 18 inches square was delivered with 3 arms (sic) 15 ft. long, suggesting a waterwheel of 31-32 ft diameter. The wheel was built by J. Lindsay, a carpenter. A new kiln was also built, and two millstones purchased at £5. 2s. 6d., including carriage.

Crowdecote mill ruins, c. 1900-1910

Accounts in the 1680s (post 1684) make no mention of Otterhole Mill. It was hardly out of use having been rebuilt, so it must have related to the nature of the miller's occupation. Perhaps the rebuilding was preliminary work prior to letting a tenancy. In 1697, the miller was Andrew Norton, paying £10 per annum rent. (16)

Both Hartington and Crowdecote Mills remained in use through the Georgian period. Otterhole Mill is referred to much less and may have become disused in the 18th century for it does not appear on a detailed map of Buxton dated 1775. (17) Hartington Mill continued in use into the 20th century, completing a remarkable period of use of at least seven centuries. Crowdecote mill features on a lantern slide (see left) of probable Edwardian age and is seen in an advanced stage of ruin.

In 1710, Hartington Mill was leased to Ralph Woodhouse at £8 per annum. In 1724, he was still the lessee. In 1724, someone with that name was keeping the manor courts. Subsequent rentals show that substantial repairs were carried out in 1732. A new waterwheel was provided together with a cog wheel (which meshed with the wallower, which provided the power to the machinery). Repairs to the leat from the river (the *'Fore Beay and Shutles'* (Fore Bay and Shuttles) was also undertaken at a total cost of £28. 10s. 0d. Further repairs were carried out in 1740 (£50. 9s. 6d.). (18)

In 1737, (just prior to the 1740 repairs), the lessee was John Wheeldon, still paying £8 per

Brund mill in the 1940s

annum. A Joseph Marchington took the mill from Lady Day 1779 at £14 per annum on a repairing basis, but the mill was out of lease in February 1785. By 1788 John Banks had taken the mill, succeeding John Fogg, who seems to have succeeded John Wheeldon. In 1793, John Banks was the miller at £28 per annum. (19)

Incidentally, a pair of millstones bought by the estate from John Lowe delivered to Booth Edge for Hoppin Mill in 1758 cost £5. 10s. 0d. A parcel of land within a third of a mile or so upstream from Otterhole Mill was called Hopping Plexckes (south-east of Plex Farm). It therefore could have been another name for Otterhole Mill (situated at GR. 048734). However, Otterhole Mill had ceased to exist by 1775 and a repair in 1758 seems unlikely.

An interesting and more likely alternative is Hopping, south-east of Booth Farm, north of Hollinsclough and west of Dowal Farm. Hopping is an area marked on Heywood's 1614 map and south-west of Hollins Farm. There is no evidence of a watermill here but calamine ore (zinc carbonate) is known to have been mined on the adjacent Chrome Hill in 1750, with the ore being sent to the calamine mill at Mill Dale on the River Dove near Alstonfield. This was being worked by the Cheadle Brass & Copper Company. Mill Dale mill was still smelting ore in 1759 and it is suggested that the Hopping millstones were edge runners for grinding the ore to remove spar, rock, etc. before being taken by packhorse down river to Mill Dale. (20)

Fairfield Mill

Although not in Hartington parish, this mill was included in the Hartington Rental Collection in the 1730s–40s. It was let in 1732 to Alexander Taylor, the lessee of Buxton Hall Inn at £10 per annum. Ten years later, the estate provided an additional building at this mill together with a pair of blackstones and the rent rose to £30 per annum. Between 1744 and

1746, Taylor was paid £600 for additional construction work at the Inn with an associated rise in rent as had happened at the mill.

The reference to blackstones is interesting for they are rare. Typically, they were lava stones from near Cologne in Germany, used for general purpose milling. They had an open, rough texture for coarse milling, such as for animal feeds. It is possible that these stones were German stones, but more likely, and more intriguing, is that they could well have been of local lava, or toadstone, which was being quarried nearby. It is persuasive to think that expensive German lava stones would have been substituted by a local manufacturer endeavouring to find an alternative supply from local lava. (21) The mill was situated near the top of Ashwood Dale.

Beresford Mill

A surprise on the 1614 Hayward Map (22) was the existence of a mill on the Staffordshire bank of the River Dove in Beresford Dale. It was situated just below the sharp bend in the river just downstream of Pike Pool. The mill was marked as being in the possession of Mr. Edward Beresford. No further reference to this mill is known, but it must have been powered by an undershot waterwheel and the plan shows a short leat from the river. Edward Beresford was the last of Beresfords who had held the estate from at least the 13th century. He was succeeded in 1623 by his granddaughter, Olive Stanhope, whose son, Charles Cotton, was the poet and contributor to the 1676 edition of *The Compleat Angler*. (23)

References

1 Chapman, S., *The Early Factory Masters*, 1967, p 331 Chapman, S., *The Early Factory Masters*, 1967, p 33

2 Bromfield, P., *Industrial Workers in a Peasant Community: Manifold Valley parishes in the 18th Century with special reference to workers at the Ecton Mine c. 1760–1820*. Keele University library

3 Porter, L., *Ecton Copper Mines Under the Dukes of Devonshire 1760–1790*, 2004, p 223

4 Dev. Coll. AS/91, p 57

5 Pilkington, J., *A View of the Present State of Derbyshire*, Vol. 2, 1789, p 289; Chapman, S.D., ibid, pp. 57 – 8

6 Dev. Coll., Chatsworth Account Book, 1801, p 114

7 Wm. Gould's diary, 18/1/1785

8 Wm. Gould, op. cit., 1/5/1785

9 *Derby Mercury*, 20/2/1800

10 pers. com. Rev. Dr. R. H. Hills

11 *Derby Mercury*, 24/12/1795

12 Weston, R., ibid, p. 34-5

13 Dev. Coll., Devonshire Collections book

14 Dev. Coll., AS/600

15 Dev. Coll., AS/182

16 Dev. Coll., AS/1610

17 Dev. Coll., Map. No. 2049

18 Dev. Coll., AS/1224, 438, 164; AS/1371

19 Dev. Coll., AS/1053

20 Dev. Coll., AS/1062, item 20; Porter, L., and Robey, J., *The Copper & Lead Mines around the Manifold Valley, N. Staffs'*, 2000, p 245. Thanks to Sue Gawkroger for reminding me of the calamine mining. There does not appear to be much visual evidence of mining on Chrome Hill, there is a level situated nearby and near to the River Dove dating from the 19th century. However there does appear to be a line of disturbed ground on the north side of the adjacent Hollins Hill).

21 Dev. Coll., AS/1371 and pers. com., Alan Stoyel re. Blackstones

22 Dev. Coll., Map 2062

23 Victoria County History, Staffordshire, Vol.7, Leek & the Moorlands, p 16

8. MINING

Lead Ore

Although there are a lot of mine shafts in the Hartington Quarters, the industry was not a large one. It is highlighted in a document detailing the estate Lot and Cope figures (these are payments made allowing the miner to sell and smelt his ore where he wished). It covers the years 1700 – 1705 and the Hartington payment was £9. 17s. 6d. For Winster, it was £1,657; north side of the River Wye it was £1,650; Ashford Manor (shown separately) was £803. The total was £4,263. (1). From this period onwards, no large lead ore deposits were located. The mine called *'Halfpenny Hole'* within Hartington mining liberty, seems to sum up the mining activity rather well.

It is likely that many of the lead mine shafts were shallow in depth, with potential veins proving of little worth. A mine called *'Deeper the Better'*, working in 1730 and 1744, came before the Barmote Court at those times. In 1744, there was a claim for wages and in 1730, a miner had removed ore *'unjustly'* – probably because he had not been paid. If this had been better capitalised and had gone deeper, the outcome seems to have been no different. Throughout the 18th century and onwards, lead ore revenues appear to have been continually very low.

This probably accounts for speculation beyond the parish by local people although probably equally without a lot of success, for example, Daniel Pett of Biggin, at Cold Eaton, south of Hartington parish in 1829 and Thomas Palfreyman, also of Biggin, and at the same Mine (*'Pett's Title Mere to Coldeaton Barn and called Middlehills Vein'* in 1835) (2). However, lead ore was produced at Cardor Lowe Mine, north of Hartington in 1755, 1766, 1785-88 and in the 19th century after 1835 (3). Small quantities of lead ore were also mined at Wheeldon Trees, Dowlow, Clay Meer, Clod Hall, Cob Seats (Newhaven) at various times in the 18th century (4).

The Devonshire Collection contains several documents relating to the Great Barmote Court for the Hartington Liberty which date from the 1720s. (5). They are basically a record of the meetings. The latter were held at Newhaven and mirrored the Great Barmote Court at Wirksworth. Like this, it had a jury of 24 people, met in April and (if required) in October. It heard complaints from miners and resolved disputes. These tended to be chiefly concerning the failure of a partner in a venture to contribute his financial share. *'Not coming and keeping company at a mine called …'* was how it was often described, although the earliest reference was clearer:

'6th October 1725. George Robinson complained … and charged James Excoll to pay £5. 15s. 10¾d. for Recconing for a 12th pt of a certain mine called ye Copseats and an eighth pt of a mine called ye Green Rake … or lose his pits.'

Fines were levied against those who did not appear (presumably as witnesses). At the Court hearings of October 1734 and 1735, various people were charged for non-appearance. Miners were charged 2d. and 'ore-burners' 1s. 0d. each. A George Lees persistently ignored the Court and was fined 5s. 4d. – *'we amercy George Lees'*, but he was still ignoring the Court in April 1737, but there was no mention of him the year after. Two different kinds of case were also heard during this period and the first must have been quite unusual. At the hearing on 28th April 1738:

'We amercy Rachel Boam ye wife of Richard Boam for making an assault of fray upon ye Mine called Noath thy Vernals Grove, and Blood Shed from the Body of Micah Newton £2. 5s. 0d.'

Goodness knows what that was all about, but it appears that Mrs. Boam was a determined lady. Two years later Micah Newton brought a case against Hezekiah Harrison for not paying his share at Copingstone Mine. The second case was brought against Isaac Marke [?] for taking and carrying away between 3 and 4 loads of ore from Zachary Pearson's Myne *'without being measured by the Lords Dish'*. This mine was seemingly still at work two years' later.

Unlike other adjacent mining liberties, Hartington Liberty was sold with the manor to the Duke of Buckingham by the King. Having purchased the estate, The Duke of Devonshire, not the Queen in her capacity as Duke of Lancaster, is therefore Lord of the Soil (owner of the lead mining rights) for Hartington Liberty.

Ochre Mining

Ochre is an iron oxide, usually occurring locally as a red or yellow colour. It was ground to a powder and mixed with lime wash to make 'paint'. It was then applied to walls, ceilings etc. to give variety to a white finish. Colour mills (where the ore was ground) existed at nearby Mill Dale, just above Viator's Bridge on the River Dove and also at Goytsclough at the northern end of the parish. Clearly they would have been common in areas where ochre was mined.

Farey (6) writing in 1811, stated that 'red mineral' – the Hartington accounts use the words 'ochre' or 'mineral' – was found south of Newhaven House Inn. In 1809, the accounts (7) record: *'To Messrs. Wheeldon and Webster by Mr. Sheffield, the royalty or duty upon $132^1/_2$ tons of mineral got by them near Newhaven House at 5s. per ton'*. Red ochre appears to have attracted a royalty at 5s. 0d. per ton and the yellow variety at 10s. 0d., perhaps because it was less common (detailed as such in the accounts for 1823). Royalty was paid up to 1812, whereupon an annual rent for the *'ochre mines'* was agreed at £80 per annum, paid in 1813 and 1814. This does not appear to have been paid in 1815, but a royalty was paid and this continued annually, but was down to under two tons (royalty 18s. 10d.) for 1824. Clearly the bulk of the deposit had been worked out by 1824 at the latest.

Although the initial account was with two partners – Wheeldon and Webster – they split up and from 1811 the account was in the name of Paul Webster only. They had a colour works in Derby and the deposit was a clay seam six inches thick between the limestone and the surface cover. A clay and colour mine and adjacent white ore mine (lead carbonate) and also an *'Iron Mine'* existed at the top of Long Dale, north-east of Hartington in 1801 and in 1806 when it was sold. (8)

Webster's mine seems to have stopped work in 1824 as no records occur in the accounts for the following year. In 1827 a Mr. Tarrend was billed for 2 tons 11 cwt. of ochre *'got in Meadow Place Farm'* (north of Youlgreave) at 5s. 0d. per ton royalty. Five years later Thomas Gosling and James Chadwick were invoiced for royalty on 8 tons 8 cwt. 2 qtrs. of iron ore and ochre raised in the Wetton Estate, again at 5s. 0d. per ton. There were, however, no Hartington references up to 1832. The yield from the Hartington mines between 1809 – 24 amounted to a total of 383 tons 12 cwt with royalty/rent accruing to the estate amounting to £300.

The existence of a colour mill at Goytsclough (9) at GR 012733, near to the car park and picnic area, would seem to infer the existence of ochre in this area. However, although Farey (10) refers to Goytsclough Quarry, he makes no mention of ochre deposits near Buxton. Yet it does seem to have existed. In 1817, Edward Ford was paid for the carriage of ochre from Whaley Bridge to Buxton. Now this could have been from the canal wharf, but a year later, Messrs. Challinor were invoiced for 8 tons of ochre *'got near Buxton'* at the rate of £5 per ton and 6 tons at £4 per ton. It was transported in casks. In 1822, Williams and Benjamin Challinor were invoiced for 3 tons 8 cwt of yellow ochre *'got near Buxton'* but at 3s. 6d. per cwt (£7 per ton). A year later, Benjamin Challinor paid for 22 tons 4 cwt but at £1 per ton, indicating a poor quality consignment.

Where was the ochre obtained from? There is no indication of payments for it being mined on the estate's behalf. This suggests that it was being quarried and the estate did have a limestone quarry near Buxton, Grin Quarry. It seems likely that the deposit was located during local quarrying operations and sold to a local colour mill; but although the more obvious candidate, it is suggested that it was not Grin, but associated with the Peak Dale Quarry. The latter was being worked on lease by the Peak Forest Canal, with the first royalty payment for limestone extracted being 1819 -20. This would account for ochre at Whaley Bridge where the connecting Peak Forest Tramway reached the canal. The lease would exclude 'other minerals' etc. Moreover, although tenuous, the Devonshire Accounts clerk always referred specifically to Grin Quarry by name, but was vague about the location of the canal's quarry, in the same manner that the ochre was recorded as being 'got near Buxton'. The early date could mean the ore was found during development work, such as in the building of the tramway to the quarry from Bugsworth Basin on the Peak Forest Canal.

The sailing boats on the River Thames and rivers in Kent such as the River Medway, had red or yellow sails. This colour emanated from using red or yellow ochre as a dye. Surviving boats still continue this tradition, a tenuous link with colour dyeing before the advent of vegetable-based dyes, originally produced in Leek, North Staffordshire, by Thomas (later Sir Thomas) Wardle and Bernard Morris, his son-in-law, and brother of William Morris, the pre-Raphaelite, in the 19ᵗʰ century.

Duke's Red Marble

An enigma in the production of local ironstone has been the story of the Duke's Red Marble. It consists of a fine-grained, limestone, impregnated with haematite (iron ore). It is deep red in colour and is capable of being carved and to a good finish. What little is known about it states that it was found near Alport and what is left of it consists of a collection of pieces in the cellars of Chatsworth. References in the Chatsworth archives are very minimal, but the existence of the stone is undeniable. Samples of it survive in commemorative plaques and in a relative small number of carvings, let alone the remaining unworked pieces.

In 1830, a payment was made to Richard Browne for his expenses *'of getting a quantity of red marble at Newhaven by His Grace's desire, £50'*. In 1832, Charles Oldfield was paid *'for going to Bonsal and Newhaven concerning the Red Marble which had been pilfered, 10s. 0d.'* (11). Also in 1832 John Thompson and Co. were paid *'for searching for larger blocks of red marble near Newhaven and for cleaning out the shafts and securing the mines from plunder, £4. 5s. 0d.'* A year later, there was a further payment to Richard Browne *'concerning the Red Marble got at Newhaven £3. 3s. 0d.'* (12).

The mine was clearly at Newhaven, not Alport, which may have been a deliberate

Packhorse/turnpike road used to carry chert from Ashford to Longnor and on into Staffordshire

distraction to put people off the scent. There was clearly some interest in the deposit from the 6th Duke, which must have a bearing on the fact that the discovery of a good sized chunk of the stone was taken to Chatsworth itself for security. It would have been of some satisfaction to the Duke with his interest in statuary.

So where was it found? No record of this exists, but the quotations above include the reference to a shaft and it was probably a mine yielding iron ore. Such a mine existed south of Newhaven according to Farey, but that is about as near as documentary evidence suggests.

Iron Ore

Much iron ore used by iron masters came from deposits associated with coal. Farey (ibid. pp. 212 and 218) states that Thatch Marsh Colliery had 'brasses' with the coal. Brasses are lumps of iron pyrites more popularly known as 'fool's gold'. In 1820, Edward Buckley was invoiced by the estate for 20 tons of 'brass lumps or pyrites from Thatch Marsh Colliery' at £1 per ton. This was repeated in 1822 for 20 tons and again in 1823 but this time for a smaller amount – 15 tons 14 cwt. This would have been a welcome addition to profits – £20 would not be far off the cost of paying a year's wage for a labourer. In 1824, the mine was taken over by Thomas Boothman and output details cease. Farey also recorded that polished haematite or 'bloodstone' was found north east of Newhaven.

Stone

Axe Edge Stone Quarry

In 1807 Zepharia, Richard and Isaac Brunt paid rent for a stone quarry on 'Ax Edge' for the year ending 1st May 1807. The amount was £3. From 1814, the amount was three guineas and they continued to pay this until at least 1824. A quarry exists at the top end of Black Clough (GR023694) which may well be the quarry referred to. There is a large quarry to the north-west, Danebower Quarry, but rentals for this have not been seen in the

Chatsworth Accounts. However, the Black Clough Quarry abuts now infilled shafts of Black Clough Colliery, which was yielding coal in 1806 – 1809 and was on Devonshire soil, if not in Derbyshire following the boundary arbitration determined as part of the Hartington Inclosure.

A Slate Delf

William Gould's diary records that he received on 28th July 1785, an application by William Billinge for a slate delf in the lordship of Hartington for two of his nephews. No further detail on this is known. A delf is a quarry and the 'slate' would be thin layers of quality gritstone for roofing. Farey refers to a saw mill for cutting stone at 'Goytes Clough' but this may be a different concern as it produced flagstones or paviers (for pavements) and may not have been on Devonshire land (13). One wonders if the three Brunts of Axe Edge Quarry (see above) were William Billinge's nephews.

Bricks & Clay

Large deposits of clay and sand have been worked at Newhaven for over two centuries. It occurs in pockets in the limestone and the Friden brickworks is the descendent of a brickworks opened nearby by the Duke for the Ecton Mine in 1786. It had one kiln and made both silica bricks (from the sand) and clay to produce both common and furnace bricks. Prior to 1786, Newhaven clay works sent unburnt bricks formed from clay to be burnt at the mine. Coal for the Newhaven kiln came from the Duke's coal mines at Hazles Cross, Kingsley and Foxt Wood Colliery, both in close proximity to Whiston smelter. The volumes despatched are not clear as they are recorded either by weight or by quantity of bricks, but they are significant. One of the earliest references to sand production is in 1758 when the estate paid for it to be sent to Chatsworth. (14). Pipe clay was also found valuable for clay pipe manufacture (15).

A further deposit of clay was found in 1796. Josiah Wedgwood and Byerley the famous potters of Etruria, Stoke-on-Trent, had taken a look at it and were (in October) waiting for the end of the harvest before stripping away the topsoil to determine the extent of it. The Newhaven area contains quite a few pockets (massive holes) in the limestone which are full of sand, clay etc.

Cornelius Flint was asked for his view on the deposit. Bearing in mind that he knew nothing about these pockets he considered that the deposit was probably a lum (or lumb). One existed in Ecton Mine and another in the Dale Mine adit level (drainage level) opposite Ecton in the Manifold Valley. There are a sort of fissure in the limestone, irregular in form, often full of clay and usually associated with mineral ore (lead at the Dale Mine, not certain at Ecton). The only thing he didn't know was how large it would be. The Newhaven pockets are much larger than a lum, but other than that, he was pretty close to the mark.

There was a clamour of interest in the discovery. A William Bourne of Belper appears to have been first out of the blocks (other than Wedgwood); then a John Coke of Brookhill Hall wrote to say that he had got some of the clay and had tried it at 'a porcelain manufactory which we are erecting at Pinxton'. This was on the Cromford Canal and he was enquiring if they could buy a quantity of the clay.

A further letter came from a B. Chisney of Liverpool. He claimed that he supplied 'about one-third of all the fine clays consumed by potters and others in the Kingdom'. He had tried to call on Cornelius Flint, but found him not at home and clearly had got his hands on some of the clay, stating that it appeared of fine quality than any so far discovered. Seeking to distribute it, he claimed that Devon clay delivered in Staffordshire fetched 34s. 0d. (£1. 70p.) per ton; Dorset clay, 41s. 0d. (£2. 05p) per ton. If the Newhaven clay proved acceptable for potters' use, it could fetch 50s. 0d. (£2. 50p.) to 60s. 0d. (£3) per ton. The expenses of getting the clay would not exceed 8s. 0d. (40p.) per ton; land carriage to the canal 17s. 0d. and canal freight 5s. 0d. per ton, totalling 30s. 0d. (£1. 50p.).

Farey noted that pipe clay existed at Newhaven. Whether this was for tobacco pipes or drainage wasn't made clear, or whether even this was the same deposit. The outcome of all this is not clear, but no revenue has been noted in the accounts. In 1808, the Inclosure Award recorded three clay pits on Great Low; at Carderlow (north of Hartington village); and at Phillimoor Edge (north-east of Hartington railway station). (16). Farey also noted that clay for mere-making was obtained from 1/4 mile north of Hurdlow and a brick kiln existed one mile south southeast of Newhaven.

Coincidentally, one of Wedgwood's potters was staying in Buxton when a further clay deposit was found in late 1812. A small quantity was shown to him and he requested that half a hundred weight (56lbs) of it be sent to their works. It was found to be 'very good clay but contained too much iron pyrites to be very valuable'. (17)

Copper

Despite the huge copper ore deposit just out of Hartington village, there was very little of it found within the parish. Other copper deposits were found, but virtually all of them are in North Staffordshire, as is the Ecton deposit. However, John Gilbert-Cooper, who took a lease from the Duke for the Ecton Mine in 1739 (for 21 years) did the same for mines in part of Hartington Common from Michaelmas 1739. The term and the royalty were as at Ecton, 21 years and one-ninth royalty. This speculation does not appear to have been successful and no revenue seems to have accrued to the estate. (18). In 1837 a small parcel of copper ore was sent to the Whiston smelter from Carder Lowe Mine, north of Hartington, but the value was under £6 (Whiston accounts, author's collection). At Halfpenny Hole Mine (see also above under Lead), copper was found in 1741-42. (19)

Barytes

A significant amount of barytes has been mined south west of Buxton around Grin Hill, especially in the period 1835-77. During this period, over 39,000 tons of it was produced, yielding a royalty to the Devonshire estate. In 1862, this amounted to 27% of the UK production. (20).

The Appointment of John Taylor

In 1818, John Taylor was appointed the Duke's Mineral Agent as part of a restructuring after the retirement of John Heaton. Norwich born, he had cut his teeth in the south-west and had been agent for Lord Grosvenor at his lead mines around Halkyn Mountain, south-west of Chester, being appointed in 1813. His success had not gone unnoticed in Derbyshire. Taylor restructured the management of the Duke's mines at Grassington in the Yorkshire Dales and replaced the Ecton manager, George Cantrell, because of a perceived 'want of science'.

However, this has since been questioned. Taylor did prefer to put his own people in places of management and a Captain Goldsworthy moved to Ecton from Cornwall. None-the-less, Ecton was to close in 1825. Thereafter a series of speculators tried their hand and lost their investment through until 1890, when the mines finally fell silent. (21).

Although Taylor's other activities are not specifically recorded, a few dates give an indication of what he was up to. In 1818, the Whiston works was put up for sale, copper ore, thereafter being smelted in Swansea, the world's main copper smelting centre at that time. Grin Quarry and its like kilns were rented out from 1818 and the Axe Edge Collieries from 1824. (22) The Peak Forest Canal Company took on limestone extraction at Peak Dale on royalty from 1819 (work may have commenced in 1818). The Heaton years of direct management were clearly drawing to a close.

References

1 Dev. Coll., AS/474

2 Dev. Coll., Barmasters Coll., Brassington Liberty Entries, Book 24

3 Rieuwerts, J.H., *Lead Mining in Derbyshire; History, Development and Drainage*, Vol. 2., 2008, p 126

4 Rieuwerts, ibid, p.125

5 Dev. Coll., AS/619, 1725 – 1744

6 Farey, J., *General View of the Agriculture & Minerals of Derbyshire*, 1811, p 265

7 Dev. Coll., T-Series, Buxton and Hartington Accounts, Box 1 – 7

8 Rieuwerts, ibid, p125

9 Harris, M., *Industrial Archaeology of the Peak District,* 1971, p 100

10 Farey, ibid, pp 402-3 and 425

11 Dev. Coll., Chatsworth Accounts, 1830, 1832

12 Dev. Coll., T-Series, Buxton and Hartington Accounts, 1832 and Chatsworth Accounts, 1833

13 Farey, ibid, ironstone: pp 212, 218; bloodstone: pp

402-3; slate depth: pp 423, 429

14 Dev. Coll., AS/1062, Item 13

15 Farey, J., *View of the Agriculture of Derbyshire* 1811, p, 448

16 Dev. Coll., L/11/20; Hartington Inclosure Award box; Josiah Wedgwood's pottery was styled Wedgwood, Sons & Byerley from 1790 – 1793, when two of Wedgwood's three sons left the business. Despite Josiah's death in 1795, the business was styled Wedgwood, Son & Byerley from 1793 to 1810, when William Byerley died; Farey, ibid, pp 453, 455

17 Dev. Coll., P Heacock's Letter Book 1812

18 Dev. Coll., H/25/4/1

19 Rieuwerts, J. *H.* ibid, p 129

20 Heathcote, C., *PDMHS Bull.*, The Barytes mines at Grin Hill [etc] near Buxton, Derbys, 1835-77, Vol. 17, pp 1-9

21 Porter, L., and Robey, J.A., 2000, ibid, pp 72, 74

22 Burt, R., *John Taylor, Mining Entrepreneur and Engineer 1779-1863,* 1977, pp 25-26

9. TRAVEL THROUGH THE MANOR

Road Conditions and Road Users

Like the unfortunate Ellen Hyne, lost on the Drystones of Axe Edge in 1571, (see below), there is a local tradition that a jaggerman and his packhorses were *'cast away'* (as old writers put it) in the area of Hurdlow – Pikehall, during a snowstorm, which probably also accounted for Ellen Hyne's death. The condition of the roads and tracks (and the weather) was clearly more tasking at times in the past. Indeed, it is claimed that many villages were often cut off in winter due to the parlous state of the nation's roads caused by mud and water (1).

In support of this is a reference to the track used to take pigs (castings) of iron to Consall Forge in the Churnet Valley, south-west of Ipstones and a dozen or so miles south-west of Hartington. Here the packhorses were often in mud and dirt which nearly reached up to their bellies; of no direct relevance to Hartington manor, it does help to focus one's mind on difficulties and dangers of travel which may now be difficult to comprehend. (2)

Even on roads one would think would be in reasonable repair, the risk of an accident was still there. On 12th August 1784 the Duchess of Devonshire wrote that *'our wagon, with two fine pier glasses and all my cloaths (sic) was overturned in Chatsworth Park. I don't know what damage was done to the goods – one maid had her arm broken and ye others head is much hurt.'* William Gould, the Hartington Rental Collector was then also managing Chatsworth and his diary records this event. The two pier glasses were valued at about £500 and broken in pieces. He also wrote that the owner of the wagon, Bright, was unable to pay for the damage. Gould made no mention about the damage to the staff (3).

Mention has been made above to the Great Drovers' Road coming through Hartington and the Duke's estate buying Scottish cattle and oxen plus both Scottish and Welsh cloth. It was common for animals to be driven long distances and there are examples of this on the estate to which attention has been drawn. It was also usual locally to see animals on the move. Hey states that *'herds of cattle and flocks of sheep that travelled much shorter distances than Scottish or Welsh drovers were a common sight on the highways leading to and from local markets and fairs'*, referring to the mid-late 18th century. Not only were people selling and buying for their personal needs but also making a living out of it. Even in the early 17th century, a Warwickshire drover travelled 45 miles to Ashbourne to buy cattle which he sold on in West Bromwich. (4).

So the reference above to Dowel Farm buying cattle in Barnsley in the 1680s fits a common practice at that time. The Great Drovers' Road would have seen animals being driven to Bakewell and Matlock markets. No doubt other packhorse roads were used similarly, such as the roads crossing the River Dove into Derbyshire at Pilsbury and Crowdecote. The saltway through Buxton and the Leek – Ashbourne road would no doubt be similar. In 1609 butter and cheese bought at Ashbourne market was sold on at Sheffield market (5).

The Great Drovers' Road also became difficult to traverse because of soft ground and mud where it rises from Upper Hulme towards the former Mermaid Inn, on Morridge west of Hartington. It was so bad that at the beginning of the 18th century, local inhabitants made a stone causeway and *'several carriers contributed towards it … to prevent their cattle and goods being damaged for the sake of having a tolerable road'*. It was claimed that over 100 packhorses loaded with salt came up this causeway each week to the Mermaid Inn (then Blakemore House Inn – where there is a traditional story of the mermaid living nearby in Blakemere, now called Mermaid's Pool). Although some of these salt-laden packhorses would have diverted to Pilsbury, heading for Bakewell and beyond, other would have continued on to Hartington (6).

The Hartington route went to the north of Warslow and then down towards Hulme End north of the current B5054. In places the route runs in a deep holloway. Having reached Hayesgate Lane (the lane running north-west from Hulme End station), it turned right to cross Archford Bridge which existed close to the later railway station. This bridge was replaced by the turnpike road bridge by the village inn which is still in use. The deep holloway is testimony to soft ground being eroded away by many packhorses in very muddy conditions.

Improvements in the roads saw turnpikes becoming highways for faster and more comfortable travel. In the latter half of the 18th century, a *'flying machine'* from Manchester, heading for London via Derby, came down the Buxton – Ashbourne road, reaching its destination in 3 days. Whether it stopped at Newhaven House is not clear. By 1776, T. & M. Pickford had *'fly waggons'* which provided a service from Manchester to London in just over four days, averaging 42 miles a day. This presumably used the established route via Buxton and Ashbourne through Hartington manor. By 1803, Pickfords had expanded their service to running 6 days a week and had 400 horses to haul their wagons. John Heaton must have had his eye on some of this trade when he rebuilt the Bulls Head Inn at Biggin, near Newhaven (see Ch. 4) (7).

Pottery manufacturers in Stoke-on-Trent became shareholders in the turnpike road from Newcastle and Leek to Bakewell. These included Josiah Wedgwood. The exploitation of chert-beds of silica in the limestone – saw a lot of it used in the grinding of flint as a replacement for bone in bone china. The chert was mined at Ashford-in-the Water north of Bakewell. It would have been a tortuous journey via Longnor with heavily laden packhorses having to descend to the River Dove at Crowdecote before climbing out of the valley to reach Longnor. There were two more climbs before the descent to Leek (or just one (but much longer) if the packhorse route by Shiningford to the Mermaid Inn was taken).

These packhorses returned with a back-carriage of pottery in crates. One carrier, a John Hayne of Hardings Booth, Longnor, carried hundreds of tons of chert from the Great Longstone area (north of Bakewell) through Hartington manor on the Bakewell – Longnor road en route to the Potteries, but chiefly to the flint mill at Cheddleton. This may well have also included the two flint mills at Consall Forge near Cheddleton, the surviving mill, and another (demolished to make way for the Churnet Valley Railway in c. 1846) just below it. (8). The pottery would appear to be bound for Sheffield and records survive to show that local carriers (including Thomas, James and John Gregory) had a business in the late 18th – early 19th centuries moving goods such as the chert as well as many other products from Longnor to Great Longstone, which were then taken on to Sheffield and Chesterfield.

This was only a small part of their activity one supposes for the entries are over the period 1789-98. In 1796 they carried 3 tons 12 cwt of cheese for instance from Longnor to *'Longstone'* and 3 tons 9 cwt in 1797. Other items included packs of wool (a pack being 2 cwt (1 cwt per pannier) at 6d. (2$^1/_2$p.) per cwt (hundredweight), 'flitches' of bacon, oats and even shoes. In 1795, they carried a box of 'snoff' (snuff) from Longstone to Longnor which had an address in Cheadle (? Staffordshire or Cheshire).

As back-carriage, they returned through Hartington parish with a variety of products including brandy, flax (for linen manufacture), sugar, malt and beans, plus 10 barrels of porter to *'Longston'* for Isaac Wheeldon (in 1797). Was this the Buxton innkeeper mentioned in

Newhaven House Inn, extended in c. 1792-93 with good accommodation to take advantage of the turnpike trade where three trust roads met. Photo: the late S Penny, taken in the 1980s

Chapter .3? An interesting item occurring in 1797 was three shipments of yarn amounting 9 cwt collected from 'Crowdey Coate' (Crowdecote) and taken on behalf of William Rogers to Longston en route to Sheffield. Was this made locally? Was it cottage produce or was it from the textile mill at Glutton, just north of Longnor or maybe the wool fulling mill at Ludwell between Crowdecote and Hartington? One wonders! Similarly, the wool could have come from the manor farms nearby.

Dodd and Dodd quote an unnamed 18th century traveller from Buxton to Matlock who saw *'a vast number of packhorses travelling, of which we counted sixty in a drove; their chief loading is wool and malt, which they carry from Nottingham and Derby to Manchester'*. (9). A little to the east of Hartington, is Alport, below Youlgreave on the River Bradford. A complaint was made in 1718 at the Derbyshire Sessions on the urgent need for a bridge here:

'Great gangs of London carriers as well as drifts of malt-horses and other carriers and passengers goe this ancient waye, which lies in a hollow frequently over-flowed by the swollen stream. Heavy rains have so scoured out the channel as to render the ford impossible for as long as 8 or 10 days, whilst at all times carriers with loaden horses and passengers cannot pass the saide road without great danger of being cast away.' (10).

Celia Fiennes rode from Haddon Hall to Buxton c. 1697. She said of the journey *'Its very difficult to find wayes here for you see only tops of hills and so many roads by reason of the best wayes up and down that's it impossible for coach or wagon to pass some of them.'* It took her six hours to complete the journey of nine miles. And we think we have problems on the road. She was referring to the deeply rutted roadway. We tend to think of a road having a defined width which came as a result of a compacted stone/hardcore carriageway capable of withstanding the weight of the transport using it and Inclosure fencing confining the roadway's width. In Celia's day, if a road became rutted it was usually with several lots of ruts churning up the soft ground over quite a width of ground. However, there were some improvements. Defoe states that by the 1720s he could find no timber bridge in the north of England. *'Even the*

Above: Newhaven Mere built in 1792. **Below:** Cardlemere Lane looking towards the A515

parish authorities now built their packhorse bridges of stone'.

With the only large river in the parish being the River Dove, plus the headwaters of the Rivers Dane and Goyt, there have been not many packhorse bridges in Hartington parish. They may still be seen at Washgate and Hoppin on the upper reaches of the Dove; Panniers Pool Bridge at Three Shires Head on the upper Dane; and Goytsbridge (rebuilt upstream when the Erwood Reservoir was constructed, drowning the hamlet of Goyts Bridge). Another bridge there remains inundated. Beggars Bridge on the old way from Longnor to Earls Sterndale no longer exists. It may have been a wooden bridge which rotted away or was destroyed in a flood. There remain several single stone bridges on the streams draining Axe Edge, including some on the infant River Dove above Glutton Bridge (the latter being built as a minor turnpike bridge).

A popular horse for packmen was the sure-footed Galloway pony. Panniers Pool Bridge at Three Shires Head is marked on an old map as Galleywood Bridge, a derivative of Galloway, often reduced to Galley. It is on the western extremity of Hartington Upper Quarter. In 1824 it was advertised on a poster that the Ipstones races included a race for Galloway ponies, so they must have still been popular after the demise of the packhorse era. Ipstones is south-west of Hartington, in North Staffordshire. The Ecton Mine used mules rather than horses. These took the copper ore and perhaps cake copper from the ore roasted at the mine to Whiston smelter, owned by the Duke. A trans-shipment depot was built on Grindon Moor two miles or so south-west of the mine. From here the mules ran ore trains to the smelter. It was six miles to the latter, where a back-carriage of coal was picked up. The smelter closed in 1818.

The sixty packhorses (tied nose to tail) mentioned above would have been a common sight in the manor as jaggermen moved large loads, sixty horses being able to carry up to six tons. However it was not necessarily just the load in transit which might have been carried. The horses would need food (bran) and water and the former would either have to be carried or purchased en route. A large village pond used by animals would be needed to enable them to drink together. Hartington's domestic supply came (prior to the installation of the pump and well) from 'The Stanner' at the top of Factory Lane. Here the fresh water from the culverted River Harding was available, with a separate meer for animals. In Monyash, to the north-west, four meres supplied the whole of the village.

At night-time both packmen and drovers sought a dedicated area where they could stop for the night, away from prying eyes, nimble fingers and annoying dogs. Land where cattle could chew the cud; paddocks where horses and their packs or sheep, pigs and ducks, could be kept together; an adjacent spot for the packman and his dog to keep out of overnight rain or wind was always beneficial too, although one suspects not necessarily available. The area of Cote Heath (see below) at Buxton on manor land was a good example of this, beyond the area of the village common field.

Village by-passes kept the drove animals together, away from dogs and the opportunity for inquisitive animals to try and wander off. Mention of the Great Drovers' Road (above) by-passing Warslow is a case in point. Inns catered for travellers and packmen alike. The Packhorse Inn at Crowdecote readily springs to mind. The Longnor – Monyash road forded the River Dove below the current turnpike bridge, affording the opportunity for animals to drink. Just beyond the ford, the inn had ale and food for the packmen (or jaggermen). The inn was originally next door to the current inn but both buildings had the advantage of a large area at the front where the train of packhorses would wait and rest.

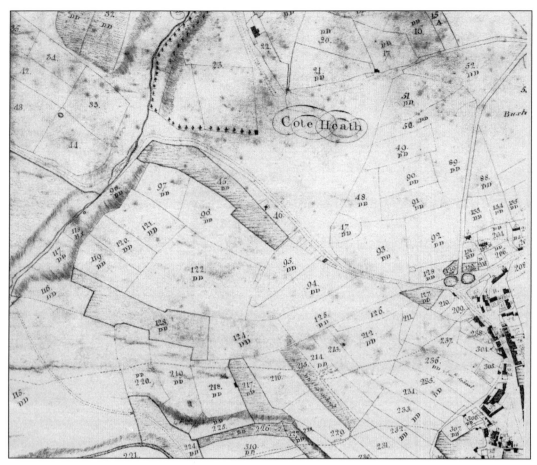

Cote Heath, Buxton. Great Salters Close was fields 96-97. Notice the two meers at the end of Green lane. Cote Heath would have provided a place to stay for drovers and packhorse teams. Salters Close probably giving an inclosed area for animals overnight etc. The street at the bottom right is High Street

Inns provided another function too. They acted as trans-shipment places. Some villages, e.g. Longnor, had the equivalent of a collection depot, where loads could be left for another packman to collect. This enabled pack trains to return home in the one day (or so). Elsewhere inns fulfilled this activity. Sieves from Abney (near Hathersage) for Ecton Mine were left at The Cock Inn, Longnor in 1785. In 1780, a John Barton (address unknown) made *'six dozen spaides'*, which were *'to be left at Thos. Besick's at The Cock'* in Longnor.

A year earlier the mine accounts record that a bill for *'sives'* from James Hodgkinson of Hathersage shows that they were left at the Red Lion in Tideswell for collection by the mine and the money was probably left at *'Thomas Armes at Tadenton'* (Taddington). Again in 1780, steel and twelve *'miner's spaides made strong'* were left by George Critchlow of Pethills Forge near Winkhill (on the Leek – Ashbourne road) at *'Botham House'*. Here was an inn where the above road was crossed by the Froghall – Warslow road. No doubt one of the carriers bound for the mine would pick up the items and take them on to the mine. The pub, The Green Man, is still there.

Other examples of trans-shipment places used by the mine were Longstone for 27 tons of

The boundary stone between Upper and Middle Quarters fronting the A515 at the junction with Blinder Lane, Pomeroy

iron plates and bars (? for the Whiston smelter) from Barnes & Co. of the Chesterfield Foundry in 1779. A few years later, nearly two tons of chains, to lower horses down the main shaft to the 34 fathoms level, were made (? At Foolow near Eyam) and delivered to Middleton, presumably Stoney Middleton. (11).

One can imagine similar activities happening in Hartington and Buxton. Even mail was left at a pub. Boulton and Watt sent plans for the Ecton steam engine to the Blackamore's Head in St. John's Street, Ashbourne in 1788 to await collection, for instance. It seems a mystery how addressees got to know that the mail was waiting for them. In 1757, Godfrey Heathcote, the Duke's attorney and agent, noted that a letter to him addressed to The George Inn in Derby was actually left at The King's Head *and it was by chance that I heard of it*! (12).

Mail coaches for the distribution of mail were introduced by John Palmer at Bristol on 2nd August 1784 and spread across the nation the following year, quickly becoming widespread and with several competitors on some routes. From 1810 – 20, the Ashbourne to Buxton road was used by four stage coaches:

Lord Nelson	(Liverpool – London)
Cornwallis	(Buxton – London)
Royal Telegraph	(Manchester – London)
Dart	(Manchester – London)

In the 1820s none of these were still running, except for the Lord Nelson (but moved to run via Bakewell, not Ashbourne). By comparison, in the 1820s, coaches were running on the Derby – Manchester route, but via Ashbourne and Leek. (13)

Another reminder of packhorse days are the few remaining packhorse inns. One is in Hartington Middle Quarter at Crowdecote, built in 1809. Another is at Little Longstone and there used to be one at Chapel-en-le-Frith. Lines of troughs for the horses remain at Wildboarclough (near Clough Hall), and at Eyam. The plague of 1656 reached this village in a bundle of cloth brought from London. A further row of troughs existed adjacent to the Mermaid Inn on Morridge on the Great Drovers' Road, west of Hartington. On the latter's limestone plateau, watertight ponds (meres) rather than horse troughs predominated and many may still be seen. One of the finest is at Newhaven at the side of the A515, opposite Newhaven House. It was built in 1792. It is in a desperate need of being cleared out, but is intact.

Although the packhorse was eclipsed by the one-ton cart or a four-wheeled wagon, it was reported in 1789 that although lime was carried great distances it was on roads, *'some of which are scarcely passable with wheeled carriages'*. (14). Even as late as 1827, the 4th Duke of Newcastle confided to his diary that on his way from a shoot on his estate at Martin, near Bawtry in Yorkshire, to his home at Clumber Park in Nottinghamshire, the post boys (i.e. the drivers of the coaches being hired for the journey) walked a quarter of the distance, *'the roads were bad.'* (15).

Additional to the state of the roads prior to the turnpike era and on minor roads thereafter, was the danger of getting lost in bad weather, especially in snow. The early parish records of Alstonfield (the parish adjoining Hartington parish on its west side) record deaths on the trackways and burials as a result:

4/3/1500 Ellen Hyne, wid., being perished in the dryestones, neire unto the marestone, upon Sonday, being the xxiiij (24th) of Febr above said

19/1/1589 John Balle, of the Fernie Ford, robbed and slayne in the nighte with theives

28/12/1591 Mary Docksaye, perished at Stanssopp

21/12/1621 Geo. Needham, perished at Lady Edge

23/2/1623 Benedict Hanthorne, perished

27/12/1658 Widowe Baylie, a poore woman of Sheen, coming from Lee Hall on Christmas Day in the forenoon was drowned in Dove in the foard at the Load End; shee ryding behind her daughter, the watter being verie bigge, her head sweed and fell backward in the watter and was carried down neare to the Milne before she was taken out.

10/3/1664 Ann W. of Thos. Hill, who was smothered in a snowy day on Calton Moor (16)

John Ball may have been killed in his bed but could have been on the road. Ellen Hyne died on the path over Axe Edge, The Drystones being an escarpment on a path east of Three Shires Head. North of The Drystones is a large rock used as a waymark called the Great Stone. It is believed that the 'marestone' is this outcrop. Widow Baylie tried to ford the River Dove at what is now Lode Mill and her body was carried down river to the mill pool at Mill Dale Mill. Stanssopp is Stanshope, south-west of Alstonfield village; Fernie Ford and Lady Edge are south-west of Newtown and Longnor (about a mile apart) and Calton Moor is crossed by the Leek – Ashbourne road north-west of Swinscoe.

It was easy to find yourself in worsening conditions, white-outs and deepening snow. In January 1809, Philip Heacock (the Duke's Buxton agent), wanted to get to Bakewell for a hearing over Youlgrave Inclosure. He rode his horse from Buxton to the Duke of York Inn at The Street (now called Pomeroy). It could surely only be because of snow that he then walked from there to Bakewell and returned in the evening. He described it as being *'a most fatiguing (sic) and unpleasant journey I never experienced'*. As we have seen above, for some people it was a journey they never did experience again. Fortunately we do not seem to have a week of continually falling snow and other extremes of weather that endangered life on the highway, although we had a taste of it in November/December 2010 and February 2012. (17).

The Hartington Coal Road

An interesting question arises in the small print of the Inclosure Award. It makes it clear that the Hartington coal road took a different route pre-Inclosure, which at least in part was abandoned following rerouting. The route of this does not appear to be recorded in surviving documents. However evidence on the ground shows holloways leaving the Thatchmarsh Colliery and dropping down from the Axe Edge ridge at right angles to the Leek – Buxton Road. The current road to Harley Cross Gate via Brand Side is the revised route of the

Above: The Great Stone or King Stone on Drystone Edge, Axe Edge, on an ancient pathway. Ellen Hyne perished near here in a snowstorm on 23 February 1571

Right: One of the stones at Five Stones north of Drystone Edge, Axe Edge, marked with a Q (Quarnford) and H (Hartington) **Below:** Five Stones

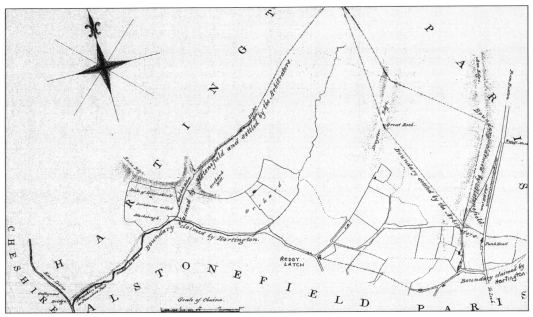

A plan attached to the Hartington Inclosure Award of 1808, showing the claims of Alstonfield and Hartington. The former had previously also been claimed by Quarnford, as the 'Q' and 'H' on the Five Stones reminds us. These are situated north east of the Great Stone, or 'Rock', as described on the plan. Note Galleywood Bridge (bottom left), now Panniers Pool Bridge. Reproduced with permission of the Trustees of the Chatsworth Settlement

former coal road. From Harley Cross Gate, the road runs almost due south past Harley Farm to Earl Sterndale, High Wheeldon and on to Vincent House at the top of Long Dale. The former coal road would have gone down Long Dale, but the new route took a more direct route from the top of that dale heading for Madge Dale. This is the dip in the road just prior to the descent down Hide Lane into the village. One wonders if the old road took a more direct route to Earl Sterndale.

Although from its name, it would appear that Hartington was served with coal from Axe Edge, the brick kiln at Newhaven brickworks used coal from Kingsley (Hazles Cross Colliery) near Froghall, brought via the Whiston smelter. The reason for this is John Heaton's policy of running the Ecton Mine and its associated works (especially the smelters at Ecton and Whiston) with coal from the estate's own mine. The Axe Edge mines were leased in 1780 when the decision to buy the Kingsley mine was taken, with some 10,000 tons being raised annually. A regular brick supply was essential to the smelters, so was coal; your own mine kept supplies moving and costs under control, that was the Heaton philosophy.

Roads Around Buxton

A plan of 1775, drawn by W. Barker (18), together with rental details and acreages related to the map's field numbers is useful in giving much detail on the roads around Buxton at that time. The road coming north from east of Hartington via Earl Sterndale and Harley Cross came through what is now Hill Head Quarry and up the current road to Harpur Hill. To the east, the turnpike road had existed from the 1740s (now the A515).

The way to Buxton from Harpur Hill continued westwards past the current turning to the industrial estate, descending down into the valley beyond. The route then went north on what is now a public footpath via Fern House, east of Grin Low. Today this path reaches Ashbourne road to the south of its former junction. This was where the current London Road reaches the traffic lights (although Dale Road the current route eastwards to Ashford Dale did not then exist). London Road did exist, going out of Buxton to reach King Street, the former Roaman Road to Derby. The road from Harpur Hill (now Green Road) had a mere either side of it at the junction. The road to Macclesfield (now West Road) also existed and from the junction a lane went up and into the current Market Place (High Street) (there was no market in 1775).

The current London Road/Ashbourne Road was the turnpike road but the road must be much older. It cut across a large open area which still existed in 1775, albeit also crossed by the way to Harpur Hill. Called Cote Heath on the plan, it was the area where drovers and jaggermen presumably kept their animals overnight. Even in 1775, a couple of the fields on the east side of the road still carried the name Great Salters Close. No doubt this area was where the packmen rested for the night. By then that area was largely inclosed. It is only as a result of this research work that this latest salters' place name has come to light. Presumably the most direct route from Burbage (now Green Road) was used by the drovers and jaggermen with their packhorses and cargo, which clearly included salt.

Along Gadley Lane and much closer to Burbage, a road turned north to reach Otterhole Mill. This continued north and then went westwards to Goyts Bridge.

New Roads at the time of Inclosure

May of the current roads in Hartington parish were set out as a result of the Inclosure. A list of some of these is given in Appendix 3.

The Cromford and High Peak Railway

Another form of travel arrived in 1831 with the opening of the Cromford and High Peak Railway. It was horse-drawn with short, fish-bellied iron rails laid on stone blocks. It ws laid between Whaley Bridge and ran for over 33 miles/53 kms. to Cromford, linking the Peak Forest Canal with the Cromford Canal. From Cromford, it entered Hartington parish roughly east of Hartington and left it on the northern boundary of the parish in the Goyt Valley. Initially it carried passengers from 1833 but this trade terminated in 1877.

The line was built chiefly to carry limestone to the canal together with coal and water up onto the limestone plateau. A station (they were known as wharfs) at Friden adjacent to the brick works was built to carry common bricks (made from local deep red clay) and silica firebricks, made from sand dug from local deposits in the pockets in the limestone. Local iron ore from the Newhaven area was also carried and there is a report (seen by your author many years ago and not noted at the time) that at one time there was 2,000 tons of iron ore stacked at Friden Wharf. It this is true, this volume is not supported from any surviving records.

The Cromford and High Peak Railway was not the first tramway in the area, for the Peak Forest Tramway had opened in 1800, a 6½ mile/10kms length of horse-drawn track between Bugsworth and Peak Dale, north-east of Buxton. Huge tonnages were soon being transported from the quarry there (still open) to the canal (see p. 23). The Froghall Tramway to Cauldon Lowe was even earlier, having opened in 1779. It is in fact the second oldest line in the country to be opened under a legislative enactment (after the Bowes Railway).

Today, the Cromford and High Peak Railway retains track at Cromford Wharf in the High

Peak Wharf maintenance shed, which opened at least by the 1850s and maybe earlier. It is probably the oldest *in situ* railway track in the world. The tonnages capable of being moved by these early tramways must have created much awe and wonder at the time. (19)

The line was built with seven inclines, four at the northern end and three at the southern end. Subsequently it was found that later more powerful engines could get up the Hopton Incline towards the southern end, despite a maximum gradient of 1:14, the highest gradient on British Railways worked by an unassisted locomotive. Gotham Curve, (with a radius of 140 feet/36 m) became the tightest curve worked on British Rail, but there were other, more sharper bends, initially. Three of the worst, near Harpur Hill, were removed by 1875. The most northerly incline, Whaley Bridge, was used fooor trials of a centre rail locomotive, later used on the Mont Cenis Pass in 1864.

With the construction of the Ashbourne – Buxton line (fully opened on 4th August 1899) the northerly section of the line to Whaley Bridge from Ladmanlow (south-west of Buxton) was abandoned in 1892. A passenger service on the Buxton – Parsley Hay section was opened in 1894, extended to Ashbourne by 1900. Although much of the Ashbourne – Buxton line was lifted in the 1960s, the northern section remains open, serving the limestone quarries at Hindlow and Dowlow. Although initially horse-drawn, the Cromford and High Peak Railway started to introduce steam locomotives in 1833 but took some eight years to change completely to steam. Even then, with several inclines requiring steam-driven, cable-hauled power to get the trains up and down, it took a long time to travel along it. The problem was that the line rose 330 yards/300 m. from Cromford to the summit level and dropped 250 yards/226 m. to Whaley Bridge.

Today, one of the engines used for haulage on the inclines survives at Middleton Top, between Wirksworth and Cromford, having been withdrawn from service in June 1963. Middleton Top may well also boast the highest surviving chimney in the Peak District. Below it, at the side of the Cromford Canal at High Peak Wharf is the steam engine which pumped water up to the canal from the River Derwent. It is the largest surviving steam-driven plunger pump in the country, part of a huge beam engine, open for visitors and occasionally steamed. Its well worth going to see: it is massive (the beam weighing something like 50 tons alone) all moving quietly and effortlessly in a most impressive manner. It is steam power at its finest.

References

1 Watson, J.S., *Oxford History of England*, The Reign of George III 1760 – 1815, 1960, p 27

2 Chester, H., *Churnet Valley Iron*, 2002, p 58

3 Dev. Coll., 5th Duke's letters, No. 637, Duchess to Countess Spencer; Hanson, M., William Gould's Diary: 9th August 1784

4 Hey, D., *Packman, Carriers and Packhorse Roads*, 2001, 2nd edit., p 126

5 Hey, ibid., p130

6 Hey, ibid., p 110

7 Hey, ibid, pp 74, 156

8 *The Day to Day Accounts of Robert Thornhill*, 1740 – 1820

9 Dodd, A.E and E. M., *Peakland Roads and Trackways'* 2000, 2nd edit., p 119

10 Dodd & Dodd, ibid. p 118

11 Porter, L., *Ecton Mine under the Dukes of Devonshire, 1760 – 1790*; ibid., pp 42-3, 181-2

12 Dev. Coll., AS/1353

13. (*Derbyshire Miscellany*, Vol. V, Pt III, 1970, pp 172 – 73, 189

14 Pilkington, J., 1789, *View of the Present State of Derbyshire*, p 312

15 Fletcher, J., (edit), Where Truth Abides, *The Diaries of the 4th Duke of Newcastle-under-Lyme (1822 – 50)*, 15th Sept., 1827, p 70

16 Alstonfield Parish Registers. Transcript of extracts made available by Tim Eades of Hope Marsh, Alstonfield, to whom many thanks.

17 Dev. Coll., P. Heacock's Letter book, 1809, 29th January 1809

18 Dev. Coll. Map 2049, and AS/1106

19 Paget Tomlinson, E., *The Illustrated History of Canal and River Navigation*, 2000, pp 111, 163-4 and 192-4

APPENDIX 1

The Boundary of Hartington Parish

A written *preambulation* of the Lordship of Shoke [Soke] of Hartington made in 1654, *by oath of severall men as well as the Jury* survives. Well, at least a copy of it, dated 25th August 1774. (1) It is a long and largely unpunctuated description of the boundary, starting at Dove Head on Axe Edge viz:

… beginning at the head of the River of Dove in the middlest clough or Stroynd thereof streight over The Mos to the Shaley Sitch at the South end of Axedg and so to the Reddelach and so to the redle Pit rake and from thence to firestone brooke and so descending down the said brook to Panniers poole otherwise called the three Shires in the River of Dane…

Nellie Kirkham started to write on the boundary, but died before it was completed, although two papers were published. (2)

She considered that the brook course coming down from Cisterns Clough and Brandside was Dove Head, the middlest clough being Cisterns Clough, as the hill to the south of the clough is Middle Axe Edge Hill. She also states that at the Dove Head spring with the initials IW/CC (Izaak Walton, Charles Cotton) was fairly recent in 1905. It exists at the point marked Dove Head on modern OS maps, although now masked from the Leek–Buxton road by trees. She was partly right for the monogram on the capstone dates from 1852. – your author has a copper plate hand written description which confirms the date – but maps, old by that date, do mark this area as Dove Head. She also states, wrongly, that seventeenth century maps are too vague to be of evidence.

The middlest clough or stroynd is easy enough to determine. Stroynd (or Strynd) means watercourse and the current county boundary on the River Dove has a branch watercourse either side of it. One goes northwards to Roundknowl and one south to Gamballs Green. The county boundary therefore follows the middle watercourse. An untitled, and somewhat crude map marks the Moss and Shaley Sitch. Support for this map being accurate however is available.

A map accompanying the Hartington Inclosure Award shows the line of this boundary and it is endorsed Boundary claimed by Hartington. This latter map shows the boundaries claimed in a dispute between Hartington and Alstonfield and that settled by the arbitrator. (3)

Boundary disputes were quite common and there were several minor ones on the Hartington parish border. This one was possibly more important, for the area included the Black Clough Colliery, owned by the Duke. Any tithes due to the manor would be important if they had to be paid to Alstonfield. One old map of 1599 accompanying details of an early boundary dispute (4) marks the area of Black Clough Colliery as *coles gott here*. Black Clough is sometimes called Orchard Clough (incorrectly). Black Clough Farm sits on the next clough to the west on a parcel of land, formerly owned by the Duke and not part of the common, known confusingly as Black Clough. A clough is another word for dale or valley. There was a boundary dispute in this area in the early part of the 17th century and in 1674, Sir John Harpur successfully claimed part of the common, including part of Black Clough Mine. (5)

Based on the Enclosure Award map, shows details from the untitled map and the 1599 dispute map. Better than words, it shows the boundary from Dove Head to Panniers Pool, The bridge there was called Galleywood bridge on the 1808 Inclosure Award map. This map shows the area from Alstonfield's point of view. The area north east of Pannier's Pool is marked as being in Staffordshire and claimed by Hartington men. It also marks Three Shires Head further up river at G.R. 017702. The name Galleywood bridge reminds us that the packhorses were usually Galloway ponies.

The Three Meerstones, Gamon Green

In 1564, Sir John Savage bought a case against various people claiming that they had taken possession of his manor of Quarnford. The record of the case gives details of the boundary of Quarnford manor, parts of which had a common boundary with Hartington. (6) At the rear and to the north east of the Travellers Rest Inn at Flash Bar is a tall stone (G Ref 033679). It used to be one of three, known as the Three Meer Stones. They are marked on the 1599 map (see above) as being adjacent to two parcels of land known as Gamons Tenement and Gamons Close. The record of 1564 states that the Quarnford boundary went … *from thence to the three meerstones at Gamon Grenehed and so to the black stone in Axen from thence to the Fetstone in the Mosse and from the Fetstone following to the three sheres at the Danehed, and from thence descending after the water to the fall in Gratbach …*

This indicates that the boundary was recorded by the three meer stones and confirms their situation at Gamon Green Head (There is a farm nearby now called Gamballs Green). The three stones presumably recorded the meeting of the Quarnford manor, Hartington and Heathylee parishes. The 1599 map marks a boundary line going from the Three Meer Stones to the Great Stone on Drystone Edge. On this line above Dove Head was the Eliot Stone at approximately G.R. 030685, which appears to be gone. From the Great Stone, the boundary went in a straight line to the acute point in the current boundary at Cheeks Hill. The 1599 map marks here *The Set Stone on the Moss*. The *black stone* of 1564 must be The Great Stone and the *Fetstone* is an error of transcription (i.e. should be Set stone). Consequently, Hartington's boundary according to a Staffordshire interpretation was as above. The Hartington interpretation would be that from the Three Meer Stones, the boundary went towards Readylatch and Panniers Pool.

What was the purpose of the Eliot Stone? It is situated where the current county boundary meets the line between the Great Stone and the Three Meer Stones, conveniently half way between the two. As early as 1614, Heyward shows the boundary coming up the Dove to the position of the (unmarked) Eliot Stone. With a bit of fudging, he indicates that the manor extended across to Panniers Pool via Readylatch. He does, however, show a line going up to the Set Stone and back to Black Cough (i.e. similar to the current boundary). Clearly by 1614, Hartington manor believed that the boundary to Dove Head was the River Dove.

Yet in 1564, Sir John Savage believed his holding of Quarnford Manor ran to the position of the Eliot Stone from the Three Meer Stones (i.e. south of the River Dove), the area between presumably being in Hartington. Later, Hartington complicated matters by claiming that the boundary from the Dove to Panniers Pool cut across below the Head of the River Dove towards the west, and south of the Eliot Stone. The more that one looks into this, the more one realises that the promotion of the boundary on Alstonfield's (or Quarnford's) contention was not just something being pursued by parish officials.

The Alstonefield parish register of 4th March 1571 records the burial of Ellen Hyne: … *being perished in the drystones, neare unto the marestone uppon Sunday being the xxiii of Febr …* In this context marestone should read merestone, which means that it was referring to the Great Stone, reflecting that it was on the Drystones and also on the boundary, i.e., a merestone. This was not a parish official recording the event, but the vicar, in a record which would not generally be read (the parish register of Alstonfield, which was in latin). He knew that the boundary went from the Three Mere Stones via the Great Stone to the Set Stone on Cheeks Hill. The 1798 arbitration finally settled the boundary as it is today, running from the now missing Set Stone to the Great Stone and turning down to Dove Head at the Eliot Stone. The vicar of 1571 was largely vindicated.

From Panniers Pool to the Goyt and Buxton

From Panniers Pool, the boundary went north:

... and so up the said River [Dane] unto the hed thereof and so streight over the moss to the head of the river of Goyte and so desending down the same river to Dernall lume and so after assending up Dernall clough to Billing Clough end and so assending up Billing Clough to the hed thereof ...

With the help of Heyward's 1614 map of the parish, (7) the boundary is easy enough to pick up down to Errwood in the Goyt Valley. Here Kirkham gets hopelessly wrong. Her annotation of numbers accompanying a map with Part 1 of her article on the boundary holds the clue as to why. She believed that Billing Clough was Berry Clough, which is south east of Goytsclough quarry. Her map marks the boundary going up Berry Clough and then eastwards towards Buxton. It was pure guesswork, but she failed to say so.

Using the 1614 map (a huge one with a considerable and an impressive amount of accurate information) as a guide, Dernall Clough is the valley rising eastwards from just north of Errwood reservoir dam. Heyward marks some enclosures just south of Dernall Clough and these may be seen on current OS maps just south of Bunsall Cob (at the east end of the Errwood dam), despite the western side of the enclosures now being under water. On the 1808 Inclosure Award map, Dernall Clough was marked as Derney Clough through which flowed the river Derney.

Billing Clough was used by MacAdam for the original Buxton turnpike road from near Longhill Farm northwards to Rake End. His road south of the brook course, rising up towards the road between Errwood and Longhill Farm, (existing in 1808) would appear to be the old parish boundary. Reaching the top (*Billing Clough hed*) confirmation is to hand, for the description of 1654 continues:

... and then following the highway leading betwixt Macclesfield and Buxstone to the wine yats and so to Watford Low Bucke [Brook] and so doune the same bruck to Watford Lowe Lumb and so to the Milneford ...

The highway referred to is the old packhorse way/saltway from the top of Longhill down to Errwood and on over Pym Chair. It now diverts down the old Cromford and High Peak Railway incline and over the dam, as the former route via Goyts Bridge has been inundated. The boundary would then have gone down the watercourse to the east of Longhill Farm and Watford Farm, to the west of Nithen End, to where the brook meets another stream coming down from Burbage Edge. Otterhole mill was located with its mill ford approximately where the two streams meet. See the section on mills herein for details of the mill.

... and so from thence keeping the High way to Wye yate and so keeping the Street way through the Town of Buxton to How way and so as ending and following the said High Street to the greening dale hedd and so up a little ould ditch of old time made of gravell to the Birrisend on the South side of the Common Way and so to Mornedale head ...

From Otterhole Mill, the boundary went south to Leek Road (the road to Burbage). South of the road in 1614 was a field called Wye Head, believed to be the Wye Yate of the description above. The boundary went along the highway towards Buxton, then a small village. This highway existed in 1614. The village of Buxton existed just to the north of this road, along what is now High Street (not to be confused with the Roman Road called High Street). As indicated in Chapter 9, in 1775, there were two large meers (ponds) at the junction of the current Leek Road with High Street, and Dale, Green and London Roads (where the traffic lights now are by The London Road public house).

Here the boundary went along the line of the current road to Ashbourne, reaching the Roman road just beyond the Duke's Drive. Then it followed *'the said High Street'* (i.e. the Roman road) towards Friden. A 1775 map (8) shows the road from Harpur Hill reaching Buxton via the Fern House. Weston records that a reference to Feunhous exists, dated 1423. (9) As this road reached Harpur Hill, the area immediately to the south was How Tor in 1614 (now largely quarried away). It is likely that the way from the traffic lights at the northern end of London Road and then the footpath from Grid Ref 061725, going south to Fern House was *How way*.

South east of Brierlow Bar, the Roman road heads for Sterndale Moor, which is between Earls and Kings Sterndale villages. *Birrisend* is spelt incorrectly. It should be Bririsend, another spelling of Briery, the old name for Brierlow. It is on the south side of the road from Harpur Hill to Chelmoreton. John Ogilvy's map of 1675 marks this way as being *'to the cole pits'*, i.e. at Axe Edge. A valley runs south from Kings Sterndale (where the King was Lord of the Manor, it being part of his High Peak estate). This valley almost reaches the Roman road. At its northen end it is now Deep Dale and further south it is Horseshoe Dale. It is the only dale to come close to the road south of Brierlow Bar and must have been called Stern Dale in 1654, at the time of this boundary description; the upper end of it being Sterndale Head. Is Mornedale an incorrect spelling for Sterndale, the inscriber reading the St as an M? Brierlow Bar tollhouse survived close to where The Bookstore now stands until 9/1/1913 when the estate sold it to Derbyshire County Council for £50, on condition that it was demolished and the site added to the highway. A year later, Portabello Cottage (the former Axe Edge Toll House) was also sold by the estate and demolished.

…following the little ditch on the north side of the common way and so to the Horedlow thorn otherwayes called the Hosdlow cross and so following the said Street to Horedlow Dick (ditch)…

The common way will be the Roman road, as it is being followed first to Briery (Brierlow) and then on to Sterndale Head. The boundary being in the ditch on the side of the old road, firstly on the south side of it and then on the north side as the road runs to Hurdlow Thorn. Thorn trees were used as marker posts, probably because of their longevity. A road is marked on Heyward's map of 1614 going between Earls Sterndale and Chelmorton, crossing the high Street at Grid Ref 104684. However this is not near Hurdlow and probably not the site of the Thorn.

The next crossing would be on a road from Hurdlow to Monyash. It crosses the High Street very close to the Bull i' th' Thorn Inn. Is this pub name preserving the place name of Hurdlow Thorn, otherwise known as Hurdlow Cross, where the local road crossed the main highway? It is quite possible, for the crossing was also where the turnpike road crossed High Street and the Earls Sterndale-Monyash roads. In 1868, this inn was known as Hurdlow House and is marked as such on the map of the area in *The Buxton Guide*. As has been seen, the turnpike (now the A515) also follows a much more ancient roadway just a little way to the south of here. If so, this would have been a more important junction than is now appreciated and the need for the marker (the thorn bush) is apparent. Horedlow Dick (or ditch) could be where the current B 5055 (Longnor–Monyash) also crosses the High Street.

...and so following the said street to Mealand mere and so to Admonslow brink and so keeping the said street leaving Harber low on the northeast side of the white cross in Oldham head ...

Passing Arbor Low, *Oldham head* was reached, perhaps not too far from Upper Oldham Farm, heading towards Oldham lane, previously the better descriptive Middleton Way. Where the *white cross* was is not so certain. The Oldham lane crosses the A515 a few yards to the north of the Jug and Glass Inn, the former way from Hartington to Middleton-by-Youlgreave.

Having followed High Street (the Roman road) for a considerable distance, the boundary veered off left and away from the old highway at the end of the former Friden Grange holding. This was just below where the Friden–Youlgrave road crosses Friden Dale, half a mile or so from Friden brickworks. The boundary went down Long Dale before turning towards Pikehall viz:

... and so following the said Street [High Street] leaving barley Flatt on the south side to frydendale mouth and so down Fridendale bottom to moos Middle hill tonge leaveing the white low; Bootherstone hill; the Radle pits; Hazleshaw; and the whorelow; on the South side and so ascending up after Mouldrige grange wall to the High Street [at Pikehall] ...

From here, the boundary took the old road to Alsop Moor; it is called Marks Lane on Heyward's 1614 map viz:

... and so asceding up after Cardle heay dick like unto the midle thereof and so over the black heath to the hore edge and so over the 5 stones in Wirksworth gate ...

The Cardle Hay ditch was followed by what is now known as Back Lane for a distance, prior to the latter heading off left. The ditch may well be a line shown on Heyward's map running roughly to the west of Back Lane beyond where the latter was crossed by the Cromford and High Peak railway. Cardle Hay was a large parcel of the common pasture. Its northern boundary was High Street and it included Alek Low. The ditch probably marked the boundary of Cardle Hay, which had previously been part of Mouldridge Grange, a holding of Dunstable Priory.

This area was formerly limestone heath land, hence the name *black heath*, turned to grassland by liming it. Two small sections were not limed however. Alsop Moor Plantation adjacent to the A515 now has tree cover, but heather and bilberry still flourish at the northern end. The other area, the Heather Moor field is referred to below and this was unlimed until c. the 1950s. The upper part of the field is fenced off and remains as coarse grass and heather. Nearby in Biggin, an area of land near Greenhead was known as The Heath in 1758. (10)

The lane followed by the boundary (now Back Lane) crossed Cardlemeer Lane, which heads from Biggin towards Wirksworth. It is marked as Wirksworth Road on the Enclosure Award. It was a drovers road coming from Cheshire via The Mermaid Inn on Morridge and clearly had a marker of five stones where Back Lane crossed it. (11)

From the five stones, the boundary continued:

...and so descending down the banck leaving the white Cliff on the right hand and so following the little greenway leaving Shackersdale on the left hand to an old grove rake within the Lordship of Hartington and so over to Eaton dale mouth ...

Thus the boundary descended to the current Biggin Moor–Parwich road, passing the

Heather Moor field on the latter's west boundary, running almost the whole way from Cardlemeer Lane to the Biggin Moor–Parwich Road (Shackersdale), the little greenway. The *white Cliff* on the right hand is passed on the south side of Cardlemeer Lane. It is a small outcrop of limestone. It can be clearly seen from the Biggin Moor–Parwich road and is at G.R. 173581. Ask locally where the white cliff is and you will be told it is the quarry fronting the road on the Parwich side of White Cliff Farm. Clearly this is wrong.

Having followed the little greenway up onto Alsop Moor, the old lead mine rake is passed as the way continues adjacent to the Alsop Moor Plantation before joining the current A515 to descend to the bottom of the hill. This must be the area of Eaton Dale mouth, the dale falling gradually towards Parwich in a south easterly direction. Various roads would have met here. What is thought to be the Via de Peco (probably) came through here; the packhorse way from Alstonfield, which ascends Cold Eaton Dale and continues on to Pike Hall via the five stones crossed the latter and then there were the two roads to Buxton, i.e. via The Liffs and Liffs Cross. And roughly the road which was turnpiked and is now the A515.

… and so following an old Dick to the Liffs Cross and so following the said Ditch to Bigginbooth ditch …

This raises a query. It would seem expedient for the boundary to be on the line of the road passed Lees Barn to reach Liffs Cross. However the boundary could have followed the (?) Via de Peco route (now obliterated by the former railway) and then struck up the side of Johnsons Knoll on the current boundary to reach Liffs Cross.

Having reached Biggin Booth ditch (Biggin Booth was a large parcel of land marked on Heyward's map of 1614, with boundaries recognisable on modern OS maps), the boundary continued:

… and so downe after the said ditch to Eaton wall and so down Durdale and so following after Eaton mall to the River of Dove …

This is easily traceable, heading for the dry dale (Dur Dale), which runs into Biggin Dale just above its junction with Wolfscote Dale. It is also the parish boundary today. The River Dove was the boundary all the way back to Axe Edge, with the exception of The Nab. This was adjacent to Parkhouse Hill near Glutton and the parish boundary, plus the county boundary, left the river at this point, on its west side.

In 1744, payment was made to Mr Taylor (of Buxton Hall) *pr Bill for ye Jurymans charges etc at going ye Boundary of Hartington £9.6.0d.* (12) Here is an example of how the Hartington men were able to make their claim to the Axe Edge land north east of Panniers Pool. Handing down the detail orally and from literally travelling along the boundary from generation to generation was considered vital at that time.

New Boundary Stones

Another way of deliniating the boundary was to mark it with stone posts. In 1774, a new set of boundary stones were erected and the list survives (13).

'Greening Dale Head
Brerely End
Nether Lane End
The corner of the encroachment of Saml. Allens
Cardley Hay Ditch (later deleted)
Shakersdale Mouth
Grove rake above Shakersdale
Eaton Dale Mouth
At Liffs Cross
At the top of the Middle Clough above Dove Head wooden boundary at the Head of the River Dane and one at the highest point of the Moss betwixt and Moss House the stone at John Wards House to be removed to one of the two last mentioned places.'

As late as 1826, the estate paid for *'stone posts as Boundary markes on Elkstones Common 16s 0d'* (14).

References

1 Dev. Coll., AS/1400. This was written before DR J.H. Riewerts advised me that the 1654 perambulation would appear to be a copy of one of 1532 surviving in Dev. Coll., Bateman M.S. scrapbooks entitled *Devonshire Collection*

2 Kirkham, N., *The Perambulation of Hartington*

3 *Dev. Coll., Copy of the Hartington Inclosure Award*, 1808

4 Nat. Archive, MPC 274(1), *John Claye v William Gilbert*. A copy of this map and the untitled map are held by the Peak Park Planning Board, copies provided by John Barnatt

5 *Victoria County History, Staffordshire*, Vol VII, Leek and the Moorlands, 1996, p 52. The map of Quarnford on p 50 marks Black Clough in the wrong place

6 *Staffordshire. Hist. Coll.*, 1938

7 Dev. Coll., Map no 2062

8 Dev. Coll., Map no 2049, by G Barker. It shows the estate in Buxton, part of Hartington Upper Quarter and in Fairfield. The accompanying terrier to this map is filed under AS/1106. Importantly, it shows Buxton prior to the building of The Crescent

9 Weston, R., *Hartington a Landscape History from the earliest times to 1800*, 2000, p 124

10 Dev. Coll., Manor Court Records, 1758, p 221

11 Dodd AE and Dodd EM, *Peakland Roads and Trackways*, 2000, pp 63, 82-84. The Dodds record that the earliest date for Cardlemeer Lane is 1276

12 Dev. Coll., AS/1371

13 Dev. Coll., AS/1399, dated 27/8/1774

14 Dev. Coll., T-Series, Bundle 14

The White Cliff adjacent to the boundary of the parish (the third wall from the left) as it descends to Shackersdale

APPENDIX 2

Hartington and Buxton Capital Expenses 1773 – 1812

Date	Activity	Cost
1776	Robert Lomas for lands in Fairfield	360
1776	John Dickenson for lands in Hartington	300
1778	Messrs. Dickenson and others for Goits Moss Colliery, Moss House and lands	2350
1781	William Gregory and John Barker for land in Biggin	
1781	Messrs. Rawlinson and others for lands in Fairfield	150
1782	Sir John Edensor Heathcote for lands at Buxton (? and Hartington)	8000
1782	John Drabble for lands at Buxton	40
1785	Sarah and Richard Foxlow for land in Fairfield	500
1786	Mr. Vernon for lands in Fairfield	600
1787	Charles Fairfield for lands in Hartington	1100
1788	Robert Longden for lands in Fairfield and Hartington	4000
1788	Edward Dakin for lands in Fairfield	1041
1788	Mr. Gould's devises for lands in Buxton, Staden and Hartington	8100
1789	Bryan Hodgson for interest in the lease of Fairfield Church & School lands	210
1790	Sarah and William Needham & Ann Goodwin for lands in Fairfield near the New Stables	1480
1790	Benjamin Priolu for land at Buxton	16
1790	John Ashman for land in Hartington	210
	Buxton new buildings to 1790 and Fairfield	63212
	Mr. Carr's Commission and his other charges respecting the same buildings	3858
1791	Edmund Wheeldon for Foxlow Farm in Hartington	3673
	Of ditto for common light there	1000
	Of ditto for land in Kingsterndale	700
	Of ditto for land in Fairfield	720
1791	Samuel Frith for lands in Buxton	40
1792	Swinscow and others for their interest in an estate at Nunfield	1125
1794	William Bott and others for lands in Hartington	700
1794	John Cowley for lands at Buxton etc.	
1794	Edward Dixon for lands at Goit	400
1798	Isherwood's Trustees for lands in Fairfield	4080
1800	John Gould of Sheen for lands in Hartington	135
1800	Joseph Brocklehurst for Houses and Land in Buxton	900
1801	Jenny Swinscow for the remainder of Nunsfield	375
1801	Messrs. Alsager's Trustees for lands at Heathcote (bought 5/4/1796)	221
1801	Phillip Gell Esq for lands and tithes	800
1801	William Johnson for an estate at Biggin	715
1801	Edmund Slater for an allotment of land on Biggin Moor	40
1801	Henry Bowman for the Bull's Head estate near Biggin	1350
1804	Edward Coke Wilmot for estates in Milnhouse Dale	4484
1804	Francis Needham's Executors for an estate at Fernhouse	310
1804	Benjamin Priolu for a house and land at Fairfield	300

1804	Messrs. Dakin for the George Inn and lands at Buxton	6000
1805	William Cheetham for messuages and lands in Buxton	1400
	Buxton and Fairfield new buildings and improvements from 1790 – 1810	59887
	Hartington Inclosure and new buildings there from 1799-1809 (below)	24044
	Hartington Manor Capital Expenses in the Current Account (below)	4999

Total   **213925**

Hartington Manor Capital Expenses in the Current Account

1792	Road from Dowal to Thercula Gate [now Thirklow]	147
1792	Diversion fence High Edge	73
1792/93	Buildings at Newhaven	2020
1792/93	Buildings at Dowal	581
1794	Buildings at Newhaven	284
1795	Buildings at Dowal	33
1795	Buildings at Newhaven	230
1810	Brierly Farm buildings	280
1810	New Bulls's Head Inn, Biggin	883
1811	Fencing Hartington Common	366
1811	New Bull's Head Inn, Biggin	22
1812	Brierly Farm buildings	50
1812	Cronkstone Farm buildings	25
1812	New Bull's Head Inn, Biggin	5

Total   **4999**

Hartington Inclosure and New Buildings there from 1799 – 1809

1799	Hartington Inclosure Commissioners first assessment	3462
1799	Fencing Hartington Common	396
1799	Additions and repairs at the house intended for Mr. Flint	11
1799	Buildings at Newhaven House	44
1800	Fencing Hartington Common	1188
1800	Buildings at Newhaven House	62
1800	Additions and repairs at the house intended for Mr. Flint	270
1801	Hartington Inclosure Commissioners second assessment	3144
1801	Fencing Hartington Common	543
1801	Fencing High Edge and Frith Pastures	50
1801	Buildings at Newhaven House	254
1801	Newhaven Farm Buildings	343
1801	Coatsfield Farm Buildings	473
1801	Additions and repairs at the house intended for Mr. Flint	13

1802	Fencing Hartington Common	889
1802	Buildings at Newhaven House	10
1802	Newhaven Farm Buildings	529
1802	Coatsfield Farm Buildings	501
1802	Pilsbury Farm Buildings	984
1803	Fencing Hartington Common	329
1803	Buildings at Newhaven House	46
1803	Newhaven Farm buildings	479
1803	Coatsfield Farm buildings	138
1803	Pilsbury Farm buildings	407
1803	Pilsbury House buildings	559
1803	Handale Farm buildings	42
1804	Fencing Hartington Common	240
1804	Fencing Hartington Common	866
1804	Buildings at Newhaven House	10
1804	Newhaven Farm buildings	46
1804	Pilsbury Farm buildings	10
1804	Handale Farm buildings	178
1804	Hartington Mill Drying House	157
1805	Hartington Mill Drying House	244
1805	Handale Farm buildings	62
1805	Cronkstone Farm buildings	459
1805	Pilsbury Farm buildings	63
1805	Newhaven House and Garden Wall	180
1806	Pilsbury Farm buildings	36
1806	Cronkstone Farm buildings	90
1807	Brierly Farm buildings	298
1807	Cronkstone Farm buildings	31
1807	Fencing Hartington Common	149
1808	Brierly Farm buildings	1000
1808	New Bull's Head Inn, Biggin	891
1809	Fencing Hartington Common	595
1809	Brierly Farm buildings	128
1809	New Bull's Head Inn, Biggin	1044
1809	Newhaven House and Farm buildings	63

Total   **24044**

APPENDIX 3

Liming of Hartington lands

		Lime Loads	Lime tons	Limestone tons	Slack loads
1777–80	Cronxton	9000	579	1158	
	Clement Seat	6000	385	770	
	Coatfield	12000	772	1544	
1778–79	Harley	12000	772	1544	
1778	How Tor	3600	232	464	
1779	How Tor	2000	128	256	
1778	to sundry places, Goit Colliery rental	7000	450	900	
1778	Hindlow	150			)
					) = 80 loads/acre
1779	Hindlow	150			)
1778	Dovehead Farm	3000			'laid in last 12 years'
1780	no further south than Cronxton Grange,	14000	900	1800	
1781–82	Goits Moss Colliery rental	28000	1800	3600	assumed
1783	Hindlow, Sticker Hill, Hill Head, 28 acres	14000	900	1800	
1787–88	Frith Pasture	15393	900	1800	
1789	Frith Pasture	47818	3074	6148	
1790	Frith Pasture	46860	3013	6026	
1791	Frith Pasture	15000	965	1930	
1789	Sherbrook	11980	770	1540	
1790	High Edge	26550	1707	3414	
1791	High Edge	14400	926	1852	
1791	Harley	14480	931	1862	
	Total	**303381**	**19204**	**38408**	**111971**

This excludes the liming of Dowal Farm.

Additional to this is the 13,192 acres received by the Duke on Inclosure of the Common. Not all of this would have been limed, but one supposes that much of it must have been. If so, the tonnage of lime involved must have been huge.

What was the value or gain to the tenant by bothering to lime the land? There had to be some incentive to make it all worthwhile. Fortunately, a document setting out a calculation which gives the figures has survived, albeit relating to inclosure of Ashford and Sheldon Common. It is dated July 1768. (Dev. Coll., AS/1517)

The cost of 'paring and burning' was	£1. 10s. 10d.
Liming with 180 loads at 7d. per load	£5. 5s. 0d.
	£6. 15s. 10d.

Charges of ploughing, sowing, harrowing and seed p.a.	£1. 0s. 0d
To reaping, carrying, stack-making	£0. 7s. 0d.
To thrashing, winnowing, selling and delivery	£0. 7s. 0d.
	£1. 14s. 0d.

Therefore if each acre produced six quarters of oats which was sold at

10s. per quarter it made an income of	£3. 0s. 0d.
with charges against this of	£1. 14s. 0d.
The profit would be (per annum)	£1. 6s. 0d.

Consequently, a profit of £1. 6s. 0d. per acre was available for a capital expenditure of £6. 15s. 0d. allowing just over 5 years to cover the outlay, there was nearly 16 years profit to be made if at the beginning of a 21 year lease. Even allowing for no crop in the first year, the profit was getting on for 400%. No wonder those with deeper pockets amongst the farmers were willing to invest in the improvements.

Mixed limed and unlimed land on Axe Edge, south east of Orchard Clough and the northern tip of Staffordshire (just above Dove Head)

APPENDIX 4

Construction of Roads

Many parish roads were laid out as a result of the Inclosures. William Fidler, the tenant of Biggin Grange, seems to have got the contract for much of the work and it was a substantial one in the event as is indicated by the table below which shows where the work was done and the cost.

Year	No.	Location	£	s.	d.
1801	1	Dale Head (Biggin) – Liffs Gate	54.	6.	7.
	2	Heathcote – Hartington Turnpike road	37.	18.	5½ (end of Long Dale)
	3	Long Dale to the Coal Road (nr. Vincent House)	134.	1.	11.
	4	Hide Lane Head – High Needham	349.	6.	4.
	5	High Needham – [Earls] Sterndale	170.	12.	6.
	6	[Earls] Sterndale – Longnor Turnpike Road	31.	19.	0.
	7	Longnor Turnpike Road – Harley Cross	121.	8.	1½
	8	Harley Cross – Dale Head	229.	12.	7½
	9	Dale Head – Leek Turnpike road	93.	9.	9½
	10	Leek Road – Congleton road	314.	7.	0
	11	Caskin Low Slack	11.	4.	6½
	12	Buxton Turnpike road – Coal Road nr. Custhouse Fields	69.	18.	3
	13	Buxton Turnpike road – Pilsbury Farm	132.	12.	6
	14	[Earl] Sterndale – Hurdlow	65.	11.	6
1803					
	15	Biggin Green	28.	8.	3
	16	Biggin Lane Head – Ashbourne Turnpike road	14.	14.	10
1805	17	Near Wolfscote	25.	13.	6½
	18	Ashbourne road – Parwich Liberty	31.	1.	2
	19	Hartington Turnpike road – Heathcote	40.	15.	9
1803	20	Repairs to New Coal Road	275.	13.	3
		Total	**£2,232.**	**15.**	**2**

William Fidler appears to have been brought in to undertake some expensive repair work shortly after the Coal Road had opened. He also undertook the building of the stone walls fronting roads and elsewhere (Dev. Coll., AS/1397 and 1247).

The former Boulton and Watt engine house, now reduced in height. See Chapter 6. Drawing by Phillip Porter

ACKNOWLEDGEMENTS

This work would not have been possible without the assistance from the (late) 11th and the current 12th Dukes of Devonshire and the Chatsworth Settlement Trustees who permitted my research at Chatsworth over several years. In particular, I have received much assistance there from James Towe, Charles Noble, Andrew Peppitt, Stuart Band and not least, Dianne Naylor. It is amazing how the collective memory of sight of otherwise unknown documents from years before has assisted my research. 'Try so and so' became a regular feature of my visits, plus an invaluable overview of some of the material I found, especially where the research pointed to a change of perceived opinion. I have also received valuable assistance from the following: Margaret Black; Roger Flindall; Albert Goodman; Marjorie Ide; Helen Maurice Jones; Trevor Osborne Property Group; the late S Penny; The late Edward Paget-Tomlinson; Phillip Porter; Brian Rich; Dr JH Rieuwerts; Alan Stoyel; Oliver Wilson, Eric Wood. My thanks to all. I have also acknowledged further assistance in the end-of-Chapter references. My apologies in advance to anyone missed from the above.

INDEX